1985

Chaucer and *The Legend of Good Women*

Chaucer and *The Legend of Good Women*

Robert Worth Frank, Jr.

Harvard University Press, Cambridge, Massachusetts, 1972

For Gladys

Preface

This book is designed to fill a gap in Chaucerian studies, though I might wish it had been done long since by another hand. I myself sat down several years ago to plot out the development of Chaucer as a narrative artist and discovered I could not make an honest assessment of that development without understanding the nature of the *Legend of Good Women* and its significance in his artistic career. Chaucer, we know, moved from *Troilus and Criseyde* to the *Legend* to the *Canterbury Tales*. For understanding the role of the *Legend of Good Women* in this dramatic sequence, however, one could choose in recent Chaucerian criticism only between silence and abuse. These are, I think, modest hyperboles. When it is not ignored completely, the *Legend* is more or less abruptly dismissed as an unwelcome task and a fragmentary failure. (The Prologue is an exception, but the Prologue is not the *Legend* proper.) The anomaly of this circumstance had to be faced head on. The *Legend* had to be anatomized; its nature had to be known. This book is the consequence.

In moments of doubt and dismay while working on the *Legend*, I have comforted myself by imagining the excitement that would greet the discovery of an unknown work by Chaucer of similar length and value. Though it lacks the drama of "newfangelnesse," the *Legend* has at times had for me some of this excitement of discovery, and I have enjoyed the experience of having a Chaucerian work almost entirely to myself. I cannot hope to have said the final word, or even the right word, about the *Legend of Good Women.* I do hope to recall scholars' attention to it. It is our responsibility to take all of an artist's work into consideration in our efforts to understand him. It is also our responsibility to reexamine the judgments of previous generations on an artist's work and — more difficult — to come to terms if possible with those works that do not easily submit themselves to our current critical predilections and enthusiasms. I hope I have not overvalued the *Legend.* I have tried not to. I have, however, no doubt whatsoever that the *Legend* is a serious work seriously treated by its author. If it turns out on further consideration to have fallen shorter of his expectations than I believe it did, I should like to think I have at least rescued it from some cavalier explanations of its shortcomings and some oversimplified evaluations of its merits.

A project such as this accumulates many debts of gratitude, especially to librarians, many of them unknown by name and responsible for kindnesses and services they do not remember; and, beyond them, to the many benefactors whose gifts ultimately brought the books he needed to the writer's hand. I should like here to thank, however inadequately, the librarians, trustees, and benefactors of the Fred Lewis Pattee Library of the Pennsylvania State University, most particularly Charles W. Mann, Jr., and Mildred Treworgy; of the British Museum; and of the Bodleian Library. Time for the research and writing of this book was in part made possible by a Fellowship awarded me by the American Council of Learned Societies; I wish to thank the ACLS for their generosity, and for their patience. The work was further assisted by means of a sabbatical granted by the Pennsylvania State University, for which I am most grateful. Funds for typing and for photostats and other expenses were made available by the Central Fund for Research and the Liberal Arts Research and Graduate Studies Office of the Pennsylvania State University; my special thanks to Dean Ben Euwema, Professor Frederick Matson, and Associate Dean Thomas Magner. Henry W.

Sams, the most imaginative of chairmen, gave assistance and good counsel in many ways on manifold occasions. Mrs. James Martini typed the manuscript cleanly and expeditiously. Hester Alison, paragon of secretaries, made everything come out right. In the final editing of the manuscript I have enjoyed the efficient and perceptive assistance of M. Rita Howe of the Harvard University Press.

University Park, Pennsylvania   Robert Worth Frank, Jr.
May 23, 1972

Contents

Preface   vii

Abbreviations   xiv

I   Chaucer in 1386   1

II   The Prologue   11

III   Cleopatra   37

IV   Thisbe   47

V   Dido   57

VI   Hypsipyle and Medea   79

VII   Lucrece   93

VIII   Ariadne   111

IX   Philomela   134

X   Phyllis   146

XI   Hypermnestra   156

XII   The Lessons Learned   169

       Excursus. The Legend of Chaucer's Boredom   189

       Index   211

Chaucer and *The Legend of Good Women*

Abbreviations

CFMA	Classiques Français du Moyen Age
CT	*Canterbury Tales*
EETS, OS	Early English Text Society, Original Series
EETS, ES	Early English Text Society, Extra Series
JEGP	*Journal of English and Germanic Philology*
MED	*Middle English Dictionary*
MLN	*Modern Language Notes*
MLQ	*Modern Language Quarterly*
MLR	*Modern Language Review*
MP	*Modern Philology*
N & Q	*Notes and Queries*
OED	*Oxford English Dictionary*
PL	*Patrologia cursus completus; series latina*
PMLA	[Publications of the Modern Language Association of America]
PQ	*Philological Quarterly*
RES	*Review of English Studies*
SATF	Société des Anciens Textes Françaises

[I]   Chaucer in 1386

The year in which Chaucer began the *Legend of Good Women* — let us say 1386 for convenience — is a propitious moment to take a searching look at his artistic career. It is one of the few moments when we have solid ground on which to stand for such an examination. Thanks to the references to his own work in the Prologue to the *Legend*, we know beyond question certain facts about the chronology of his writings, a privilege we enjoy at no other moment in his lifetime. We know what he had and what he had not written by this date, and we can therefore place the project of the *Legend* precisely in the sequence of his work. We can also look at what went before and consider what was to follow this critical moment in his career.

The word "critical" may seem both melodramatic and superfluous. Superfluous because in a sense every moment in an artist's career is critical. Melodramatic, certainly, if the word suggests some spiritual conflict or some dark shadow of the soul. We know nothing of the kind about Chaucer, and nothing of the kind is intended. But the word will be useful for emphasizing the fact that Chaucer, as an artist, did certain things in the years before 1386 that he would never do again and that after 1386, beginning with the *Legend*, he would do certain things he had never done before. It is some of these changes, as they appear for the first time in the *Legend*, that I wish to examine in the process of analyzing the legends themselves. I shall flirt with melodrama to the extent of suggesting that the time was ripe for changes and that, failing these changes, Chaucer's achievement might have been markedly less lustrous.

All this may have a distressingly familiar sound. In the old division of Chaucer's career into a French, an Italian, and an English phase, 1386 was the year to ring the bell announcing the inauguration of the English phase. Or if one plotted his history as a movement from artificial and conventional to realistic modes, this was about the time to rule the new column labeled "realism" and begin making entries. These descriptions of Chaucer's career are no longer acceptable; in any event, they are directed toward aspects of his work which do not concern me here for they are based on the fact that the inception of the *Canterbury Tales* dates from about this period. What interests me is that Chaucer set to work on the *Legend of Good Women* at this time.

Certain innovations in genre, in theme, in technique, and in verse form begin with the *Legend* and give that work thereby more significance than critics have hitherto accorded it. I wish to examine these innovations which suggest that this period was a time of change and, as I have said, a time of crisis. Why does the *Legend*, a work generally ignored and largely condemned as a failure, come at just this moment? What is its attraction for Chaucer, and what is its meaning in his history? What, in fact, do we have in the *Legend*? These would all seem to be questions that demand an answer.

When he began the Prologue to the *Legend of Good Women*, Chaucer had completed a body of work that might have satisfied a less energetic or creative man. His translations aside, he had written the *Book of the Duchess*, the *House of Fame*, the *Parliament of Birds*, *Troilus and Criseyde*, the *Knight's Tale* ("al the love of Palamon and Arcite / Of Thebes"), and "the lyf also of Seynt Cecile." Though it has been suggested that still other titles, from items in the *Canterbury Tales*, should be added to this list, one can legitimately ask, where Chaucer told so much, why would he fail to tell us all? The vagueness of "balades, roundels, virelayes" needs no explanation. "Anelida and Arcite" must be added, I believe; but his failure to mention a work not only incomplete but obviously abandoned at a very early stage is understandable. The list, with this addition, is thoroughly instructive for our purposes without further modification.[1]

As one studies the list, what emerges is an impression of Chaucer's restless versatility. There are triumphs in this record — the *Parliament of Birds, Troilus and Criseyde,* the *Knight's Tale* — but no one of them is quite like another. Each is a triumph in a particular genre or mode. Having found the way to success in a form, Chaucer never repeated the pattern. Indeed, his habit seems to have been to toss a particular kind of poem aside once he had explored its possibilities and solved the problem it posed.

This restlessness can be clearly seen in the history of Chaucer's use of the dream vision. The accepted order — the *Book of the Duchess,* the *House of Fame,* and the *Parliament of Birds* — is surely correct. Chaucer's order in the Prologue to the *Legend,* which puts the *House of Fame* before the *Book of the Duchess,* is probably dictated by the exigencies of rhyme and an indifference to chronological precision. He does put the *Parliament of Birds* last, which is where the metrical evidence suggests it must go. The *Parliament* reveals a brilliant mastery of the vision genre. In its firmness of structure, the complexity of its treatment of theme, its sustained ironic point of view, it is clearly superior to the two earlier poems. Having mastered the form in the *Parliament,* he abandons the dream vision thereafter; *Troilus,* "Anelida," the *Knight's Tale,* and the life of St. Cecilia are not in the genre. The apparent return to the vision in the Prologue to the *Legend* is a self-conscious, possibly mocking resumption of the form. More important is the fact that the narratives that make up the

---

1. The list is based, of course, on the Prologue to the *Legend of Good Women* (F 328–332, 417–430; G 254–266, 405–420). Line references and quotations for all Chaucerian texts, unless otherwise noted, are based on F. N. Robinson, *The Works of Geoffrey Chaucer,* 2nd ed. (Boston, Houghton Mifflin Company, 1957). Permission to quote has been granted by Houghton Mifflin Company, copyright 1933; renewed 1957 and 1961 by F. N. Robinson.

body of the work are presented outside the frame and outside the sanction of the dream form.

In abandoning this form, Chaucer is doing something more than jettisoning a device. He is moving into a new kind of poetry, the narrative mode, and away from the lyric-narrative and discursive-narrative modes of his vision poems. Narrative movement, that is, movement from one moment or place or condition to another, is not generally characteristic of vision poetry. Movement in vision poetry is primarily from one mood to another (the mood often being established by explicit lyric expression) or from one position in an argument or exposition to another or from mood to exposition to mood. There may be narrative movements, but generally they function as exempla, as part of the frame, or as transitional devices to shift agents within the vision from mood to mood or from stage to stage of the discourse. Religious visions frequently have narrative movement, but here the events must normally be the dream experiences of the narrator or agent and relate to him in some direct and specific fashion; in addition, the relation must be doctrinal.

Relatively pure narrative, extended or complex narrative, or narrative from literature or history is not ordinarily appropriate for the dream vision. Such narratives — and the term "pure narrative" will cover them all — lack the elements which the dream is peculiarly adapted to exploit: namely, the ultrafantastic experience (the meeting with personifications, the journey through hell or through space), discursive or reflective or doctrinal content, and the uniquely personal experience which becomes a validating and dramatistic "witnessing" of the message. Relatively logical or chronological linear movement is not necessary within a dream; indeed, it may be said to be wasted there. Narratives from literature or history can be used within the vision as exempla, for example, the story of Narcissus in the *Roman de la rose*, the belling of the cat in *Piers Plowman*, or the narratives told by Genius in the *Confessio Amantis*. But there is no point in telling the story of

Palamon and Arcite or of Pyramus and Thisbe as such within a dream. The expository purpose of the *Confessio* justifies (barely) Gower's use of the vision form, but, practically speaking, the reader is outside the dream experience during the narrative portions of the *Confessio*. When the expository purpose is minimal or disappears, the teller of a narrative or narratives had best dispense with the dream. Chaucer puts the story of Ceyx and Alcyone outside the dream in the *Book of the Duchess*. Gower's experience reveals the awkwardness inherent in trying to accommodate pure narrative within the vision. To get at the immense world of story Chaucer had to discard the polite French vision form completely.

At the same time that Chaucer was transforming himself into a narrative poet, he was also trying a new pattern of verse. Whether or not we assume the poem he referred to as "Palamon and Arcite" was essentially like what comes down to us as the *Knight's Tale*, that is, a poem written in five-stress couplets, we have the Prologue to the *Legend* and the legends themselves as evidence of Chaucer's experimentation with a new verse form.[2] It is, of course, a form especially adaptable for narrative poetry, as its subsequent long history amply demonstrates. We can wonder at the ease with which Chaucer manipulates the rhyme royal stanza in the *Parliament* and in *Troilus*, handling dialogue and action with no sense of strain or artificiality, but there need be no wonder that he should experiment with and use to the full a less restrictive, more flexible form as he moved more and more into the writing of pure narrative.

There was need, however, for yet more novelty, yet more change. *Troilus* and the *Knight's Tale* suggest a problem we may imagine Chaucer to have been facing with special concern in 1386, the problem of subject matter. The com-

2. See Paull F. Baum, *Chaucer's Verse* (Durham, North Carolina, Duke University Press, 1961), pp. 48ff.; also Tauno F. Mustanoja, "Chaucer's Prosody," in *Companion to Chaucer Studies*, ed. Beryl Rowland (Toronto, Oxford University Press, 1968), p. 68.

plete, the exhaustive treatment of courtly or romantic or polite love — call it what you will[3] — in *Troilus*, together with the judgment pronounced upon the limits of that experience in the conclusion, left Chaucer limited possibilities for further treatment unless he were content to repeat himself. What indeed remains to be said, within the perspective of the code, after *Troilus*?

The wonder is that he was able to use the code once again, freshly and magnificently, in the *Knight's Tale*. But even so there are signs of the exhaustion, or at least the attenuation, of the theme of idealized human love. It is only a slight exaggeration to say that Chaucer's perspective there is that of Troilus from the eighth sphere. We have a sense of love viewed from a great distance, with amusement and in a spirit of tolerant irony. Love is not the subject of the *Knight's Tale* as it is of *Troilus*. We can learn a great deal about love, or at least about one kind of love, from *Troilus*. We can learn almost nothing about love from the *Knight's Tale*. It is a convenience there, it is used to set matters in motion and to illustrate the dilemma of human experience within the Boethian prison house. But the *Knight's Tale* is not really about idealized, codified love.

The subject is exhausted — perhaps not for his audience, but for Chaucer. It could offer no further great imaginative challenge once that challenge had been met as directly and as comprehensively as it was in *Troilus*. The question of what to write about now must have been a very real concern for Chaucer in 1386.

At the same time a question of technique might also have troubled him, though he had turned already toward a possible solution in the *Knight's Tale*. Amplification had been Chaucer's primary method for treating a theme in his earlier poetry; his aim seemed clearly to be elaboration,

3. For a recent challenging of the validity of the term "courtly love" and its existence in Western literature from the twelfth to the fifteenth century, see the discussion in *The Meaning of Courtly Love*, ed. F. X. Newman (Albany, New York, State University of New York Press, 1968).

not brevity.[4] If we examine the *Book of the Duchess*, for example, we can see that the basic framework, the "plot," is simple and slight. The poem is an exercise in amplification, a method obviously congenial, even irresistible, to an enormously creative young poet. There are moments in the *Book of the Duchess*, indeed, as when the narrator is tossing about the gifts of pillowcases and featherbeds he will offer Juno, that suggest an exuberant and expansive imagination threatening to run wild. Similarly, the "plots" of the *House of Fame* and the *Parliament of Birds* are comparatively slight. We move to three or four stages in the course of the poem, and at each stage pause to watch the poet elaborate, decorate, or expand the immediate thesis, mood, or situation. Though there is skillful use of the art of abbreviation in the telling of the tale of Seys and Alcyone, in the recounting of the Dido-Aeneas story, in the summary of the *Somnium Scipionis*, the passages are none the less amplifications within the framework of the poems.

In *Troilus and Criseyde* the art of amplification reaches its culmination. The expansion by one-third of the narrative he found in Boccaccio's *Il Filostrato* added depth and comprehensiveness to Chaucer's poem. The expansion is bold and surehanded, but Chaucer carries the method about as far as it can go without destroying the artistic unity of the poem. Some, indeed, would say it has been carried too far. Mutterings about Troilus' soliloquy on predestination and critics' difficulties with the poem's conclusion reveal how close to the dangerous edge the method of amplification has been pushed. Ahead lies giantism, the fatal inability to cease expansion that ruins, for example, so much of the work of Lydgate.

One might cite the collapse of "Anelida and Arcite" —

4. The most convenient collection of a number of the rhetorical texts in which the devices of amplification and abbreviation are discussed is Edmond Faral, *Les arts poétiques du XII* *et XIII* *siècle* (Paris, É. Champion, 1924). On amplification, see also J. W. H. Atkins, *English Literary Criticism: The Medieval Phase* (London, Methuen & Co. Ltd., 1943), pp. 102–107. Alan Gunn's discussion of amplification in *Le roman de la rose* is a useful case study: *The Mirror of Love* (Lubbock, Texas Tech Press, 1952), pp. 63–138.

whether one puts it before or after *Troilus and Criseyde* — as another warning against excessive amplification. We can only speculate, of course, but, standing back and looking at the poem, I see it as an enterprise in which the overly elaborate lyrical amplification has choked the poem, has caused it to founder. It is difficult to see how Chaucer could have succeeded in setting the poem in motion again, how he could have returned to the narrative mode after that complex and extended complaint.

In any event, in the *Knight's Tale* Chaucer turned abruptly in the other direction. His method here is for the most part abbreviation. He transformed a narrative of nearly 10,000 lines into one of 2,250, dropping entire sections of the original and cutting consistently and skillfully throughout. There are amplifications, but they are comparatively few. This change comes none too soon. It was high time that he began to appreciate the value and to learn the art of abbreviation.

Abbreviation has more than a negative virtue for the narrative artist, it does more than avoid excessive length, padding, or prolixity. If it is to be done properly, it requires that the artist distinguish between the essential and the nonessential, that he know precisely what effect he wishes to create by his narrative in order to know what to keep and what to cut away. It demands also that he attend to the question of proper length or magnitude. A particular narrative aiming at a particular effect has certain limits as to size; it must not be too long, it must not be too short. Above all, abbreviation of narrative materials requires the artist to focus on narrative as such, to be aware of action and event, of movement and pace.

These considerations are especially demanding if the narratives are to be relatively brief. Chaucer turns, quite deliberately, to the short narrative after the *Knight's Tale*.[5]

5. The evidence shows that Chaucer completely abandoned the long narrative after the *Knight's Tale*, that is, for the last fourteen years of his career. The longest tales in the *Canterbury Tales* (except for the *Knight's Tale* with its 2,250 lines) are the *Man of Law's*, 1,029; *Clerk's*, 1,106; and *Merchant's*, 1,134.

The God of Love asserts that in these legends he will be content "That thou reherce of al hir lyf the grete . . ." (F 574).
One would give a great deal to know exactly why. Had his
audience found *Troilus* uncomfortably long? Was there a
newly developed taste for the short narrative? The many
brief narratives in Gower's *Confessio Amantis*, coming at
about the same time as the brief narratives in the *Legend*
and the, for the most part, comparatively brief narratives in
the *Canterbury Tales*, hint at a possible shift of taste, but
we can only guess.[6] Was it that, for the kinds of material
Chaucer was becoming interested in, brief narrative treatment was more appropriate? The God of Love, in Prologue
F of the *Legend*, gives a kind of commonsense reason for
brevity: "For whoso shal so many a storye telle, / Sey
shortly, or he shal to longe dwelle" (576–577). The remark
applies immediately to the project of the *Legend* itself, but,
without undue distortion, we can expand the remark to

The figures for the other tales are instructive: *MillT*, 668; *RvT*, 404; *WBProl*,
828; *WBT*, 408; *FrT*, 364; *SumT*, 586; *SqT*, 672; *FranklT*, 896; *PhyT*, 286;
PardProl, 134; *PardT*, 432 + 24; *ShipT*, 434; *PrProl*, 34; *PrT*, 224; *SirThop*, 206;
MkT, 776; *NPT*, 626; *SecNProl*, 119; *SecNT*, 434; *CYProl*, 166; *CYT*, 762;
MancProl, 104; *MancT*, 258. *Melibee* and the *Parson's Tale* are not narratives
and so are omitted, as is the *General Prologue*; the several tale prologues should
also probably not be listed, though some might wish to include them in the
line count for the narrative proper. It is worth noting that the tale of the
Canterbury narratives which is potentially of greatest length, the *Squire's Tale*,
is incomplete. Recent criticism suggests that Chaucer deliberately left it unfinished and is, in fact, poking fun at the romantic ineptitudes of the Squire.
See John McCall, "The Squire in Wonderland," *Chaucer Review*, 1 (1966),
103–109; also Robert S. Haller, "Chaucer's *Squire's Tale* and the Uses of Rhetoric," *MP*, 62 (1965), 285–295, esp. 293; and Harry Berger, Jr., "The F-Fragment
of the *Canterbury Tales*: Part I," *Chaucer Review*, 1 (1966), 88–102. Among
other matters, Chaucer may have been satirizing one kind of inordinately long
narrative. The line count for the narratives in the *Legend*, to complete the
record, is as follows: Prologue(F), 579; Prologue(G), 545; *Cleopatra*, 126; *Thisbe*,
218; *Dido*, 444; *Hypsipyle and Medea*, 312; *Lucrece*, 206; *Ariadne*, 342; *Philomela*, 166; *Phyllis*, 168; *Hypermnestra*, 162 (within a few lines of completion).
   6. John Fisher has recently re-examined the question of the interrelationships
between the *Confessio Amantis* and the *Legend*. See *John Gower: Moral Phi-
losopher and Friend of Chaucer* (New York, New York University Press, 1964),
pp. 235–250. He does not, however, discuss the matter of the brief narrative.
His statement (p. 235) that the *Confessio* and the *Legend* "appear to stem from
the same royal command" is highly speculative.

cover the *Canterbury Tales* also. If an artist in his forties wishes to tell a great many stories, he will probably opt for the brief narrative. There is not enough time to tell many more narratives on the scale of the *Troilus*, or even, perhaps, of the *Knight's Tale*. The large-scale work will be the cluster of short narratives themselves, a *Legend*, a *Canterbury Tales*. But certainly the most interesting implication of the God of Love's remark, an implication borne out by Chaucer's subsequent career, is that Chaucer is now intensely interested in narrative, in stories — as many of them as possible.

Leaving all speculation aside, we retain some interesting facts. Chaucer has ceased writing dream poems and instead is writing narrative poetry. He has written one very long narrative poem and a shorter one of 2,250 lines. In the course of writing them, he treats the theme of idealized, codified love so thoroughly as to leave very little more to say; up to this point, except for the *House of Fame*, love has been his constant theme. Beginning with the second, shorter narrative, he has dropped his customary method, amplification, and turned to abbreviation instead. (He may have noticed certain dangers in amplification.) At the same time that he switched his method, he began experimenting with a new verse pattern, the decasyllabic couplet.

There is some justification, therefore, for suggesting that 1386 was a critical year. To continue writing precisely as Chaucer had been writing did not seem a promising course. Although he had made some moves in new directions, they were still tentative and not sufficiently advanced to say whether they were promising or not. The uncertainty of his artistic future compels us to examine the work he turned to at this moment, the *Legend of Good Women*, with less than languid interest. We should not be too surprised to find Chaucer, in the Prologue to the *Legend*, reflecting at some length on his poetic career and on the work he is about to undertake.

[II]   The Prologue

The much admired Prologue to the *Legend of Good Women* is all of the *Legend* that the mid-twentieth century is willing to take to its bosom. It is famous for its charm. Or it is if one selects the proper passages. This is not a sneer; I simply wish to point out that some of the time Chaucer appears to be talking seriously so charm is not the whole business of the Prologue. Unfortunately, the charm both distracts us from the seriousness and encourages us to read only the Prologue, making it an end instead of what it really is — a beginning.

The Prologue is also famous because for many years it was the object of controversy. It exists in two versions, labeled nowadays F and G, and the question of which came first has received an extraordinary amount of attention.[1]

1. For an admirably succinct review of the controversy over the question of priority up to 1907, see Eleanor P. Hammond, *Chaucer: A Bibliographical Manual* (New York, Macmillan Company, 1908), pp. 381–382. For later bibliography on the controversy, see Dudley David Griffith, *Bibliography of Chaucer: 1908–1953* (Seattle, University of Washington Press, 1955), pp. 272–282. The case for the priority of F (formerly called B) over G (formerly called A) was argued by John Livingston Lowes in two magisterial articles: "The Prologue to the *Legend of Good Women* as Related to the French *Marguerite* Poems and the *Filostrato*," *PMLA*, 19 (1904), 593–683, esp. pp. 635–683; and "The Prologue to the *Legend of Good Women* Considered in Its Chronological Relations," *PMLA*, 20 (1905), 749–864. The latter assigns dates for the two Prologues: the summer or autumn of 1386 for F (see pp. 753–779); sometime, possibly soon, after Anne of Bohemia's death on June 7, 1394, for G (see pp. 780–781). Lowes's additional supporting arguments for this approximate date of G (see pp. 782–801) are less substantial; his argument that the legends themselves were all or largely written before the (F) Prologue to the *Legend* (pp. 802–818) is subjective and has never been accepted. The argument for the priority of F, however, has never been convincingly challenged.

There is today a consensus that F is the earlier, and I shall act on that assumption, basing my discussion primarily on F and referring to G only when necessary. The debate over priority is another factor that has tended to isolate the Prologue from the legends.

The main function of the Prologue in the total although incomplete work we call the *Legend of Good Women*, would seem, however, to be that of introduction. It is this function which I wish to discuss. This is not to deny the Prologue some of the qualities of an aesthetic entity; it is merely that this matter is not my concern. I wish to examine the Prologue for such clues as it may give us as to Chaucer's purposes in the legends themselves, in the project as a whole. What he felt to be the significance of this work may in some part be revealed here, and that would be worth knowing.

In the chronology of the Chaucer canon the Prologue appears to be a throwback; as a dream vision it is a momentary regression to a form and manner already abandoned in the *Troilus* and the *Knight's Tale* and never used in the *Canterbury Tales*. Critics have commented on the Prologue's conventionality,[2] but the appearance of orthodoxy is misleading, probably deliberately so, for Chaucer's apologia in the Prologue, his explanation and defense of what he is about to do, is not merely conventional. True, the Prologue has its conventional furniture: the reference to books, the typically Chaucerian figure of the comically placed narrator, the talk of love and the God of Love, and the dream form itself. But Chaucer has not made merely servile use of these elements on other occasions, and he does not humbly crook the knee to them here. The conventions are, in fact, cajoled into performing services never dreamed of.

The reference to books has its customary function: it suggests a learned substructure for what is to be the fabric of his

2. For example, George Lyman Kittredge, *Chaucer and His Poetry* (Cambridge, Mass., Harvard University Press, 1915), p. 152; John Livingston Lowes, *Geoffrey Chaucer* (Oxford, Eng., Clarendon Press, 1934), p. 126.

creations. Just how seriously we are to take this defense of
"olde appreved stories" may not at once be clear. Since its
immediate purpose seems to be to contrast with the arti-
ficially "natural" world of May mornings and simple daisies
("Farewel my bok, and my devocioun!"), the first reaction
may well be to take lightly the bookish talk by this bookish
writer. But the daisy blooms here only for a summer's day,
we should observe. Critics sometimes talk of the Prologue
as if it were nothing but daisies, daisies, daisies all the way,
but it is not. Books win out in the end. There will be a
balade about famous ladies to be met only in story; the conversation in the vision is to center on Chaucer's writing; the
Prologue is a prelude to an open raid on the literature of the
past. Perhaps the first thirty-five lines should be taken more
seriously rather than less.

There is good reason for thinking Chaucer might have
been writing these opening lines in other than a flippant
mood. He was about to retell stories from the classical
treasury of myth and poetry; he would be using Ovid extensively, and the Virgilian tale of Dido, if not Virgil himself.
His love and reverence for writers of the classical past were
deeply felt. The devout mood at the conclusion of *Troilus
and Criseyde* is revealing:

> But litel book, no makyng thow n'envie,
> But subgit be to alle poesye;
> And kis the steppes, where as thow seest pace
> Virgile, Ovide, Omer, Lucan, and Stace.
>
> (V, 1789–1792)

Then, too, in Chaucer's day the reworking of classical
material was in some part an act of piety, for it was an act of
preservation and propagation. In telling of Dido and Thisbe, Lucrece and Medea, Chaucer would be helping to keep
a heritage alive. It is unlikely that he was emulating the
scholarly and educative performance of Boccaccio in *De
Casibus Virorum Illustrium* and *De Claris Mulieribus;*[3] his

3. Aage Brusendorf suggested that the Latin titles of the individual legends
were modeled on Boccaccio's chapter headings in *De Claris Mulieribus;* see

free treatment of sources implies no concern for a comprehensive erudition, no intention to create an encyclopedic
work of reference like Boccaccio's. And yet he knew he
was serving as a transmitter of the past, even if his method
was only to "reherce of al hir lyf the grete." His book, too,
would become in its fashion a key of remembrance.

It is not as a historian or scholar, but as an artist that
Chaucer demands to be taken seriously here. The demand
is made obliquely, but it is revealed in the larger strategy of
the Prologue as a whole. The demand appears in the opening lines, and it determines the "plot" of the Prologue. The
attention paid to "stories" and the writing of them and the
artful pressure exerted on his audience to persuade it to follow him in what he as a writer of stories is about to do suggest sincerity of intention and an awareness of innovation.

What he is about to do, to put it quite baldly, is to tell a
series of tales coming out of the classical pagan past and tell
them for their own sake. The fiction of a martyrology of
lovers supplies a very general theme, but it does not really
explain the act of composing these tales. It helps to place
them within a recognizable and acceptable convention, that
of idealized love, which ostensibly explains their creation
and makes easier their reception. But the rituals of courtly
love rarely intrude in the narratives themselves.

The theme of "the praise of good ladies" will operate to
the extent that Chaucer will make Cleopatra an innocent
such as she never was before or has been since, and he will
pass in silence over events in Medea's history which reek
too much of blood or witches' brew. But he does not so treat
his material that the characters emerge transformed from
their classical originals into recognizably medieval agents
in a courtly love drama. Pyramus and Thisbe are not a
Tristram and Isolde; the story of Lucrece illustrates no principle from Andreas Capellanus. One has only to compare
Chaucer's treatment of the Thisbe story with the Anglo-

The Chaucer Tradition (London, Humphrey Milford, Oxford University Press, 1925), pp. 144–145.

Norman version incorporated into the *Ovide moralisé*, or his telling of the tale of Philomena with Chrétien de Troyes's *Philomena*, also absorbed into the *Ovide*, to see what metamorphoses can be wrought in Ovid's materials by medievalization in the cause of *fine amours* and to distinguish what Chaucer himself did and did not do with his material.

If the offering of the narratives on the altar of the God of Love is at best a pretence, it is nonetheless the only nod to didactic convention which Chaucer makes. He eschews completely any moral or theological purpose and claims for his tales a purely secular intention. Two fourteenth-century treatments of much the same material that he used here make an instructive contrast. The *Ovide moralisé* retells the *Metamorphoses*, medievalizing freely as it goes. The Ovidian narratives, when they are on stage, are quite obviously presented for the sheer enjoyment and fascination of the stories themselves. But the narratives are at the same time embedded in a moralistic matrix: the figures and events of the narratives are given allegorical interpretations, and moral comment is provided. Similarly, Chaucer's friend John Gower, in his *Confessio Amantis*, placed his tales, many of them from Ovid, in a double framework of convention: courtly love and morality. Though Gower normally allows the narrative to go its own way during the telling, it is always accompanied by comment which makes it an exemplum of a principle in either courtly love or orthodox morality, or both.

This treatment of Ovid was not only completely acceptable to medieval taste, it was also in harmony with one medieval view of Ovid, and for practical purposes we may take Ovid as the core of the *Legend*. There were divided attitudes toward Ovid in the later Middle Ages, and as a consequence there were several Ovids.[4] One was the

---

4. For a quick glance at medieval attitudes toward Ovid, see L. P. Wilkinson, *Ovid Recalled* (Cambridge, Eng., Cambridge University Press, 1955), pp. 366–398. See also F. Munari, *Ovid im Mittelalter* (Zurich, Artemis Verlags-AG, 1960), and Simone Viarre, *La survie d'Ovide dans la littérature scientifique des*

"moral Ovid." This is the Ovid we see in the Ovidian allegorizations, of which the *Ovide moralisé* is only the most extended example,[5] and in the sententious comments culled from his writings.[6] Even the plain Latin text of the *Metamorphoses* could be accompanied by moralistic glosses or prefatory *accessus* introducing him as a moralist whose "final cause" was to urge us toward virtue and deter us from vice and showing us through his stories of transformation that worldly things are but transitory.[7] The *Heroides* might be met in similar guise.[8]

Chaucer's Ovid, however, is not this moral teacher, but the master of poetic narrative. The absence from the *Legend* of the kind of moral comment or allegorical interpretation so often found with Ovidian material is sufficient indication that Chaucer is not presenting the moral Ovid here. I am not suggesting that this makes the *Legend* superior to the poetry of moral comment, only that this

---

XIIᵉ et XIIIᵉ siècles, Centre d'Études Supérieures de Civilisation Médiévale (Poitiers, 1966).

5. For details, see Lester K. Born, "Ovid and Allegory," *Speculum*, 9 (1934), 362–379, esp. 370–379. The attitude toward allegory expressed there is somewhat out of date.

6. See *ibid.*, p. 371, for one instance. In the *Speculum Historiale* of Vincent de Beauvais, chaps. cvii to cxxii of Book VI consist of *flores* and *flosculi* from Ovid's writings.

7. Some of these *accessus* are printed in Karl Young, "Chaucer's Appeal to the Platonic Deity," *Speculum*, 19 (1944), 1–13, specifically 4–10. See also Gustaw Przychocky, *Accessus Ovidiani*, in Polska Akademia Umiejetnosci Cracow, Wydzial Filologiczny, Rozprawy Akademia Umiejetnosci, ser. III, 4 (1911); Edwin A. Quain, "The Medieval Accessus ad Auctores," *Traditio*, 3 (1945), 215–264; and R. B. C. Huygens, *Accessus ad Auctores*, Collection Latomus, XV (Berchem-Bruxelles, 1954).

8. Born, "Ovid and Allegory," p. 377, provides one example. And a brief moral lesson directed to the business of love is suggested in the "Prologo" which introduces almost every epistle in the Italian translation of the *Heroides* by "Filippo," which Chaucer may have used: *Volgarizzamento delle Pistole d'Ovidio* . . . (Florence, 1819), pp. 1, 27, 40–41, 49, 60, 80, 100, 107, 121, 139, 156, 171(?), 196. An example from the prologue to Medea will suffice: "La 'ntenzione d'Ovidio principalmente ene di riprendere li sperguiri amanti, i quali sono piu vaghi della grolia vana, che di mantenere la chiara veritate. E spezialmente intende di riprendere li nobili e possenti uomini, le cui opere sono tutte in essemplo . . ." (pp. 107–108). Chaucer's martyrology is not this tendentious, even within the framework of its concern for love.

makes it different. When, as in Gower, moral poetry accompanied narrative, it could add a useful and enriching
dimension to the work as a whole and, often, to the narrative itself. Aside from its qualities as moral verse — a distinctive type of verse to be judged by distinctive standards
— it had a supportive value for audience and artist. It made
what might seem troubling or offensive comfortable and
pleasing, what might seem strange ultimately familiar,
what might seem pointless or irreverent happily instructive.
But Chaucer abandons such support for his performance.
He sets out to achieve independence of treatment, relying
on "these olde appreved stories" with no extraneous prop-
ping. All that his stories will "prove" is that particular
women, and by implication many women, are faithful.
Since there are playful overtones to this dictum throughout
and since in the development of some of the tales even this
moral is subordinated, his audience will enjoy precious few
moments of moral *frisson*, however ardently they worship
the God of Love.

To illustrate the point at issue, let us anticipate by taking
a passage from the last story he tells, the *Legend of Hypermnestra*. On her wedding night Hypermnestra has been
ordered by her father under pain of death to slay her bridegroom, Lyno.

> The nyght is wasted, and he fyl aslepe.
> Ful tenderly begynneth she to wepe;
> She rist hire up, and dredfully she quaketh,
> As doth the braunche that Zepherus shaketh,
> And hust were alle in Argon that cite.
> As cold as any frost now waxeth she;
> For pite by the herte hire streyneth so,
> And drede of deth doth hire so moche wo,
> That thryes doun she fyl in swich a were.
> She rist yit up, and stakereth her and there,
> And on hire hondes faste loketh she.
> "Allas! and shal myne hondes blody be?
> I am a mayde, and, as by my nature,
> And bi my semblaunt and by my vesture,
> Myne handes ben nat shapen for a knyf,

As for to reve no man fro his lyf.
What devel have I with the knyf to do?
And shal I have my throte korve a-two?
Thanne shal I blede, allas! and me beshende!
And nedes-cost this thyng moste have an ende;
Or he or I mot nedes lese oure lyf.
Now certes," quod she, "syn I am his wif,
And hath my feyth, yit is it bet for me
For to be ded in wifly honeste
Than ben a traytour lyvynge in my shame.
Be as be may, for ernest or for game,
He shal awake, and ryse, and gon his way,
Out at this goter, or that it be day" —
And wep ful tenderly upon his face,
And in hyre armes gan hym to enbrace,
And hym she roggeth and awaketh softe.
And at a wyndow lep he fro the lofte,
Whan she hath warned hym, and don hym bote.

(F 2678–2710)

The passage, whether a success or failure (to my mind, it is admirable), is surely what we can call total narrative. It stands or falls on the author's ability to compel our awareness of the scene and create a sympathetic or empathetic reaction by a selective visualization of the event, by action, by speech (a kind of soliloquy or interior monologue here), and by language. There is no appeal to any handy external code to secure a reaction. To be sure, the tale is a few lines short of conclusion, but there is no reason to think this ending would have been different from the others. It would have been another comment on the faithfulness of women — a sentiment obviously inadequate to support the tale. Hypermnestra stands in an area of imagined experience outside the code of courtly love and outside the dogmas of Christian morality. She is interesting and moving, if at all, as a fragile, isolated, frightened creature trapped in a fearful dilemma. There is perhaps some general, external motivation in her decision "to be ded in wifly honeste." But the reflection is part of the internal drama and serves mainly to show the movement of her thought. The next lines discard

even this, however: "Be as be may, for ernest or for game, /
He shal awake" — so that the decisive action seems finally
to spring from some instinct of devotion below consciousness.

I repeat, the success or failure of the scene is not the issue
here. The issue is the method Chaucer has deliberately
chosen: to present a narrative without reference to the conventions or moralizings ordinarily appealed to. The drama
inherent in the human experience being witnessed and the
skill with which the experience has been realized for our
witnessing are his sole counters in the game.

To move now to the opening lines of the Prologue is to
see what Chaucer is preparing the ground for. He is about
to tell stories from a past and alien age outside ordinary experience, certainly outside ordinary literary experience. If
the phrase were not so hackneyed and an appeal to it not so
grotesquely anachronistic, one might say he is suing for
the willing suspension of disbelief. Certainly it is belief he
is pleading for.[9] He puts the matter quite explicitly some
lines later, when he is repeating his argument:

> But wherfore that I spak, to yive credence
> To olde stories and doon hem reverence,
> And that men mosten more thyng beleve
> Then men may seen at eye, or elles preve, —
> That shal I seyn, whanne that I see my tyme. . . .
>
> (F 97–101)

In the opening lines, very boldly, he alludes to the common
belief in heaven and hell in spite of the absence of ocular
proof — boldly, because there will certainly be no appeal to
Christian faith in the legends which follow.[10] But belief in
things not seen is a fact in men's lives, and he appeals to it
now to claim a hearing for his narratives:

9. For example, "men shulde leve," "Yeve credence," "yive I feyth and ful
credence": F 10, 20, 31.

10. Cf. G 296–300, where he calls attention, through the God of Love, to the
fact that the women he is being urged to write about were pagans: "And yit
they were hethene, al the pak. . . ."

> But God forbede but men shulde leve
> Wel more thing then men han seen with ye!
> Men shal not wenen every thing a lye
> But yf himself yt seeth, or elles dooth;
> For, God wot, thing is never the lasse sooth,
> Thogh every wight ne may it nat ysee.
> Bernard the monk ne saugh nat all, pardee!
>
> (F 10–16)

In petitioning for belief in the tales found in old books, Chaucer seems particularly interested in a range of human experience found there somewhat wider than was normally accommodated in courtly literature:

> Than mote we to bokes that we fynde,
> Thurgh whiche that olde thinges ben in mynde,
> And to the doctrine of these olde wyse,
> Yeve credence, in every skylful wise,
> That tellen of these olde appreved stories
> Of holynesse, of regnes, of victories,
> Of love, of hate, of other sondry thynges,
> Of whiche I may not maken rehersynges.
> And yf that olde bokes were aweye,
> Yloren were of remembraunce the keye.
> Wel ought us thanne honouren and beleve
> These bokes, there we han noon other preve.
>
> (F 17–28)

"These olde appreved stories" — note the skillfully loaded participle — "Of holynesse, of regnes, of victories, / Of love, of hate, of other sondry thynges. . . ." It is a challenge, and at the same time a waving of most attractive bait to an audience he wishes to lure onto unfamiliar territory. And they are, I insist, asked to believe, to "yeve credence." The pseudoauthority of the dream will not be invoked for the narratives themselves. Praise of ladies and in some general way of the power of love there will be, but not the familiar French courtly love poem. Later in the Prologue he makes this explicit:

> Ne I not who serveth leef, ne who the flour.
> Wel browken they her service or labour;

> For this thing is al of another tonne,
> Of olde storye, er swich stryf was begonne.
>
> (F 193–196)

And finally, as I have said, he was discarding the moralizing matrix which might ease these stories into acceptance
and transform them into didactic dramas whose substantiality could be denied once the pleasure of their telling had
been enjoyed. These were to be presented as stories of real
events occurring in the past. They were to be accepted as
records of believable human experience, wondrous and perhaps troubling because human and because strange. The
range of this experience and its substantiality and secularity
are insisted upon: "Bernard the monk ne saugh nat all,
pardee!"

But what of the worship of the daisy? There is no gain-
saying the charm of the marguerite passages, and no wish to
gainsay it. One must, however, suspect Chaucer most when
he is being most guileless and simple-seeming. The Prologue, and especially the daisy sequence, we know with the
wisdom of hindsight, was a farewell performance. He
would never use the vision form again; he would never
write "courtly" poetry or treat courtly love seriously again.
The sequence is reminiscent of some of the most delight-
ful moments in the *Parliament of Birds* and might suggest
that he is still preoccupied with the phenomenon of courtly
love, however amused his attention may be. There is some
of that.

But note one thing. The daisy passages skirt dangerously
close to the shoals of parody. We may allow for the ritual
of the flower and the leaf and still find an exaggeration here
that flirts with mockery. He does, in fact, entreat us to consider his case apart from these playful cults. If his plea
avoids the necessity of taking sides, it also denies involvement. Further, the rival cults were related to forms of love
and ultimately to certain values.[11] The narrator's worship

11 See Derek A. Pearsall, "Introduction," *The Floure and the Leafe* . . .
(London, Thomas Nelson and Sons, Ltd., 1962), pp. 22–33.

of the daisy, however, has no such dimensions; it appears to be an end in itself. Unlike the French "Marguerite" poems, there is no evidence of a lady hovering in the background. What is most to the point, the daisy sequence serves to keep the narrator within an area cleanly removed from the experience of courtly love. The sequence uses all the language and postures of courtly love, not for the proper object of love, but for a daisy.[12]

It is possible, it seems to me, to read the praise of the daisy both as a beguiling tribute to a modest, charming flower and as a sly and cheeky mockery of the worshipful lover and the worship of love. The hyperbolic language and postures are typical for devotion to ladies, but comic for devotion to daisies. He is up at dawn to see the flower unfold in the sun: "That blisful sighte softneth al my sorwe" (F 50). He does her reverence, "As she that is of alle floures flour, / Fulfilled of al vertu and honour" (53–54). Here the hackneyed metaphor acquires a comic truth — this really is a flower.[13] He will love it till he dies, he swears he will, he is not lying: "Ther loved no wight hotter in his lyve" (59). And at eve-

---

12. If the passage expresses a devotion to Queen Anne, as has been suggested (see F. N. Robinson, *The Works of Geoffrey Chaucer*, 2nd ed. [Boston, Houghton Mifflin Company, 1957], pp. 839–840), she also is an object removed from the realm of courtly love, and the language is a recognizable rhetoric for praising her, nothing more. That Chaucer is referring to *his* lady, whoever this might be, seems an unlikely reading of the text. Those few lines which might suggest a real woman (i.e., F 94) do not necessarily bear this meaning. The whole weight of Chaucer's talk of love is directed toward the daisy. No real lady ever emerges from behind the flower; if she was there, she was sadly ignored. Nor is Alceste, the figure related to the daisy, his lady. See below, n. 14. Dorothy Bethurum's cry of vexation is understandable but mistaken; it reveals how far beyond the believable toward parody Chaucer has pushed matters: "The daisy is, of course, some woman; not even Wordsworth could find in that miserable little English daisy 'the clernesse and the verray lyght / That in this derke world me wynt and ledeth'." See "Chaucer's Point of View As Narrator in the Love Poems," *PMLA*, 74 (1959), 516.

13. It is repeated at F 185, but omitted in G. Peter Dronke discusses the history of the image, with many examples, in *Medieval Latin and the Rise of European Love Lyric*, 2 vols., 2nd ed. (Oxford, Eng., Clarendon Press, 1968), I, 181–192. (On the range of experience encompassed by Ovid's *Heroides* [and *Amores*], see ibid., I, 163.)

ning he runs to see her go to rest. Alas, he has not sufficient English, rhyme or prose, to praise it properly!

> She is the clernesse and the verray lyght
> That in this derke world me wynt and ledeth.
> The hert in-with my sorwfull brest yow dredeth
> And loveth so sore that ye ben verrayly
> The maistresse of my wit, and nothing I.
> My word, my werk ys knyt so in youre bond
> That, as an harpe obeieth to the hond
> And maketh it soune after his fyngerynge,
> Ryght so mowe ye oute of myn herte bringe
> Swich vois, ryght as yow lyst, to laughe or pleyne.
> Be ye my gide and lady sovereyne!
> As to myn erthly god to yow I calle,
> Bothe in this werk and in my sorwes alle.
>
> (F 84–96)

It is the familiar lexicon of love, with more to come: "gledly desir," fire in the heart, "dredful hert and glad devocioun." He kneels before it (117), he sinks down leaning on his elbow to gaze at it all day (178–183) and rushes home once more when the flower closes so that he can be out in the morning to see it open. But in this last detail, as in one or two others, the daisiness of the daisy emerges through the ritualistic language. We are not far from the technique employed for Pertelote, where the language of gallantry competes frantically with the gallinaceous.

If there were ultimately some transference of this intensity of devotion to a lady or to the cause of Love in some fashion, all might yet be well. But there is none. The daisy worship, to be sure, has a function in the necessary psychology of the literary dream. It is the waking preoccupation which, acting as a tripping mechanism to set the dream in motion, will appear splendidly transformed but still recognizable within the content of the dream. The daisy becomes, of course, the key figure, Alceste, whose "habit grene," gold fret in the hair, and white crown with "flourouns smale" make of her a living, walking daisy. But she is never presented as the object of the kind of personal feeling presumably expressed in the adoration of the daisy before the dream begins. The dreamer's relationship with Alceste is formal. He praises her beauty, but his attitude is not the tribute of an adoring lover. Indeed, since he is represented as not knowing who she is until he is told, there can be no question of anything of the kind. He is grateful for her intercession (F 271–281, 455–474), and he reverences her goodness when he learns who, in fact, she is.[14] Throughout the scene, however, the issue is Chaucer's role as a poet, not his relationship with Alceste or any other lady. What is established between the daisy and Alceste is a pictorial equivalence, not an emotional one.

The daisy unquestionably plays a role in the vision as a whole. It dissolves into Alceste and explains in part her intercession for the poet: "Wel hath she quyt me myn affeccioun, / That I have to hire flour, the dayesye" (523–524). But it is questionable whether these functions demand the kind of language and the intensity of feeling expressed. Since the emotion is not transferred to a more worthy object but remains focused on the daisy, the suspicion of parody remains.

Working against these considerations, however, is the welcome to spring passage which in F comes between the morning and the evening worship of the daisy, immediately preceding the dream (125–177). I can find no mockery in the rejoicing of the birds at winter's end and their survival, in their mating, or in the brief survey of key values in the code of love: Danger, Pity, Mercy, Right, Courtesy.[15] In G,

14. The "my lady" of the refrain in F (255, 262, 269) and the phrase "my lady sovereyne" used by the poet a few lines later (F 275) is either a direct translation of the "ma dame" in his French original (see Robinson, *Chaucer*, note on these lines, p. 843), or more probably the formal "my lady"; she is not his "lady" in the courtly love sense. The G text does not contain this possible ambiguity. Elsewhere in F Alceste is "a quene" (213), "this lady" (248, 341), "his quene" (302). The God of Love calls her "my lady" at 454.

15. In the context of the "natural" world evoked by the daisy itself, it is just possible that these other elements from the natural world, the birds, are in some danger of shedding their conventional character and becoming real birds again. In which case, the conventions of love are set against realities of nature, and their artificiality is threatened with comic exposure. There is some insistence in

the personifications are removed, and the coming-of-summer passage is shifted to the opening moments of the dream proper. The passage then becomes introductory background and prepares appropriately for the entrance of the God of Love and Alceste. This may have been the intended function of the passage in F; if so, it is rather awkwardly placed. If taken seriously, that is conventionally, as part of the pre-dream experience, it reduces the sense of parody lurking about the daisy passages. (The changes in G make parody a stronger possibility, I should say.) We shall have to settle for the smaller portion: The daisy sequence, however much it may invoke the language of love, places Chaucer quite outside any involvement with love. His involvement, like Ferdinand the Bull's, is with flowers. And this artfully contrived separation from love is of some importance in understanding the meaning of the dream itself. The parody, if it be there, merely pushes harder in the same direction.

The dream — Chaucer's last literary vision — is the most paradoxical of all Chaucer's creations. It is more paradoxical than the daring, experimental dream in the *House of Fame*, for that vision, once it sets off in its novel manner in an unexpected direction, follows a consistent course. (Coincidentally, perhaps, in that poem, too, we are invited to consider, though much more briefly, Chaucer the poet.) The paradox here, however, is more extreme. All the trappings are conventional for the love vision and are conjured up with dazzling mastery: the glittering God of Love with his two fiery darts as red as coals and his wings spread angellike; Alceste, the delicate, beautiful, and tenderhearted

---

the passage on their bird nature: e.g., the reference to the fowler (conventional enough in other contexts but not inevitably so here), and especially the lines whose tone is otherwise rather puzzling:

> Yeldyng honour and humble obeysaunces
> To love, and diden hire other observaunces
> That longeth onto love and to nature;
> Construeth that as yow lyst, I do no cure.

(F 149–152)

The illusion does seem at moments to be under attack.

queen, green and gold and white, with her crown "of o perle fyn, oriental"; the charming *balade*; the troop of ladies making their gracious obeisance to the daisy; the easy ordering of the whole company according to rank; the dramatic and sustained silence. Never had Chaucer created with such strokes the milieu of the courtly love poem and the exquisite ambiance peculiar to that literary mode.

But this delicate, sugary creation is allowed to go to waste, like an elegant wedding cake left melting in the hot sun. The substance of the vision is the charge against the poet, the discussion which ensues, and the imposing of penance. It is a literary conversation concerning the work of a particular writer, and it might have been conducted against any background. This setting is perhaps the most appropriate for the specific topic of conversation, but it needed only a sketching in. The unusual magic Chaucer creates in evoking the world of love promises an experience that is never realized. It sustains the fictional figures of the God of Love and Alceste and the fiction of a charge of heresy against love. It also helps sustain the fiction that the tales which follow are comfortably within the courtly love tradition; that, perhaps, is its most potent purpose. The magic of the early moments of the dream is such that it has led readers, including most scholars, to overestimate the subservience of the legends to the code. Agreed, the legends tell of true women and faithless men, but they speak of love not as it is envisioned in the code or in the *Book of the Duchess*, the *Troilus*, and the *Knight's Tale*, or in Froissart and Machaut, but as a force more powerful and more protean in its forms and consequences than Troilus, or Criseyde, or even Diomede had dreamed of. Rape, suicide, abandonment, despair, callous abuse, and cynical seduction are the matter of his legends. The lady's Mercy and Pity and Danger have nothing to do with the world Chaucer is about to unfold. The rose garden has vanished, and the green meadow of the Prologue will win by its illusory art the pardon that he needs to escape over the garden wall from what has threatened to become a prison.

The contrast between the promise and the performance is not ironic. The fact is simply that the vision is largely preoccupied with matters alien to the surface considerations that have preceded it. Having shown how well he could do the old soft shoe number, Chaucer goes on to what here really concerns him, his career as a writer, and the kind of material he wishes to be free to work on. The basic image of the vision is suggestive: he is charged with heresy against love, and he is obliged to do penance. The image suggests feelings of guilt: he has to a degree violated the code, he wishes to be even more free of its limitations, and he will be. And the image suggests feelings of restriction: to write within the code is punishment. This is to be heavy-handed about a very light matter indeed, but if the basic images have any deeper significance than the merely playful, this is the direction in which it seems to me they point.

The literary discussion in the vision goes rather more directly toward much the same issue: what a writer may or should write about. Beneath the metaphor of heresy is a serious literary question. We know nothing about specific censorship or a royal directive or a queen's request. Even if we did, the conversation would still be worth analyzing for it shows us Chaucer's mind at work on a matter of great concern to him as an artist. The charge is that he has spoken against Love (322–331) and that he has slandered women (332–334). The form his penance takes is to write about true women and thus presumably to support Love (435–441, 481–491). The defense Alceste advances for the poet is, as Robert Payne has observed, really no defense at all.[16] It is all a glorious wriggling out from under. A god should be merciful. Perhaps Chaucer has been slandered; perhaps, since he is rather simpleminded ("nyce": 362), he didn't realize what he was doing or he was simply obeying someone's command; perhaps he repents now. After all, he was only translating what older clerks had written, which is not the same as writing it himself out of malice. Rather

16. Robert Payne, *The Key of Remembrance: A Study of Chaucer's Poetics* (New Haven, Connecticut, Yale University Press, 1963), p. 103.

more pertinent is her observation that in many of his poems he has served the God of Love and that he also has translated works of "holynesse." Chaucer's own defense is still more to the point: he is not guilty. Whatever his author meant (that is, the man whose work Chaucer was translating), in *Troilus and Criseyde* and the *Romance of the Rose* his intention was to further "trouthe" in love and to warn against falseness. But his rational observation is cut short in a manner typical of the arbitrariness and irrationality of love:

> Lat be thyn arguynge,
> For Love ne wol nat countrepleted be
> In ryght ne wrong; and lerne that at me!
>
> (475–477)

Perhaps we can take this as a self-contained if playful argument and let it go at that. But the issue that runs through the argument and that appeared earlier, before the dream began, is the issue of the writer's material and the role of the writer in relation to his matter. Robert Payne is surely correct when he observes that the Prologue is preoccupied with literary matters, that it is what he calls something close to a treatise on the art of poetry.[17] I do not agree, however, that the issue is the quality of Chaucer's artistry.[18] That is not a subject he can properly write about, and he dismisses that question with a joke as always: "Al be hit that he kan nat wel endite . . ." (414). I do agree with Payne that Chaucer is discussing the matter which the artist uses, but I do not think that the question is the relation of reading or tradition to experience. Or, if so, it is only indirectly or incidentally. The question is rather the proper or allowable matter which a writer may use in his composition, the source materials he may work with. In practical terms, this becomes the question of what a writer may write about, "may" meaning what he finds important as a subject for imaginative treatment and what he can persuade

17. *Ibid.*, pp. 56, 63–66, 91–111.
18. *Ibid.*, pp. 99, 101.

his audience to accept as an important and allowable subject for their attention.[19] Literary history is in part a record

19. We know very little about Chaucer's relationship with his audience and about the composition of that audience. Ruth Crosby worked out some of the influences of oral presentation on his poetry in two articles, "Oral Delivery in the Middle Ages," *Speculum*, 11 (1936), 88–110, and "Chaucer and the Custom of Oral Delivery," *Speculum*, 13 (1938), 413–432. So did Bertrand Bronson in "Chaucer's Art in Relation to His Audience," in *Five Studies in Literature*, University of California Publications in English, Vol. 8, No. 1 (Berkeley, University of California Press, 1940), pp. 1–53. A strong sense of Chaucer's sensitivity to his audience emerges from the studies, but we learn very little about the nature of his audience, except for Bronson's praise of its sophistication (pp. 52–53). There are some revealing moments in his poetry, however, in which we catch Chaucer being very much concerned about his audience's reaction and working adeptly to win their acceptance or at the very least to ward off their displeasure. *Troilus*, based on an Italian original (not something from the familiar and accepted French literary culture) and studying with unusual intensity and detail a courtly love affair without the usual accompaniment of battle and adventure, apparently struck Chaucer as sufficiently unfamiliar fare to make advisable meeting the objections he anticipated; hence his comments to his audience at the beginning of Book II, lines 22–49. For all his lightness of tone, he is clearly concerned about the reaction of the women in his audience to his story of Criseyde's unfaithfulness when the narrative is ended (V, 1772–1785). Pushing into unknown waters in the *Canterbury Tales*, he prepares his audience more carefully for the novel kinds of narrative and especially for the crude action and crude language of some of the tales to come in his apology at the end of the *General Prologue*, A 725–746. When the first of these ungenteel narratives, the *Miller's Tale*, is about to begin, he prepares his audience again, making it quite clear what kind of story this and the *Reeve's Tale* following will be, repeating his apology and warding off any objection by suggesting to his audience that they can choose another tale instead (A 3167–3186). There is no mistaking how intently and how ingeniously Chaucer labors here to lead his audience into his material and to control their reaction. When the *Miller's Tale* is finished, he is very careful to say that the tale amused most of the pilgrims (several of whom were "gentils") and grieved none but Oswald the Reeve, and that was of course for purely personal reasons. Thereafter he feels no need to intervene. All of this suggests that, when Chaucer did something new, he felt obliged to persuade his audience to move with him. It also suggests a somewhat conservative audience or a Chaucer not completely confident that he can present anything he wishes to his audience, or both. Alfred David has some interesting comments on this question in "The Man of Law vs. Chaucer: A Case in Poetics," *PMLA*, 82 (1967), 217–225. Boccaccio's defense, at the opening of Book IV of *Il Decamerone*, of the kind of tales he was telling, and his "apology" in his Epilogue, both directed especially at hostile comments from the ladies in his audience, are a tempting parallel. See Aldo D. Scaglione, *Nature and Love in the Later Middle Ages* (Berkeley and Los Angeles, University of California Press, 1963), pp. 102–113,

of the struggle with their audiences which writers must periodically engage in to get a hearing for unfamiliar or unwelcome material. In our time it has been the battle by twentieth-century writers to include sexual experience as a legitimate subject for treatment, but the long struggle from roughly the 1740's to the 1840's to secure a hearing for poetry focusing on personal, private emotion is equally dramatic.

For Chaucer (and for late medieval writers in general), the evidence suggests that this question took a special form. The poet is not so much an "inventor," a spontaneous creator, as he is a transmitter and reworker of already existing materials. He provides "the key of remembrance," as Robert Payne has reminded us, and the phrase is Chaucer's in this Prologue. The attitudes expressed and the language used in the Prologue are revealing on this score and lead to the heart of the issue. "Translating" is an important activity of a medieval writer; in a sense, it *is* the activity of the writer. The distinction between Chaucer's translation of the *Roman de la rose* and his creation, from Boccaccio's *Il Filostrato*, of the *Troilus* is, we should notice, blurred. The charge is that Chaucer has hindered Love's servants with his "translacioun":

> For in pleyn text, withouten nede of glose,
> Thou hast translated the Romaunce of the Rose,
> That is an heresye ayeins my lawe,
> And makest wise folk fro me withdrawe;
> And of Creseyde thou hast seyd as the lyste,
> That maketh men to wommen lasse triste. . . .
>
> (328–333)

There is perhaps a slight distinction in the language used about the two works here, but Chaucer's responsibility is the same for both. Alceste's language, however, suggests no distinction between the two:

198–201. But Italian culture is too distant in space and tradition to permit us to draw any hard conclusions.

And eke, peraunter, for this man ys nyce,
He myghte doon yt, gessyng no malice,
But for he useth thynges for to make;
Hym rekketh noght of what matere he take.
Or him was boden maken thilke tweye
Of som persone, and durste yt nat withseye;
Or him repenteth outrely of this.
He ne hath nat doon so grevously amys,
To translaten that olde clerkes writen,
As thogh that he of malice wolde enditen
Despit of love, and had himself yt wroght.

(362–372)

Here, both works appear to be things "made," and also things "translated." A distinction between these two works (*Troilus* and the *Romance*) and things he himself might have "wroght" is suggested, but it is not clear what things "wroght" would be. Entirely original works? Such works as the *House of Fame*, perhaps? A few lines later, however, Alceste makes no distinction between this work and a number of others, including Chaucer's reworking of Boccaccio's *Il Teseide*: "He made the book that hight the Hous of Fame," and also the *Book of the Duchess*, the *Parliament of Birds*, "And al the love of Palamon and Arcite," and "many an ympne . . . / That highten balades, roundels, virelayes" (417–423). In matters of holiness "He hath in prose translated Boece, / And maad the lyf also of Seynt Cecile." The distinction implied by the language here is almost meaningless. The Life of St. Cecilia, at least as we have it in the *Second Nun's Tale*, is a poetic translation.[20] It is, to be sure, a somewhat free, poetic translation, as opposed to the more literal prose translation of Boethius, but any hope that this fact will fully account for the verb "maad" is somewhat dashed when we note that elsewhere Chaucer himself (or, rather, the Second Nun) calls it a "translacioun."[21] And in

20. For Chaucer's sources see G. H. Gerould, "The Second Nun's Prologue and Tale," in *Sources and Analogues of Chaucer's Canterbury Tales*, ed. W. F. Bryan and Germaine Dempster (New York, The Humanities Press, 1958), pp. 664–684.

21. *Canterbury Tales*, G 24–25; see also 79–83.

the next line of the Prologue Alceste says, "He made also, goon ys a gret while, / Origenes upon the Maudeleyne," a lost work which almost certainly was a translation.[22] Finally, in the G version (344) Alceste says, "he wrot the Rose and ek Crisseyde."

This blurring of distinctions which a nineteenth-century writer, say, would certainly maintain implies a somewhat different attitude toward the literary process from our attitude today. It does not necessarily imply that Chaucer was not aware of any difference between translating the *Roman de la rose* and transforming *Il Filostrato* into *Troilus and Criseyde*. But it does imply that in some way he thought of the two activities as similar, even identical. One important similarity, I suggest, is that both involved transmission of already existing "matter" from another language, with such additions and subtractions as might seem necessary.

This in turn suggests the importance of the "matter" for the medieval writer, and an attitude toward it. It consists, roughly speaking, of the written materials — literature, history, moral writings, and so forth, inherited from the past, both distant and recent. The literary artist is the transmitter of this heritage. Or, to put it less passively, this heritage is a principal source of his own art and his own inspiration. He selects what he will write about, not from "experience" or "imagination," but from this accumulated body of tradition. The act of "creating" is not primarily the creating of the material. Chaucer, in his greatest poetry, has clearly not set out to "invent" in this sense. The creative activity, or at least an important part of it, is of another kind. The artist must *find* his material, somewhere, somehow. The act of finding material involves not merely the poet's learning or the act of discovery through reading but the act of selecting, the act of choice. What this becomes, finally, is an act of intense imaginative response. It is, in its own way, much like "inspiration." In a long addition to G (267–

22. Robinson, *Chaucer*, p. 845, note on 417ff. See also John P. McCall, "Chaucer and the Pseudo Origen *De Maria Magdalena*: A Preliminary Study," *Speculum*, 46 (1971), 491–509.

312), the God of Love very pointedly discusses this problem of choice:

> Was there no good matere in thy mynde,
> Ne in alle thy bokes ne coudest thow nat fynde
> Som story of wemen that were goode and trewe?
>
> (G 270–272)

He proceeds to enumerate some of these sources, noting particularly the Roman and Greek authors in his library of sixty books, and concludes by emphasizing the problem of choice once more:

> But yit, I seye, what eyleth the to wryte
> The draf of storyes, and forgete the corn?
>
> (G 311–312)

In F, Alceste's charge of simple-sooth foolishness implies the same problem, though more obscurely: "Hym rekketh noght of what matere he take" (365). *Take* is the operative word here.[23]

The matter an artist takes is an important part of the creative process. It still is, of course. But for a medieval writer intent on "creating" a work of some value, more frequently than for writers of later generations, the choice would be from traditional matter, "olde bokes." So talk about the sources to be used involves also the themes and

---

23. In the F Prologue the God of Love touches on the problem of the writer's choice just before the vision ends:

> Thise other ladies sittynge here arowe
> Ben in thy balade, yf thou kanst hem knowe,
> And in thy bookes alle thou shalt hem fynde.
> Have hem now in thy legende al in mynde;
> I mene of hem that ben in thy knowynge.
> For here ben twenty thousand moo sittynge
> Than thou knowest, goode wommen alle,
> And trewe of love, for oght that may byfalle.
> Make the metres of hem as the lest —   (F 554–562)

This passage is omitted in G, and I suspect that the lengthy passage added in G, the one I have been discussing, replaces it and expands upon it. The issue is also present by implication from the beginning of the Prologue in F as well as G in the introductory discussion of "olde bokes."

the areas of human experience which a writer will be treating and which he will be asking his audience to accept as worthy of their attention. It is also, as I have said, a question of what his imagination responds to most intensely. This is the issue, I believe, in the heresy scene.

The weight of this scene, the sheer amount of time spent reviewing what Chaucer has written and discussing what he ought to write (for *ought*, read what he is *planning* to write), demands such an interpretation. Ordinarily Chaucer is dramatically self-effacing. Here, even though he makes himself the butt of a joke, I cannot believe he thrusts himself forward merely to prance about comically in the limelight. He is using himself in this way in order to announce what he is going to do in the *Legend* and to justify it. There would be no need to spend all the time he does on the announcement if the legends were, in fact, what he makes them appear to be, merely orthodox items in the literature of courtly love. The G addition suggests several characteristics in his material which might disturb his audience. One is the violence of the tales (see F 22–24):

> They chose to be ded in sondry wyse,
> And deiden, as the story wol devyse;
> And some were brend, and some were cut the hals,
> And some dreynt, for they wolden not be fals.
>
> (G 290–293)

Another is their purely pagan character; they operate outside the familiar morality of both Christianity and courtly love:

> And this thing was nat kept for holynesse,
> But al for verray vertu and clennesse,
> And for men schulde sette on hem no lak;
> And yit they were hethene, al the pak. . . .
>
> (G 296–299)

The charge of heresy and the imposition of penance work then to this purpose: They suggest impatience with the more orthodox poetry of courtly love, and a "guilty" intention to abandon this for other kinds of writing (an abandonment already foreshadowed in the *Troilus*). The device enables him to suggest some of his problems as an artist, primarily the problem of "creative" choice. It lends an illusion of orthodoxy to the new kind of story he is introducing, which is written at the command of the God of Love and his queen as an act of penance. Unless he behaves too outrageously in the stories that follow, he can, under cover of the fiction he has contrived, do almost anything he wishes. The selection of the theme of "faithful women" permits him to use freely material in Ovid and other writers, gives him the frame he needs as a vehicle for the "publication" of a series of tales, and leaves him with a toehold on the old orthodoxy of courtly love. He apparently has achieved the maximum maneuverability he felt he could win for himself, granted the character and tastes of his audience and the role he had played as a writer heretofore. All in all, it seems a successful, even a brilliant device, but we must see it for what it is and not be deluded by it.

We should be careful, also, not to minimize the importance of the strategic victory which Chaucer wins by this means. It is a quiet declaration of independence on an issue of central importance in the creative activity of a medieval writer. The material Chaucer selects for the legends which follow is essentially alien to the code of courtly love. By ignoring its prescriptions and treating love as a varied human experience rather than a ritualized process (however psychologically relevant this may be), the tales are an oblique challenge to the code. Once freed, Chaucer could work with material yet more alien, material even richer in possibilities for an artist of his widely ranging interests and varied talents: secular legend, folk tale, beast fable, fabliau. The *Legend* does reveal the development of several techniques of his art, as we shall see. But if we consider for the moment only the kind of material used, we can see that to step from the *Troilus* to the *Legend* to the *Canterbury Tales* is easier than to step from the *Troilus* directly to the *Canterbury Tales*. A struggle for freedom of choice in the materials of his art is waged and, under the guise of capitulation, won in the Prologue. Charm is used here, as it has been used on many occasions, in the interests of seduction and conquest. And Chaucer's battle sign has been not a dragon or a lion or even a rose, but the ordinary daisy. Some centuries later Walt Whitman went him one better and used grass for much the same purpose. The analogy, I suggest, is worth reflecting on. In its simplicity and "naturalness," in its commonplace quality, the daisy is not unlike Whitman's leaves of grass. It serves to break through not to a democratic poetry, but to a poetry more of the world and less of the garden, to a realm of experience beyond the patterned and polite, the limited and predictable emotions and movements of courtly love. Given this significance, the daisy is a proper object for Chaucer's passion, the artist's passion for his freshest vision.

[III] Cleopatra

Chaucer began his series of legends with an odd choice and what seems on several counts an unfortunate choice. *Cleopatra*, the shortest of the narratives, is one of the least successful, in some part because of its extreme brevity. The hero and heroine are whisked on and off the stage and the curtain is lowered almost before we have settled in our seats. We troop out feeling that a great opportunity has been bungled and that Chaucer has been untrue to his material. History, drama, and romance have all been cheated. What went wrong?

One misfortune he is not responsible for: Shakespeare also chose Cleopatra. Shakespeare's seductive creation glides wantonly between Chaucer's page and our reading of it, and, glancing at her, we can see only that Chaucer has denied her charms and made a failure of what we know can be a triumph. We must invoke a historical perspective if we are to see what Chaucer actually did in his first narrative, and we must begin by accepting the simple fact that Shakespeare's Cleopatra is not there, either for Chaucer's audience or for Chaucer himself. What we are in fact looking at is her modest debut.

This is the first serious treatment of Cleopatra in the English language. There may be earlier references to her, but I know of none and they must be few indeed. She is not a member of the repertoire of ladies commonly referred to in the courtly literature of France. Dante, Petrarch, and Boccaccio knew her, and perhaps to them must go the honor of introducing the serpent of old Nile to modern Western literature.[1] Chaucer may first have noticed her in the *Inferno*, where, in the second circle, whirling among the lustful, she can be seen for a second between Semiramis and Helen of Troy: "poi è Cleopatras lussuriosa" (v, 63). This tantalizing glimpse apparently fascinated him, for almost immediately he borrowed her, along with Semiramis and Helen, from this section of the *Inferno* and incorporated them into his pantheon of lovers painted on the walls of Venus' temple in the *Parliament of Birds* (291). Cleopatra is unaccompanied by Antony, as in Dante's line, so presumably Chaucer did not yet know her story, but she obviously interested him.

Where Chaucer found her love story or, more to the point, what source or sources he used for his telling are matters of debate. The candidates are Plutarch, Florus' *Epitome Rerum Romanorum*, Orosius, Boccaccio's *De Casibus Virorum Illustrium* and *De Claris Mulieribus*, and Vincent de Beauvais' *Speculum Historiale*.[2] This uncertainty is frustrating.

1. John Livingston Lowes, in "Is Chaucer's Legend of Good Women a Travesty?" *JEGP*, 8 (1909), 513–569, attempted to determine the attitude of Chaucer and his contemporaries toward the heroines of the *Legend*. He could find, however, very few references to Cleopatra. Boccaccio knew her; in addition to the accounts in *De Casibus Virorum Illustrium* and *De Claris Mulieribus*, he refers to her in *La Fiammetta* (chap. viii) and in the *Amorosa Visione* (chap. x). She appears among the ladies in Petrarch's *Trionfo d'Amore* (I, 89–91), and his *Trionfo della Fama* (I, 106): Lowes, "Is Chaucer's Legend a Travesty?" pp. 558–564.

2. For Plutarch, see Walter W. Skeat, *The Complete Works of Geoffrey Chaucer* (Oxford, Eng., Clarendon Press, 1894), III, xxxvii, 310–314; for Florus, see *ibid.*, pp. xxxvii, 312–314, and M. Bech, "Quellen und Plan der 'Legende of Goode Women' und ihr Verhältniss zur 'Confessio Amantis,' " *Anglia*, 5 (1882), 314–318; for Orosius, *Historiarum libri septem adversus paganos*, VII, 19, see P. C. Ghosh, "Cleopatra's Death in Chaucer's 'Legende of Gode Women,' " *MLR*, 26 (1931), 332–336; for Boccaccio, see Skeat, *Oxford Chaucer*, III, xxxvii, and Edgar F. Shannon, *Chaucer and the Roman Poets* (Cambridge, Mass., Harvard University Press, 1929), pp. 179–190; for Vincent de Beauvais, see Ghosh, "Cleopatra's Death"; W. K. Wimsatt, "Vincent of Beauvais and Chaucer's Cleopatra and Croesus," *Speculum*, 12 (1937), 375–381; Pauline Aiken, "Chaucer's Legend of Cleopatra and the Speculum Historiale," *Speculum*, 13 (1938), 232–236; and Ernest Schanzer, "*Antony and Cleopatra* and *The Legend of Good Women*," *N&Q*, new ser. 7, 205 (1960), 335–336. The strongest candidate at the moment is Vincent de Beauvais. For the relevant passage, see *Speculum Historiale* (Venice, 1591), VI, liii.

Not knowing precisely what materials he used, we cannot determine their effect on the narrative he created. Boccaccio's accounts in *De Casibus* and *De Claris* are not flattering to Cleopatra; if Chaucer used these, he had to cut them so extensively that only the shreds of a narrative remained. If he used Vincent de Beauvais, then he worked with more neutral material,[3] but the *Speculum Historiale* provided not much more than a scenario (including, however, the "purpre sayl" — "veloque purpureo"). In either event, he had the sketchiest of narratives to work with, and, one would have thought, not the most promising of ladies with which to begin his book of legends.

Considering these difficulties, one might be tempted to take literally the God of Love's injunction at the close of the Prologue — "At Cleopatre I wol that thou begynne" (566) — and assume that Chaucer was acting under orders, obeying, perhaps, a royal command. But the speculation raises its own difficulties. If Cleopatra was virtually unknown, how did Anne, or Richard, or the Earl of X know of her?[4] Since the *Parliament of Birds* reveals that Chaucer had already made her acquaintance, it makes better sense and creates fewer problems to assume that the God of Love's command is a device for introducing someone who had caught Chaucer's eye, his excuse for putting this unknown in a starring role. Instead of carping over what he failed to do, we should give Chaucer credit for sensing the romantic possibilities of her story and for launching her on her English career.[5]

3. Not completely neutral; for example, "Lasciuus Antonius correptus amore Cleopatrae Ægypti Reginae"; and "Reginae vero ad pedes Augusti prouoluta tentauit oculos eius, sed spreta ab eo disparuit."

4. J. S. P. Tatlock suggested a diplomatic reason for the choice. Cleopatra is the only queen among the martyrs and the only woman except Thisbe (the second legend) whose lover is quite blameless toward her: "Chaucer may have felt a lack of delicacy in celebrating his own enamoured queen in the *Prologue*, and then immediately recounting the tales of other queens and women basely betrayed by their lovers." *The Development and Chronology of Chaucer's Works*, Chaucer Soc., 2nd ser., No. 37 (London, K. Paul, Trench, Trübner & Co., Ltd., 1907), p. 113n. But the point of view established in the Prologue calls for faithless men. And why *this* queen, the unknown Cleopatra?

5. His treatment here did establish her. We begin to see references to

He also glimpsed the essential themes: the opposition of Rome and Egypt, war, exoticism, and the world well lost for love:

> But love hadde brought this man in swich a rage,
> And hym so narwe bounden in his las,
> Al for the love of Cleopataras,
> That al the world he sette at no value.
> Hym thoughte there nas nothyng to hym so due
> As Cleopatras for to love and serve;
> Hym roughte nat in armes for to sterve
> In the defence of hyre and of hire ryght.
>
> (599–606)

Chaucer makes, I would say, a halfhearted attempt to bring the two elements, war and exoticism, within the familiar forms of chivalry and love. But the fit is imperfect and the will to mold his matter in this fashion wavers. Antony is *almost* a chivalric figure. He is "a ful worthy gentil wer-reyour" (597) who loves with a proper intensity, as the passage just quoted reveals; his credentials are impeccable:

> This noble queene ek lovede so this knyght,
> Thourgh his desert, and for his chyvalrye;
> As certeynly, but if that bokes lye,
> He was, of persone and of gentillesse,
> And of discrecioun and hardynesse,
> Worthi to any wyght that liven may. . . .
>
> (607–612)

This passage also places Cleopatra within the code, for she

Cleopatra immediately thereafter. Gower places her among the company of lovers in the final book of the *Confessio Amantis* (VIII, 2571–2577), and she is a symbol of faith and constancy in two poems by Lydgate: "The Floure of Curtesye" (194–195) and "A Ballade of Her That Hath All Virtues" (19), in *The Minor Poems of John Lydgate*, ed. Henry Noble MacCracken, EETS, OS 192 (London, Oxford University Press, 1934, reprinted 1961), II, 416, 380. Translating *De Casibus*, Lydgate omits the story ("The pitous deth and the hatful caas / Of gret Antonye and Cleopatras," VI, 3618–3619) since Chaucer has told it already and it would be presumptuous to redo what he has done. Lydgate does say enough, however, to reflect the unflattering impression given in Boccaccio: *The Fall of Princes*, ed. Henry Bergen, EETS, ES 121 (London, Oxford University Press, 1924, reprinted 1967).

is shown loving Antony for the right reasons. The next
lines face her directly:

> And she was fayr as is the rose in May.
> And, for to make shortly is the beste,
> She wax his wif, and hadde hym as hire leste.
>
> (613–615)

The flat formula of the first line, however, and the brevity
of the treatment amount to no more than a perfunctory bow
to the conventions. She will receive more attention later,
when she will emerge as innocent, loving, and faithful unto
death.

Chaucer falsified his materials to achieve this impression,
radically if his source was Boccaccio, slightly if it was Vincent de Beauvais. The narrative is handled so that Cleopatra has no responsibility for Antony's abandoning his
wife (see 592–594, below) and no responsibility for his flight
at Actium:

> Tyl at the laste, as every thyng hath ende,
> Antony is schent, and put hym to the flyghte,
> And al his folk to-go, that best go myghte.
>   Fleth ek the queen, with al hire purpre sayl,
> For strokes, whiche that wente as thikke as hayl;
> No wonder was she myghte it nat endure.
>
> (651–656)

She seems equally free of the charge of faithlessness to
Antony after his death: "His wif, that coude of Cesar have
no grace, / To Egipt is fled for drede and for destresse"
(663–664). She seems, indeed, a gentle, timorous creature,
properly passive and colorless.

But there was only so much that Chaucer could do, or was
willing to do, with his material to transform it into the
popular blend of love and chivalry. History is perhaps too
intractable, and Chaucer's eagerness to move on beyond
completely familiar actions and emotions is too strong for
convention finally to triumph. Antony, let us note, is not
the ideal courtly lover:

> Rebel unto the toun of Rome is he.
> And over al this, the suster of Cesar,
> He lafte hire falsly, or that she was war,
> And wolde algates han another wyf;
> For which he tok with Rome and Cesar stryf.
>
> (591–595)

And he is defeated and dies in despair.

In the two "big" scenes, the battle and Cleopatra's death, however, we can see most clearly the unsolved problems of the poem. The battle scene is presumably the opportunity to dramatize the chivalric dimensions of Antony and his world. Actium is, of course, history, but the treatment is all Chaucer's, not that of any source. This one famous passage in the poem, which encompasses the most vividly imagined moment, is not at all chivalric. It is not that this naval battle lacks the customary associations of knightly combat. The threat of invasion by the French in the autumn of 1386 and the English victory in the spring of 1387 over a fleet of foreign vessels commanded by the Flemish admiral Sir John de Bucq may, as William Schofield has suggested, have stirred the English imagination and given an added heroic dimension to the battle at sea.[6] It is rather that Chaucer, in his immensely effective handling of the battle, chooses to ignore Antony throughout. Indeed, it seems to be presented from the point of view of the ordinary fighting seaman, not the chivalrous knight and certainly not Antony:

> Up goth the trompe, and for to shoute and shete,
> And peynen hem to sette on with the sunne.
> With grysely soun out goth the grete gonne,
> And heterly they hurtelen al atones,
> And from the top doun come the grete stones.

6. William Henry Schofield, "The Sea-Battle in Chaucer's 'Legend of Cleopatra,'" *Anniversary Papers by Colleagues and Pupils of George Lyman Kittredge* (Boston, Ginn and Company, 1913), pp. 139–152, esp. 140. Schofield even suggests that the contemporary interest in naval affairs in England may account for Chaucer's including Cleopatra, since it "gave him an opportunity to describe one of the decisive sea-battles of the world . . ." (p. 152). There seems no need to go this far.

In goth the grapenel, so ful of crokes;
Among the ropes renne the sherynge-hokes.
In with the polax preseth he and he;
Byhynde the mast begynnyth he to fle,
And out ageyn, and dryveth hym overbord;
He styngeth hym upon his speres ord;
He rent the seyl with hokes lyke a sithe;
He bryngeth the cuppe, and biddeth hem be blythe;
He poureth pesen upon the haches slidere;
With pottes ful of lyme they gon togidere;
And thus the longe day in fyght they spende. . . .

(635–650)

The sea battle in the *Alliterative Morte Arthure* is evidence
that such scenes could be handled to retain the heroic strain
and focus on a central figure (Arthur).[7] There is no reason
to think Chaucer could not have done the same if he had
wished. Instead, he writes a passage in which detail and
diction both violate high style. It strives to be "history"[8]
rather than romance. At no moment do the values of chivalry emerge; there is no sense that they control the scene.

Though Antony fails to dominate the battle scene, the
first two-thirds of this rather masculine narrative are about
him. Cleopatra emerges in the final third, and the death
scene focuses on her exclusively. It is the occasion in the
poem where love must have its say. It is, however, a rather
feeble say that is not a complaint but a reaffirmation of her
faithfulness. It has one evocative romantic passage:

nevere wakynge, in the day or nyght,
Ye nere out of myn hertes remembraunce,
For wel or wo, for carole or for daunce. . . .

(685–687)

This is the most "courtly" moment of her speech and in the

---

7. *Alliterative Morte Arthure*, ed. Edmund Brock, EETS, OS 8 (London, 1871), lines 3598–3705. See also Schofield, "The Sea-Battle," p. 144n3.

8. See Schofield's quotations from Froissart and others and his conclusion that the "methods of naval warfare that he [Chaucer] depicts correspond in the main to those actually used by mariners of his own land when he wrote his poem. . ." ("The Sea-Battle," pp. 142–151).

scene. There is no review of their wooing, none of the language or gestures of courtly love; the talk is of her "wyfhod" and her "covenant." Chaucer's sources gave him nothing for this speech, and he seems to have been unwilling to invent within familiar terms and unable to invent outside them.

The exotic scenes before and after the speech are more effective.

> [She] made hire subtyl werkmen make a shryne
> Of alle the rubyes and the stones fyne
> In al Egypte, that she coude espie,
> And putte ful the shryne of spicerye,
> And let the cors enbaume, and forth she fette
> This dede cors, and in the shryne it shette.
> And next the shryne a pit thanne doth she grave,
> And alle the serpentes that she myghte have,
> She putte hem in that grave. . . .
>
> (672–680)

And her death —

> And with that word, naked, with ful good herte,
> Among the serpents in the pit she sterte,
> And there she ches to have hire buryinge.
> Anon the nadderes gonne hire for to stynge,
> And she hire deth receyveth with good cheere. . . .
>
> (696–700)

Both tomb and death are acts of devotion. But their appeal is their exoticism, their suggestion of opulence and passion, and the devotion envisioned here seems hardly a mode of courtly love.

The poem is a failure, finally, because it lacks imaginative unity. Possibilities in the material, though apparently sensed, are not realized. The emotional situation of Cleopatra is undeveloped and lacks intensity. The same is true of the treatment of Antony. The battle scene is, by contrast, full of power and exuberance; it is highly masculine poetry, using rhetoric to rush forward, not to tarry. Its crowded, almost "impressionistic" use of detail (a narrative development of the catalogue, I would suggest) is even more successful than his use of the same method in the tournament scene of the *Knight's Tale*.[9] This impressive technical achievement, in its sense of rapid movement and its skillful selection of relevant moments of action, anticipates such triumphs as the chase in the *Nun's Priest's Tale* and the chaotic melee in the *Reeve's Tale*. The passage works to no purpose here, however. At most, it might have been intended to heighten the pathos of the gentle queen, caught in a brutal, masculine world of war and cruelty. The effect is never achieved, if it was intended, and it seems significant that Chaucer's imagination soared most successfully here, when it was most distant from the world of the walled garden. The poem lacks an ethic to bind it together: the courtly ethic is only feebly and intermittently gestured at, and no substitute replaces it. Alternately, it lacks a strong central emotion to make it coalesce. It remains a heap of fragments. But the rejection of courtly love was necessary for Chaucer's continued development, and it is better for the poem to fail in this way than to have succeeded routinely in the old manner.

If it fails also in some part because of its brevity, that, too, is a virtue. This is not said out of the conviction that, if a poem is a failure, the shorter the better. Brevity was a technique Chaucer had set about mastering here. We can see him beginning the mastery, for example, in Antony's death:

> And whan that Antony saw that aventure,
> "Allas," quod he, "the day that I was born!
> My worshipe in this day thus have I lorn."
> And for dispeyr out of his wit he sterte,
> And rof hymself anon thourghout the herte,
> Or that he ferther wente out of the place.
>
> (658–662)

No long speech, no unconscionable time a-dying. One

---

9. The two scenes are linked by Chaucer's use of alliteration in both, a practice unusual for him, another evidence of his experimentalism.

might argue that the poem might have been more effective if this scene, and others, had not been so brief. Brevity is responsible for the flat, and so almost comic, last line! But the willingness to be brief, the concentration on the essential actions, "th' effect," difficult and costly lesson though it might be, would ultimately serve Chaucer well. The poem deserves some commendation as an exercise somewhat ineptly performed but conscientiously carried through to honest completion.

[IV]   Thisbe

Choice, which involves the artist's freedom to choose the material he finds significant and involves also the nature of that material, is one of the larger issues behind the creation of the *Legend*. It was unfortunate that Chaucer chose to begin the series with Cleopatra, but his second selection, the tale of Pyramus and Thisbe, is, consequently, all the more miraculous. As though he were aware of every mistake he had made with the first legend and had profited by the experience, Chaucer turned in the second legend to material perfect for his purpose, Ovid's telling of the Thisbe story in the *Metamorphoses*.[1] Where the Cleopatra ma-

1. Ovid, *Metamorphoses*, iv, 55–166. See M. Bech, "Quellen und Plan der 'Legende of Goode Women' und ihr Verhältniss zur 'Confessio Amantis,' " *Anglia*, 5 (1882), 318–320; Walter W. Skeat, *The Complete Works of Geoffrey Chaucer* (Oxford, Eng., 1894), III, xxxviii, 314–317; Edgar F. Shannon, *Chaucer and the Roman Poets* (Cambridge, Mass., Harvard University Press, 1929), pp. 190–196. The only "source problem" is one raised by Sanford Brown Meech, "Chaucer and the *Ovide Moralisé*: A Further Study," *PMLA*, 46 (1931), 203n, namely, the question of where Chaucer learned that the city of Semiramis ("Semiramis urbem," 58) was Babylon. It was not so identified in the *Metamorphoses* nor in Gower's telling of the story (*Confessio Amantis*, III, 1332). Meech points out that it is identified as Babylon in the *Ovide moralisé*, IV, 229, and suggests Chaucer might have learned it there, or, since Chaucer shows no signs of knowing the version in the *Ovide*, from Lactantius' famous commentary on the *Metamorphoses* or from a medieval gloss. But possibly a mystery is being manufactured needlessly. In line 99 of Ovid's story, Thisbe is referred to as "Babylonian Thisbe" ("Babylonia Thisbe"), and the connection would not be difficult to make. Also, in Boccaccio's *De Claris Mulieribus*, chap. xii, the Thisbe story is headed "De Thysbe Babylonia Virgine," and Babylon is mentioned twice in the opening lines. Semiramis is identified with Babylon in an allusion in "Le Lay Amoureux" by Machaut: "De Babiloine la roine / Semiramis": *Oeuvres de Guillaume de Machaut*, 3 vols., ed. Ernest

terial created difficulties, Ovid's narrative eased the way by providing a narrative of proper length and congenial theme brilliantly treated. Choosing it was an inspiration;[2] translating and reworking it may well have been an education. What Ovid had to teach him was, above all, the virtue of a straightforward narrative uncluttered by irrelevancies or elaborations. The tale itself has a straight story line, which Chaucer faithfully preserves, and the narrative is of a proper magnitude. Treatment is full enough, so that incident, scene, emotion, and character of a simple kind are adequately developed. Chaucer scarcely tampers with this. There are no uncalled-for expansions, no fatal excisions.[3] Chaucer seems to have realized that the length and the density of the treatment were just right for the material. He demonstrates a restraint remarkable for a medieval poet. My guess is that Ovid's Pyramus and Thisbe taught Chaucer the art of the simple poetic narrative. If he had fears that the form would not succeed, Ovid's tale must have quieted them; if he needed a model, it was there.

He found in Ovid's work a beautifully proportioned narrative, and he preserved this in his version. There are two parts, the scene in the city and the scene in the fields. Each part can be subdivided, the first into a brief exposition, the lovers at the wall, and the plan to run away; the second into the scene of Thisbe alone in the field, Pyramus' discovery of

---

Hoepffner, SATF (Paris, É. Champion, 1908–1921), II, No. CCCVI, IIIe Lay, lines 150–151. Perhaps the information was more generally known than Meech suspected. On Semiramis, see Irene Samuel, "Semiramis in the Middle Ages: The History of a Legend," *Medievalia et Humanistica*, 2 (1944), 32–44, and Johnstone Parr, "Chaucer's Semiramis," *Chaucer Review*, 5 (1970), 57–61.

2. This is not to imply it was a daring choice. The story was very popular in the Middle Ages. For some references see Lydgate, *Temple of Glas*, ed. Josef Schick, EETS, ES 60 (London, 1891), p. 75. Gower (*Confessio Amantis*, III, 1331–1494) was telling the story at about the same time as Chaucer. It is referred to in the thirteenth-century Provençal *roman* titled *Flamenca* (line 621) as one of the popular stories, and it is told briefly as one of the *exempla* in Machaut's *Le Jugement dou Roy de Navarre*, 3171–3186 (*Oeuvres*, I).

3. Shannon, *Chaucer and the Roman Poets*, pp. 190–196, notes Chaucer's cuts and additions. For perceptive comments on Chaucer's handling of Ovid here, see Norman Callan, "Thyn Owne Book: A Note on Chaucer, Gower, and Ovid," *RES*, 22 (1942), 272.

the bloody scarf and his suicide, Thisbe with the dying Pyramus, and her final speech and death. Chaucer does not follow Ovid slavishly, but such minor cutting and expansion as he does are beautifully skillful. He drops the explanation of the mulberry's color (red because stained with the lovers' blood). Ovid's metamorphoses are not relevant for the *Legend*.[4] The somewhat artificial and jarring image in Ovid of Pyramus' blood pouring out like water from a broken pipe (IV, 122–124) is cut from three lines to one (852). The few expansions are equally tactful. Occasionally he supplies a line or two of explanation (721–723, 786–787), he gives the lovers a slightly longer speech to the wall (756–766), and he adds the touching note of Thisbe's fear, as she is hiding in the cave, that Pyramus, not finding her, may think her false (855–857).[5] These are almost the only real additions to his source. The consequence of these slight changes, interestingly enough, is that all the scenes are of approximately the same length. There is no necessary virtue in giving equal time to all parts of an action, but it does suggest an ability to give each phase a full but disciplined development. This balance of the individual scenes probably creates in considerable measure the impressive sense of steady, forward movement in the narrative.

4. If he knew Boccaccio's *De Claris Mulieribus*, chap. xii, he would have found there a version which omitted the metamorphosis also. Sanford Brown Meech, "Chaucer and the *Ovide Moralisé*," p. 187, comments that it was Chaucer's practice, in reshaping Ovidian material, to leave out the metamorphosis which is the climax of the story and calls attention to his treatment of the story of Ceyx and Alcyone in the *Book of the Duchess* and of the stories of Philomela, Progne, and Tereus in the *Legend of Philomela*. On the other hand, it should be pointed out that at the conclusion of the *Ariadne*, Chaucer mentions that the gods took pity on Ariadne and the stars of her crown may be seen in the sign of Taurus (2221–2223).

5. Though Boccaccio's *De Claris Mulieribus* has not been suggested as a source, there is a similar touch there: "Nec mora Thysbe potam leaenam abiisse rata, ne decepisse videretur amantem aut diu expectatione suspensam teneret." Guido A. Guarino translates the passage thus: "Shortly afterwards, Thisbe, thinking that the lioness had drunk and left, returned cautiously to the spring so that it should not seem as if she scorned her lover and kept him waiting a long time." See *Concerning Famous Women* (London, George Allen and Unwin, Ltd., 1964), p. 26.

There is only the simplest characterization in Ovid, and the same is true in Chaucer. The narrative is not concerned with character but with an emotion — love — and a condition — youth. The action does not evolve from the kind of people Pyramus and Thisbe are; it evolves from the emotion they feel and the simplicity and intensity with which they respond to it. A certain kind of character may be implied by the action, but it is left largely undefined, except by such comments as "trewe and kynde." What really matters is that two young people love with equal ardor: "And bothe in love ylyke sore they brente" (731). This ardor, and its shared intensity, is communicated by the author's comments, the handful of speeches, and the lovers' actions.

Chaucer may have learned something from Ovid, also, about the art of narrative diction, the art of phrasing a detail in language which combines both action and emotion in the single detail. Time and again a striking detail strikingly phrased turns out to be Ovid skillfully translated: Thisbe's running to the cave "with dredful fot" is Ovid's "timido pede" (100); Pyramus casting up at Thisbe "his hevy, dedly yen" (885) is Ovid's "oculos a morte gravatos" (145).

This careful attention to the original could hardly help but be profitable, provided it led to a release of fresh powers of Chaucer's own possession and not to slavish imitation. What is *Thisbe*, a brilliant translation and nothing more? Or is it an independent, self-contained entity, a created thing, and, thereby, a poem? For all its fidelity to the original, *Thisbe* is a narrative poem noticeably different from Ovid's tale. The story from the *Metamorphoses* has been itself transformed, and the process of transformation is the result of a number of shifts and alterations in Chaucer's telling.

The simplest and least important change is one of time and locale. The name and date are the same — the Babylon of Semiramis. Ovid's story transpires in his own world and its past. Chaucer's work occurs neither there nor in his present world, but in a believable blend of both: that special region where Babylon and England meet, in that special time where the calendar simultaneously marks the mysterious classical past and the fourteenth-century present. One finds this same peculiar localizing in other medieval poetry involving distant time and place,[6] but rarely so convincingly as here, or so simply done:

> At Babiloyne whylom fil it thus,
> The whyche toun the queen Semyramus
> Let dychen al aboute, and walles make
> Ful hye, of hard tiles wel ybake:
> There were dwellyng in this noble toun
> Two lordes, whiche that were of gret renoun,
> And woneden so nygh, upon a grene,
> That there nas but a ston-wal hem betweene,
> As ofte in grete tounes is the wone.
>
> (706–714)

The names and the walls of "tiles" (brick) are exotic, but the ditch about the town — a detail not in Ovid — makes it a familiar medieval city, and the two lords living side by side upon a green could be found in any English town of good size: "As ofte in grete tounes is the wone. . . ." The time and scene are a blend of then and now, of here and there. It is not Ovid's world.

Much more important as a transforming force is the language of the poem. It is, first of all, an easy, idiomatic, unstrained English, with none of the awkward, spastic quality of the translation about it. The native English manner is illustrated by Chaucer's treatment of Ovid's line, "Quoque magis tegitur, tectus magis aestuat ignis." For Ovid's proverb he has found an English equivalent, or invented one: "Wry the glede, and hotter is the fyr" (735). In

6. For perceptive comments on the medieval attitude toward and treatment of antiquity, see W. S. Hecksher, "Relics of Pagan Antiquity in Mediaeval Settings," *Journal of the Warburg Institute,* 1 (1937–38), 204–220; and Erwin Panofsky, *Studies in Iconology* (New York, Oxford University Press, 1939), pp. 27–28. Morton Bloomfield argues persuasively for an untypically developed historical sense in Chaucer ("Chaucer's Sense of History," *JEGP,* 51 [1952], 301–313).

fact, he has found two, for the next line adds, "Forbede a love, and it is ten so wod."

Chaucer's poem is written in a slightly different style from Ovid's work. There is a somewhat wider range, from the colloquial to the rhetorical, and the colloquial is a much more important element in Chaucer than in Ovid. Chaucer makes relatively little use of rhetoric, and most of it comes, as might be expected, in the final, more emotional scenes. But even here there is a deliberate exploitation of the colloquial. After Pyramus' rhetorical monologue culminating in suicide, the speeches Chaucer added for Thisbe are contrastingly, and ironically, low pitched and familiar in tone:

> If it so falle that my Piramus
> Be comen hider, and may me not yfynde,
> He may me holde fals and ek unkynde.
>
> (855–857)

And coming forth to find him she thought,

> I wol hym tellen of my drede,
> Bothe of the lyonesse and al my deede.
>
> (860–861)

And in Thisbe's speech resolving suicide we find this:

> "My woful hand," quod she,
> "Is strong ynogh in swich a werk to me;
> For love shal yeve me strengthe and hardynesse
> To make my wounde large ynogh, I gesse."
>
> (890–893)

The ironic understatement of the last line is reinforced by the colloquial quality of the phrase and also by the rhyme tag, "I gesse," for it gives us the unexpected combination of death and the casual manner.

The language of the poem can also be poetic in its own right, independent of Ovid. The line, "How kysseth she his frosty mouth so cold!" (878) is Ovid's "gelidis in vultibus oscula figens" (141), but it is Chaucer's word "frosty" that elevates the line to magnificence. It communicates both dedication and loss. It has not only the chill of death but the whiteness of the mouth from which the blood has fled. The early frost that kills is here, and the delicate, transient rime that evokes a sense of the delicate, transient youth and life and love which are melting away. Or again, a few lines earlier in this same rhetorical passage, there is "And how she wep of teres ful his wounde. . . ." The impact of the line, apart from the dramatic extravagance of the detail itself, is derived from two uses of language. The placing of "ful" is ambiguous, so that there is not only a wound full of tears (extravagant), but also a fullness of tears, a complete grief (natural). And the verb "wep" is especially powerful. Chaucer's line is superior to Ovid's "vulnera supplevit lacrimis" (140). The act of weeping is more natural than filling a wound with tears; at the same time the object of "wep" is "wounde," and the sense of weeping a wound communicates the laceration of Thisbe in her grief. Chaucer's language is independently poetic and is used to create emphases and to evoke emotions not identical with those of Ovid.

The effect of these differences and changes is finally, I believe, to shift the theme of the narrative. The overall theme of both narratives is love, the simple, natural love of two young people, the impossible amalgam of innocence and desire that youth finds unendurable and middle age finds incredible. It is, for the first time in Chaucer, not courtly love. He obviously believed in it even while wondering at it.

The paradox and conflict of innocence and desire are dramatized in the action by means of a pattern of separation and union. The lovers live side by side, but they may not meet; the parents refuse marriage, and the children seek each other the more ardently; the wall separates, but it also brings them together; they flee to meet, but they are parted; death both divides and unites them. The conflict is also contained in many of the images, most importantly in images of hot and cold: the conventional image of love as burning, as fire (731–735), the sword warm with Pyramus' blood; and the "cares colde" (762), "The colde wal they wolden kysse of ston" (768; this "cold" is not in Ovid), and the echo later, in the line already discussed, "How kysseth she his frosty mouth so cold!" The paradox is repeated in the trysting place, the grave of Ninus, by the well of living water.

This conflict assumes both an outer form and an inner form. The outer struggle is nominally with the parents, but it is actually with a whole world that is hostile — a world not only of parents but of walls, dangerous fields, ravenous lions, and death. The inner struggle is even more poignant. It is the conflict of innocence and desire; not only is it a struggle between these forces, in which each is at the same time both urging on and frustrating the other, but it is also essentially a struggle to preserve both in a world where innocence too long maintained will kill desire and where desire if successful will destroy innocence. This conflict is dramatized and resolved, first in the wall scene and finally in the scene of the death in the fields.

This inner struggle becomes the theme in Chaucer's poem; only the outer struggle emerges in Ovid. Chaucer shifts the emphasis to innocence. In his poem, the lovers' deaths are a triumph of innocence; in Ovid's, they are a triumph of desire. Chaucer has made this shift by creating a slightly stronger sense of the lovers as people and of their feelings for one another through the effective use of the colloquial level of language to humanize the material and to suggest innocence and naïveté and through the intensifying effect of some of his language.

A comparison of Ovid's and Chaucer's treatment of the wall — a relatively mundane moment, one would assume! — may suggest the differences between the two poems, and perhaps also some of what Ovid could teach Chaucer:

> fissus erat tenui rima, quam duxerat olim,
> cum fieret, paries domui communis utrique.
> id vitium nulli per saecula longa notatum —
> quid non sentit amor? — primi vidistis amantes
> et vocis fecistis iter, tutaeque per illud
> murmure blanditiae minimo transire solebant.

saepe, ubi constiterant hinc Thisbe, Pyramus illinc,
inque vices fuerat captatus anhelitus oris,
'invide' dicebant 'paries, quid amantibus obstas?'

(IV, 65–73)

(There was a slender chink in the party-wall of the
two houses, which it had at some former time received
when it was building. This chink, which no one had
ever discovered through all these years — but what
does love not see? — you lovers first discovered
and made it the channel of speech. Safe through
this your loving words used to pass in tiny whispers.
Often, when they had taken their positions, on this
side Thisbe, and Pyramus on that, and when each in
turn had listened eagerly for the other's breath,
'O envious wall,' they would say, 'why do you stand
between lovers?') [7]

This wal, which that bitwixe hem bothe stod,
Was clove a-two, ryght from the top adoun,
Of olde tyme of his fundacioun;
But yit this clyfte was so narw and lyte,
It nas nat sene, deere ynogh a myte.
But what is that that love can nat espye?
Ye loveres two, if that I shal nat lye,
Ye founden first this litel narwe clifte;
And with a soun as softe as any shryfte,
They lete here wordes thourgh the clifte pace,
And tolden, whil that they stode in the place,
Al here compleynt of love, and al here wo,
At every tyme whan they durste so.
Upon that o syde of the wal stod he,
And on that other side stod Thesbe,
The swote soun of other to receyve.
And thus here wardeyns wolde they deceyve,
And every day this wal they wolde threte,
And wisshe to God that it were doun ybete.
Thus wolde they seyn: "Alas, thow wikkede wal!
Thorgh thyn envye thow us lettest al."

(737–757)

7. Translation by Frank Justus Miller, in Ovid, *Metamorphoses*, 2 vols., Loeb
Classical Library (Cambridge, Mass., Harvard University Press, 1951), p. 183.

The effect of the colloquial style — "deere ynogh a myte," "if that I shal nat lye," and so on — in creating a sense of intimacy with the lovers is evident. Their attitude toward the wall has more of the childish and, hence, of the innocent about it. The wall — its lime and stone — is more vividly realized, and so the separation is more real and moving. A line not in Ovid shows us Chaucer taking the poem and making it his own: "And with a soun as softe as any shryfte," where the sibilants echo the whispering and the image "softe as any shryfte" implies the sacredness of the love and the innocence.

It is reassuring to see Chaucer his own man here, and his poem about innocence may be said to be in considerable part his own creation. But the passage also reveals what Ovid had to teach him. A stone wall, a mere stage property, is dramatized and becomes part of the action. The story and the characters in it move forward by means of the property and are not delayed by it. The rhetorical possibilities are not scanted — Ovid gives us the lover's address to the wall, and Chaucer follows him — but everything is cut to the discipline of the narrative and used only to meet its demands. For Chaucer to see clearly, as Ovid most particularly could show him, that a narrative could depend on its own action to achieve realization and should so depend, rather than on elaboration and amplification, was the boldest and most revolutionary lesson he could learn. With Ovid leading the way, he paces through a simple narrative here and emerges with a complete action that is realized by virtue of the skill with which its events and agents are presented and the effectiveness of its language — nothing more.

[V] Dido

If Chaucer had completed his legendary, he presumably
would have told the story of Alceste as the final narrative,
the *chef-d'oeuvre* crowning his series.[1] Of all the famous
women he was to treat before Alceste, however, none can
have loomed so imposingly as Dido. She was for the Middle
Ages *the* heroine from the classical past. Virgil had im-
mortalized her passion in the *Aeneid,* and in the *Heroides*
Ovid had made her a pathetic and betrayed victim of love.
Ovid's influence on the medieval attitude toward Dido was
in some ways greater than that of Virgil; Ovid is largely responsible for the unsympathetic treatment of Aeneas and
the exaltation of Dido. Her prestige was further inflated
because many of the medieval adaptations of the *Aeneid*
gave added emphasis to her unhappy story.[2] Several Latin
"complaints" by Dido are also witness to her emotional
appeal for the age.[3] The magic of her name is reflected in
Chaucer's handling of her martyrdom: *Dido* is the longest
of the legends and in some ways the most remarkable.

The story's length is, of course, in part a consequence of
its length in the original. If we assume that Virgil's telling
of the love of Dido and Aeneas is the basis of Chaucer's

1. F 548–550, G 538–540.
2. See Louis Brewer Hall, "Chaucer and the Dido-and-Aeneas Story," *Mediaeval Studies,* 25 (1963), 148–159, esp. 148. This is a very helpful study. On
Ovid, see p. 154, where Hall points out that the seventh letter of the *Heroides*
was an integral part of the Dido story in the Middle Ages.
3. See *The Oxford Book of Medieval Latin Verse,* ed. F. J. E. Raby (Oxford,
Eng., Clarendon Press, 1959), Nos. 235, 236 (pp. 359–362, 494).

legend, the assumption that makes the best sense,[4] then he was working with a narrative which ran to at least 1,300 lines of Latin verse.[5] There were abbreviated versions of Virgil, and Chaucer may have known and used them. His poem gives every sign, however, of being the result of his own very skillful and poetic cutting and reworking either of the *Aeneid* or of a close translation of the *Aeneid*. His problem here is not improvisation, as in *Cleopatra* (or, what is less likely, remodeling inappropriate material); nor is it sympathetic translation, as in *Thisbe*. It is the art of ab-

---

4. M. Bech, "Quellen und Plan der 'Legende of Goode Women' und ihr Verhältniss zur 'Confessio Amantis,' " *Anglia*, 5 (1882), 320–324, asserted the sources for *Dido* were Books I–IV of the *Aeneid* and the seventh epistle of the *Heroides*. He saw no trace of Boccaccio's treatment of Dido in *De Claris Mulieribus*, which in any event departs from the traditional account of her history. Edgar F. Shannon accepted Virgil and Ovid as the sources and discussed in detail Chaucer's rearrangement of Virgil's story and his omissions (*Chaucer and the Roman Poets* [Cambridge, Mass., Harvard University Press, 1929], pp. 196–208). E. Bagby Atwood, "Two Alterations of Virgil in Chaucer's *Dido*," *Speculum*, 13 (1938), 454–457, while suggesting the influence on Chaucer's version of several passages in later books of the *Aeneid* (i.e., after Books I–IV, which cover the period spanned by *Dido*), also proposed that Chaucer used the *Excidium Troiae*. See also *Excidium Troiae*, ed. E. Bagby Atwood and Virgil K. Whitaker, Mediaeval Academy of America Publication No. 44 (Cambridge, Mass., the Academy, 1944), pp. lxix–lxx. D. R. Bradley argues that Virgil's text can explain the details in question and that the *Excidium Troiae* need not be invoked ("Fals Eneas and Sely Dido," *PQ*, 39 [1960], 122–125). Albert C. Friend has suggested that the *Ilias* of Simon Aurea Capra or Chevre d'Or provided the arrangement of the Dido story which Chaucer followed in the *House of Fame*, but he has made no argument for its utilization in the *Dido*. Louis Brewer Hall, "Chaucer and the Dido-and-Aeneas Story," says there is no satisfactory immediate source for the adaptations of the *Aeneid* in either the *House of Fame* or *Dido* and adds that whether Chaucer consulted Virgil directly "cannot be decided with specific assurance until we know a great deal more of a specific nature about the level of Chaucer's linguistic accomplishment." The fourteenth-century Italian translation of the *Aeneid* by Andrea Lancia would have provided Chaucer, he says, with "a reasonably accurate rendering of Virgil's narrative content" (p. 148). That Chaucer knew Virgil and Ovid seems reasonably certain. There may be a question about details and the possible use of translations. According to Sanford Brown Meech, lines 1357 and 1360 of Dido's final lament from *Heroides*, vii, are translated directly from the fourteenth-century Italian translation of the *Heroides* by one Filippo: "Chaucer and an Italian Translation of the *Heroides*," *PMLA*, 45 (1930), 114–115.

5. Omitting Books II–III of Virgil's *Aeneid*, in which Aeneas recounts his adventures to Dido, and lines 1–156 of Book I, the storm at sea.

breviation and adaptation, and *Dido* posed a major challenge to his artistry.

There is nothing to be gained, it must be said at once, in comparing Chaucer's treatment with Virgil's, to Chaucer's disadvantage. His version of the Virgilian story, not radically different in outline from conventional medieval versions,[6] is quite different in artistic purpose from Virgil's — and from Ovid's. He was not writing epic; nor was he writing a lyrical epistle. Here and elsewhere in the *Legend* he was writing the narrative of sentiment [7] — no better phrase comes to mind. His method is narrative, the linear relating of events. The events of the narrative are unfolded to describe a relationship or situation involving intense feelings, one or another of the emotional conditions attendant on the sentiment of love. His *Legend of Dido* narrates the passions of the Carthaginian queen: her emotions when she falls in love with Aeneas and her emotions when she is betrayed by him. The method, I repeat, is narrative, the use of detail, incident, and scene in a meaningful sequence.

A comparison of the legend with Chaucer's earlier telling of the story in the *House of Fame* reveals his considerable development as a narrative artist in the intervening years. One of the striking differences between the two tellings is Chaucer's mastery, in *Dido*, of the art of abbreviation. The *House of Fame*, most scholars would agree, has something to do with fame or reputation, and the Aeneas-Dido story is told as a decorative *amplificatio* in Book I in relation to the theme of "fame." It is Aeneas' involvement with Dido that is presumably the reason for summarizing the *Aeneid* or some retelling of it. The passage devotes 206 of its 325 lines to this part of his story. Dido laments her ruined reputation (315–360), and the story is amplified by a catalogue of betrayed women and false lovers (based largely on the

6. Hall, "Chaucer and the Dido-and-Aeneas Story," pp. 153–154.
7. Hall's description of *Dido* (*ibid.*, p. 158) as an *exemplum* teaching that "in love – and by implication in life as well – one should not make final judgments on the basis of outward appearance" seems a great oversimplification and misjudges the poem both as to genre and to theme.

Heroides (388–426)). It takes Chaucer 78 lines to move
Aeneas from Troy to the shores of Libya, and after Dido's
death he continues the narrative, summarizing in 41 lines
the hero's adventures and triumphs after he leaves Carthage. No great harm is done thereby, but if the Dido story
was his business, as it seems to have been, he could have
managed his abbreviating much more skillfully. *Dido*, however, is a masterpiece of cutting. Even with a six-line invocation to Virgil, which announces his theme, and five lines
of *occupatio* in order to cut the story of Aeneas' adventures
at sea, he moves from the fall of Troy to Aeneas' arrival in
Libya in 34 lines. The 23 lines of narrative summary cover
the salient details, many of which suggest the subthemes
and images of the story he is about to tell — treachery, betrayal, fire, and death. His narrative, moreover, ends where
it should end, with Dido's suicide. All that we hear of
Aeneas' later career is a single detail that underlines his betrayal: he sailed to Italy "And wedded ther a lady, hyghte
Lavyne" (1331). To his narrative Chaucer appended a skillfully excised fragment from the *Heroides* to raise the narrative to an emotional climax, and he was done.

Perhaps this seems more a matter of artistic control than
abbreviation. Perhaps the two come to the same thing here.
The fact remains that in the *House of Fame* his book seems
rather to master him; whereas, in *Dido* Chaucer is clearly
the master of his book. The art of merciless omission and of
poetic selectivity is part of that mastery. The aesthetic importance of that art, with all due respect to the *House of
Fame*, is demonstrated by the incomparably superior cutting
evidenced in *Dido*.

Something yet more interesting and significant also
emerges from a comparison of the two versions: a vivid
sense of Chaucer's development as a narrative poet. If one
looks carefully at the telling of the story in the *House of
Fame*, one finds precious little narrative content. Chaucer
provides narrative summary for earlier and later events, but
he can offer nothing more than summary and sometimes
not this much when he must tell the actual story of Dido

and Aeneas. What he provides instead is emotionalized moral commentary (265–292), a series of complaints uttered by Dido (300–360), and more authorial commentary, primarily a catalogue of faithless men and their betrayed ladies (383–426). A defense might be that straight narrative is not Chaucer's purpose here, that his purpose is decorative and that he is after a combination of emotion and morality. Even if this be granted, one can nonetheless see that Chaucer avoided narrative as a means of achieving these ends and instead chose devices of rhetoric at once easier, more explicit, and less effective. A lack of confidence in his narrative powers and perhaps a sense of embarrassment before an intense and complex emotional situation are suggested, for example, by his handling of Dido's falling in love:

> And, shortly of this thyng to pace,
> She [Venus] made Eneas so in grace
> Of Dido, quene of that contree,
> That, shortly for to tellen, she
> Becam hys love, and let him doo
> Al that weddynge longeth too.
> What shulde I speke more queynte,
> Or peyne me my wordes peynte
> To speke of love? Hyt wol not be;
> I kan not of that faculte.
> And eke to telle the manere
> How they aqueynteden in fere,
> Hyt were a long proces to telle,
> And over-long for yow to dwelle.
> (*House of Fame*, 239–252)

We must not make the mistake of reading too literally and autobiographically the language of an *occupatio*. He is telling us, first of all, that he is cutting his sources. But even if we do not take "I kan not of that faculte" as a confession of failure, we are left with the fact that the method he chooses does sadly attenuate the scene and, really, mangles the event on which the emotional and moral effects of his story depend. It is difficult to believe that an artist who had mastered the art of telling a story would have so thoroughly evaded the narrative demands and watered down the narrative potential of his material. *Dido* is quite a different story — literally. Between the *House of Fame* and *Dido* there lies, of course, most notably *Troilus and Criseyde*, and that may seem to make further comment pointless. For the man who created the *Troilus* would appear to have already demonstrated his mastery of all the skills we might want to talk about in discussing *Dido*. He knew how to present interesting and believable characters; he could create the illusion of their movement into emotional involvement; he could present dramatically as well as rhetorically the intense emotional reactions of these imaginary characters. What more is needed? Indeed, is not what we have in *Dido* a regression rather than development?

I think not. It would be foolish, in fact it would be mistaken, to argue that *Dido* is a better poem than *Troilus and Criseyde*. It is a much more modest poem than the *Troilus*, and it can claim nothing like its complexity. It invites comparison, if at all, only because it involves a woman falling in love and a person in love betrayed and in despair. The most useful purpose a comparison can serve, however, is to underline the essential differences between the two poems, in particular to appreciate the brevity and concentration of *Dido*. Different techniques are made obligatory by this brevity. An analysis of these techniques suggests that *Dido* is an achievement of a different kind from the *Troilus* and reveals in Chaucer new capacities as a narrative artist.

Dido is hardly reminiscent of the *Troilus*. It is reminiscent at moments of the *Knight's Tale*, and it was probably closer in time of composition to that poem than to the *Troilus*. It is sometimes like the *Knight's Tale* in its externalities. The "worlds" of the two poems are not too different from one another, a chivalric world of hunts and ceremonies, of lordly generosity and display. There is nothing quite like this in the *Troilus*, where the action takes place for the most part in a private, subjective world and where the objective world is not so glittering or idealized but, rather, is a "diplomatic" world where people must be maneuvered and moved about.

Dido does not plunge into the subjective world as does the *Troilus*. It has some passages of subjective analysis or description, but it lacks the space and leisure to explore this world and to achieve a sense of movement at this level. This is one of the primary differences between the two poems, and from this springs one of the differences in technique.

If *Dido* is like the *Knight's Tale* in its greater objectivity, it puts that objectivity to a different use. The *Knight's Tale* by and large avoids the subjective aspect of experience completely. Emotions are a *donné* in the poem. We see the consequences of emotion in the violent actions of Palamon and Arcite, but the emotion is without a real history, nothing more than the conventional miraculous birth of love at first sight. There are, likewise, few glimpses of an emotional relationship. Instead we concentrate on the external forms of the Knight's world which the young men's emotions disturb, and we observe the process by which these external forms — duels, prayers, tournaments, parliaments, and philosophical discourse — channel feeling and, finally, restore order, rationality, and a seamless surface.[8] In *Dido*, on the contrary, emotion is the heart of the poem, and the external world of the narrative is used as a way of suggesting and dramatizing emotion. The technique is not symbolism, but in its skillful deployment of externalities and details it comes very close to symbolism.

The technique is employed for the delicate business of showing the falling in love of Dido, the very matter Chaucer had avoided in the *House of Fame*. He could get very little help from Virgil here, for Virgil was not interested in the development of Dido's love but in the consequences of her passion. Dido's actual entanglement is accomplished, as is fitting in an epic, by Olympian manipulations. Cupid is substituted by Venus for Aeneas' son Ascanius; he is fondled by Dido, and thereupon he implants a hidden fire and his

---

8. I follow here the interpretation of the *Knight's Tale* presented by Charles Muscatine, "Form, Texture, and Meaning in Chaucer's *Knight's Tale*," *PMLA*, 65 (1950), 911–929. See also his *Chaucer and the French Tradition* (Berkeley, University of California Press, 1957), pp. 175–190.

own potent poison.[9] The scene, though it may be emblematic, is not descriptive of the process. In Virgil we must believe in Dido's love because of this *Cupido ex machina* and because of our sense of Aeneas' heroic worth and the appeal of the heroic adventures which he relates to the entranced queen.

Chaucer's interest, on the other hand, is in the whole history of Dido's emotions. He begins by talking of her beauty and her great reputation for all noble qualities (1004–1014):

> she regneth in so gret honour,
> That she was holden of alle queenes flour,
> Of gentillesse, of fredom, of beaute. . . .
>
> (1008–1010)

We (and Aeneas) first see her at her devotions in the temple, an original detail [10] that suggests a chastity and devoutness of soul which Aeneas is soon to destroy. Dido's beauty and goodness (the familiar "beautee and bountee" of medieval heroines) is asserted a second time, interrupting the account of Aeneas' first moments in Carthage. This seems in part Chaucer's strategy for shifting attention as soon as possible to Dido, after the necessary concentration in the opening lines on Aeneas. Quite properly, he had cut short Venus' account to Aeneas of Dido's earlier history;[11] his business is with her present, not her past. But this denies him an early opportunity for turning the spotlight on her. Now, these interruptions shift our attention and diminish Aeneas' claim on us (1035–1042). The missing comrades appear (another tribute to the queen, for they have come to her for help because of her reputation for goodness; 1053–1054),[12]

9. Virgil, *Aeneid*, I, 688; see also 644–722.

10. In Virgil, Aeneas sees Dido in the temple, but in her role as ruler and law-giver (*ibid.*, I, 496–508).

11. *Ibid.*, I, 340–368.

12. In Virgil, they come to Dido because the Phoenicians have refused to allow them to beach their ships, a harsh security measure Dido had commanded (*ibid.*, I, 522–564, esp. 539–541, 563–564). The effect of Chaucer's alteration is obvious. (In Virgil, Dido welcomes the men warmly when she knows who they are and offers to send out scouts to search for Aeneas [*ibid.*, I, 565–578]).

Aeneas sheds invisibility and is revealed, and Dido can
begin falling in love.

The technique for handling this process is not in any
sense realistic. This legend is not, even metaphorically
speaking, a psychological short story. The technique is
"narrationally" convincing, however, and enormously skillful. The problem is a delicate one: he must show Dido
falling in love without suggesting that she is a wanton
woman. She must fall overwhelmingly in love, but, since
the magical love at first sight is being eschewed, there must
be some sense of time elapsing before she is completely
enamored of Aeneas. Yet leisure is denied him by his commitment to brevity. What Chaucer does, therefore, is to
create a kind of double time. He creates the impression that
Dido falls in love almost at once, though it is not the blind-
ing lightning flash that smites Troilus. From the time references he provides, one has the sense that no more than
forty-eight hours elapse between her meeting with Aeneas
and her surrender in the cave (see 1092, 1112, 1154, 1164,
1188). Contrariwise, however, Chaucer also creates the
impression that her love evolved gradually though power-
fully and that we move rather slowly before we come to the
scene in the cave.

He manages this double sense of Dido's falling in love
most adroitly. Within a few lines after she sees Aeneas
(1061–1079), Chaucer tells us Dido is in love with him:
"And with that pite love com in also" (1079). This suggests
a precipitous emotional involvement. But then Chaucer
seems to forget all about what he has said. For sixty lines he
does not so much as mention love, and he treats Dido with
complete objectivity.[13] We see her acting as queen and
generous host and are told nothing of her subjective reactions. (We are, I believe, led to an awareness of her feelings,

13. The line from the feasting scene, "Of many an amorous lokyng and
devys" (1102), seems completely generalized and is not applied specifically to
Dido. It seems merely a detail to suggest courtly festivity. Cf. CT, F 272, 285–
286 (the dancing and festivities at the feast of Cambyuskan's nativity): "Now
dauncen lusty Venus children deere. . . ." "[Who could describe] Swich sub-
til lookyng and dissimulynges / For drede of jalouse mennes aperceyvynges?"

but it is communicated obliquely.) Then Chaucer reintroduces the topic with Venus' substitution of Cupid for Ascanius in order to set Dido's heart aflame with love. This, of course, had been Virgil's device to explain and initiate Dido's passion. Chaucer is much more reticent. Our author tells us, he says, that this was done

> This noble queen enamored to make
> On Eneas; but, as of that scripture,
> Be as be may, I take of it no cure.
>
> (1143–1145)

Though discarding the pagan explanation, the passage does reintroduce the question of Dido's enamorment. Now Chaucer can show us for a second time Dido falling in love. For that is what in effect happens: she falls in love with Aeneas twice (1150–1158). In the process, we have achieved a sense of time, of duration. Dido is both impetuous and steady: love comes swiftly as passionate love must; love comes slowly as enduring love must. But even now he continues to be ambiguous. How quickly did Dido announce her love to Anna and give herself to Aeneas? By the rapid time scheme, everything transpires within two days after they meet. But by the slow time scheme, the climax is indefinitely retarded: the scene with Anna, on the eve of the cave scene, begins with the words, "it fil upon a nyght" (1162). What night? There is no knowing. And so Dido has been saved from a charge of unseemly haste. It has been beautifully managed, and now Chaucer is free to show us the consequences of her love:

> Now to th'effect, now to the fruyt of al,
> Whi I have told this story, and telle shal.
>
> (1160–1161)

Double time is only one of Chaucer's techniques in this first sequence with Dido (1061–1159). The first falling in love of Dido (1061–1081) is worth examining. It is a long, loosely organized collection of phrases, clauses, and sentences linked by the simple device of *repetitio*; "and" is used twelve times. The structure of each linked unit is, with one or two exceptions, completely simple. The effect is of unity and rapidity. We follow Dido's eyes and occasionally her reactions or thoughts on seeing Aeneas for the first time. What we observe her seeing and reacting to are those aspects of Aeneas that a woman of her rank and *gentilesse* would properly be impressed by. Much of it is visual and objective: she observes that his men honor him, that he has the appearance of a knight (a warrior), that he is handsome and has a noble countenance and a powerful and muscular form, that he looks like a lord. Seeing what she sees, Chaucer's audience would clearly expect emotional involvement. Of her subjective reactions we see little, but what we see is significant. As a sensitive woman she pities him; "in hire herte she hadde routhe and wo" that so noble a man as he should be "disherited." As a vulnerable woman, she is attracted to him because he is a stranger, someone new and exotic. Chaucer chooses to comment on this reaction in particular:

> And, for he was a straunger, somwhat she
> Likede hym the bet, as, God do bote,
> To som folk ofte newe thyng is sote.
>
> (1075–1077)

It helps to explain his attraction for her.[14] It suggests a weakness, a flaw, but the comment is hardly a censure. He returns to her pity as the first cause of her susceptibility (urged on, no doubt, the "anon" suggests, by a woman's fondness for "newfangleness"):

> Anon hire herte hath pite of his wo,
> And with that pite love com in also;
> And thus, for pite and for gentillesse,
> Refreshed moste he been of his distresse.
>
> (1078–1081)

Her pity and her *gentilesse*, of course, are all to her credit.

---

14. He comes back to this (line 1158), telling us Dido is now aflame "With Eneas, hire newe gest, to dele. . . ."

The pity, note, is not the pity of the lady for the beseeching lover but a more general, humane quality of heart. The whole passage, without quite saying so, places us behind Dido's eyes and, briefly, within her thoughts. When it has finished, love seems an understandable and, almost, proper consequence.

For some lines thereafter we watch Dido as she makes Aeneas and his company welcome and at ease. The report of her generous hospitality, of the feasting and dancing and giving of rich gifts, handled as events in the story, is, together with the hunting scene, the main source of courtly atmosphere, the shimmer of regality and gorgeousness with which Chaucer invests the tale. Nothing contributes to this effect so much as the account of the lavish gifts which Dido showers on Aeneas. Hints in Virgil to suggest the incident have been found by scholars,[15] but the fact remains that as an incident it is apparently original with Chaucer. In Virgil we see only Aeneas presenting gifts to Dido. It was this, of course, which suggested Dido's offerings. Chaucer retains the gift-giving of Aeneas, but whereas in the *Aeneid* his gifts were a source of admiration and wonder and underlined the magnificence and generosity of the hero, in the *Legend* the effect is quite otherwise. Aeneas' gifts come after Dido's; they are listed in a single line with no description, and they seem no more than a response to Dido's hospitality and an inadequate response at that. The pathetic imbalance between Dido and Aeneas operates in the gift scene. The lavish outpouring of bridled coursers, steeds for jousting, large palfreys for easy riding, jewels, sacks of gold, rubies shining by night, a "gentil hawtein faucoun heroner," hounds, and cups of beaten gold shows us not merely the largesse of a truly noble queen, "she that can in fredom passen alle"; it represents objectively that cascading emotional involvement of Dido, her heedless giving of self. It continues metaphorically the process of falling in love. And the imbalance is significant, for the tragedy is one in

---

15. See Atwood, "Two Alterations of Virgil," pp. 454, 455–456; Bradley, "Fals Eneas and Sely Dido," pp. 122–124.

which Dido is the giver and Aeneas is the niggardly re-
turner, the taker, *l'autre qui tend le joue.*

This relationship and the gift-giving motif with its associations of regality and splendor are continued in the hunting scene. It is a thoroughly medieval hunt, a skillful mosaic
of bits and pieces from Virgil [16] and details of sight and
sound from fourteenth-century experience. The hunt is in
his source, but reinforcing its presence is the medieval association of hunting with the courtly life and with love,
Froissart's "l'amoureuse chace." [17] Chaucer treads on dangerous ground, making his "amorous queene" initiate the
hunt ("An huntyng wol this lusty freshe queene, / So
priketh hire this newe joly wo" — 1191–1192), thereby suggesting she is the pursuer. In fact, she becomes almost immediately the quarry. The scene before the hunt begins is
magnificently pictorial in Virgil. It remains this, but becomes something more in Chaucer: it is not static; it advances the dramatic situation. Dido, all in gold and
precious stones sitting on a red saddle barred with gold and
on "a thikke palfrey, paper-whit," is the beautiful object,
the last and richest gift of all that she has to give. The handsome Aeneas on a prancing horse is the man in absolute
control:

> Upon a courser stertlynge as the fyr —
> Men myghte turne hym with a litel wyr —
> Sit Eneas, lik Phebus to devyse,
> So was he fressh arayed in his wyse.
> The fomy brydel with the bit of gold
> Governeth he, ryght as hymself hath wold.   (1204–1209)

Nothing will move him unless he chooses. After this scene
the events in the cave and the ultimate tragedy can come
as no surprise.

16. Virgil, *Aeneid*, IV, 129–159. Most of the scene is Chaucer's own. He
omits the epic simile (143–149), gives Dido's steed to Aeneas (135), and transforms Ascanius' wish for a boar or a lion into a general sentiment mingled
with hunting cries.

17. The hunting scene with the God of Love: Froissart, *Le Paradys d'Amour*,
916–956.

These passages of largely objective description not only encrust the narrative with a rich and glittering enamel and flash forth the magnificence of courtly life; they also reveal the nature of the two main characters (the emotional intensity of Dido, the lack of feeling in Aeneas) and the quality of their relationship. The technique is ideal for the short narrative. Though the scene is vividly realized — and realized, as I have said, not only for background but to suggest the rich gift of self which Aeneas receives from Dido — the forward movement of the events of the narrative is not slowed and the inner life of Dido is revealed.

For this reason Chaucer needs to provide remarkably little direct description of Dido's thought and feelings. We have only three such dramatized scenes, and they are comparatively brief. The first is the scene with Anna (1162–1187). Chaucer has compressed two nights in Virgil's description of Dido into one, perhaps combining details from both nights [18] and abbreviating and speeding up the action in the process. In the scene with Anna we see, by moonlight, Dido turning and tossing and sighing in her bed and finally announcing her love to her sister. Because he is handsome, manly, "And therwithal so moche good he can," she must be wedded to him. Virgil has been switched about. There, in spite of her love, Dido resolves to be true to her dead husband's memory, and it is Anna who argues, on personal and political grounds, for an alliance with Aeneas. It will do Chaucer's cause no good to show Dido talking about her dead husband. And simplicity of scene, not complication, makes for speed. Chaucer suggests in a summarizing phrase that Anna opposed Dido's declaration — "somdel it withstod" — but was won over. We thus see the strength of Dido's passion: "Love wol love, for nothing wol it wonde" (1187).

But Dido's love is an honest love: "I wolde fayn to hym

18. Virgil, *Aeneid*, IV, 1–55, 80–89. It is morning in the first scene in Virgil, night in the second, with the moon sinking (81), a detail which may have given Chaucer his rising moon (1163). Dido's sleeplessness is perhaps implied in the first scene in Virgil (1–8), but it is more strongly implied in the second (82–85).

ywedded be" (1179). This motif of marriage runs throughout the remainder of the narrative. In the cave scene we
hardly see Dido, except as a loving woman giving herself
in marriage — to her sorrow:

> And here began the depe affeccioun
> Betwixe hem two; this was the firste morwe
> Of hire gladnesse, and gynning of hire sorwe.
> ....
> ... Sely Dido rewede on his peyne,
> And tok hym for husbonde, and becom his wyf
> For everemo, whil that hem laste lyf.
>
> (1229–1231, 1237–1239)

Her "marriage" is at the heart of her grief in the second
of her dramatic scenes. We lose sight of her for a time as
we hear the rumor of her liaison spreading and watch the
false Aeneas woo her. Only as Aeneas is about to desert her
does she reappear (1290–1326). The scene is handled with
great skill. It is not Chaucer's transformation of Dido from
Virgil's raging, vengeful, betrayed woman into a much
gentler creature that is so remarkable. It is his restraint, his
ability by suggestion in summary or by a brief speech or
even a fragment of speech to create her despair and grief in
so short a span. It begins with a single line of direct discourse:

> She axeth hym anon what hym myslyketh —
> "My dere herte, which that I love most?"
>
> (1293–1294)

And when Aeneas confesses his intention of leaving and
gives his reasons, she bursts forth:

> "Is that in ernest?" quod she, "wole ye so?
> Have ye nat sworn to wyve me to take?
> Allas! what woman wole ye of me make?
> I am a gentil woman and a queen.
> Ye wole nat from youre wif thus foule fleen?
> That I was born, allas! What shal I do?"
>
> (1303–1308)

The summarizing passage, with its rapid sequence of verbs, conveys without direct comment her desperation:

> To telle in short, this noble quen Dydo,
> She seketh halwes and doth sacryfise;
> She kneleth, cryeth, that routhe is to devyse;
> Conjureth hym, and profereth hym to be
> His thral, his servant in the leste degre;
> She falleth hym to fote and swouneth ther,
> Dischevele, with hire bryghte gilte her. . . .
>
> (1309–1315)

And she is allowed one final plea:

> And seyth, "Have mercy! and let me with yow ryde!
> These lordes, which that wonen me besyde,
> Wole me distroyen only for youre sake.
> And, so ye wole me now to wive take,
> As ye han sworn, thanne wol I yeve yow leve
> To slen me with youre swerd now sone at eve!
> For thanne yit shal I deyen as youre wif.
> I am with childe, and yeve my child his lyf!
> Mercy, lord! have pite in youre thought!"
>
> (1316–1324)

The speech, passionate and contradictory, is aimed as much at the audience as at Aeneas. It begins and ends with a plea for mercy; it shows us Dido isolated in a hostile world, Dido willing to die if only she can die an honest woman, that is, as Aeneas' wife, Dido carrying Aeneas' child. More, it shows us a queen on her knees, reduced to a fundamental feminine condition, begging for love and life and reputation.

The effect comes very close to pathos, a mode Chaucer explores in several of the legends to follow. But Dido is too positive, and for all her gentleness she has been too much the queen, even when being pursued and betrayed, to evoke a truly pathetic response. Chaucer has made several moves to achieve this effect of pathos. She is seen in a largely passive role throughout the love affair (in the cave and after), and he stresses her innocence ("sely Dido," 1157, 1237, 1336, and "O sely wemen, ful of innocence," 1254ff.).

She is also, however, the "noble queen" (1143, 1164, 1222, 1309), the ruler of a city, the giver of gifts. The reticence and brevity of his treatment preserve her dignity and allow us to admire more than pity her. She is not quite a tragic figure, either, but in her final scene she is more tragic than pathetic. Her kissing the "cloth" left behind by Aeneas and her twenty swoons are overt appeals by Chaucer for our tears, but her last speech, a brilliant selection from Virgil,[19] by its brevity suggests control and strength:

> O swete cloth, whil Juppiter it leste,
> Tak now my soule, unbynd me of this unreste!
> I have fulfild of fortune al the cours.   (1338–1340)

The aura of the heroic in the Latin is even stronger here since Dido's earlier frenzy has been cut away and we get a sense, albeit flickering, of tragic resignation. This note is maintained to the end, for she takes her fate in her own hands and without further speech or display slays herself. The final action is presented in objective summary.

Even the coda, Chaucer's translation of the opening eight lines of "Dido to Aeneas" in the *Heroides*, does not spoil this mood. It seems to be there because Ovid, having also written of Dido, must, therefore, be included. By limiting himself to the opening lines, Chaucer does not become involved in the more emotional passages. The mood here is quiet and lowers the tension, but it reveals Dido acknowledging the hopelessness of her cause and seeing Aeneas and his love for what they were. Again, it suggests strength rather than weakness:

> For thilke wynd that blew youre ship awey,
> The same wynd hath blowe awey youre fey.
>
> (1364–1365)

Dido shares the stage, of course, with another character

19. *Ibid.*, IV, 651–653, where the relics (*exuviae*) become the "cloth." In Virgil, the relics were "once dear while God and Fate allowed." In Chaucer the cloth is still "O swete cloth" and "dum fata deusque sinebat" is attached to the next phrase, "whil Juppiter it leste, / Tak now my soule, unbynd me of this unreste!" ("accipite hanc animam meque his exsolvite curis").

who played an archetypal role in the medieval imagination. Chaucer's handling of Aeneas, that "light o' love," is fascinating to watch. He is cast from the beginning in the role of villain, and Chaucer does everything he can to make him the villain he never was in Virgil. (We have noted how Chaucer reverses the effects of Aeneas' gifts in his original.) In the opening sections of the narrative, where he must relate Aeneas' earlier adventures, he does so objectively; he does not stress his sufferings, and he offers him very little sympathy. The one moment of warmth for the hero appears when, retaining the scene in Virgil, Chaucer allows Aeneas to burst into tears upon seeing the destruction of Troy painted on the walls of Dido's temple. Even here, however, he will not let Virgil alone. In the *Aeneid*, Aeneas, weeping, exclaims that the world is full of their sorrow (*laboris*) and the scenes of their suffering are evidence that men pity them (I, 456–463). In Chaucer, Aeneas weeps because their shame is known throughout the world; once having lived in prosperity, they are now digraced (*desclandred*). Such reminders as he does provide of Aeneas' sorrows and suffering seem intended not to win sympathy for him but to remind us of his debt of gratitude to Dido (for example, 1103–1105). This debt is put most strongly before us just as Aeneas is about to abandon her:

> There as he was in peril for to sterve
> For hunger, and for myschef in the se,
> And desolat, and fled from his cuntre,
> And al his folk with tempest al todryven. . . .
>
> (1277–1280)

Ingratitude compounds Aeneas' sins against Dido. He is also, specifically, the false love in quite un-Virgilian fashion. True to the original, the narrative shows only Dido in love before the cave scene and suggests that Aeneas had no interest at all in Dido.[20] Once in the cave, however, Aeneas

20. The *Eneas* uses Cupid-Ascanius to explain Aeneas' love as well as Dido's. As a consequence of Venus' power, Aeneas and Dido (but they alone) are inflamed with love when they kiss Cupid: *Eneas*, 2 vols., ed. J. Salverda de Grave, CFMA (Paris, É. Champion, 1925–1929), lines 769–780, 801–822.

falls on his knees before her vowing eternal devotion and lamenting "as a fals lovere so wel can pleyne," till she has pity on him for his pain, "And tok hym for husbonde, and becom his wyf" (1238), a scene straight out of Chaucer's imagination. By a further sleight of hand Chaucer now shows us Aeneas playing the suitor, though exactly when this transpires is not completely clear. The passage occurs after the cave scene but just before Aeneas abandons Dido — a moment chronologically all wrong but rhetorically perfect, for the effect is of pursuit and betrayal all at one blow. The passage grows out of an *exclamatio*, the only considerable rhetorical interruption of the narrative in the poem: "O sely wemen, ful of innocence" (1254–1263). The citation of Aeneas' treachery seems an *exemplum* within the *exclamatio*: "Tak hede now of this grete gentil-man, / This Troyan, that so wel hire plesen can. . . ." There follows an inventory of his crimes: doing his obeisances, waiting on her at feasts and dances and when she goes to the temple and when she returns (echoes of the *Ars Amatoria*?), fasting till he sees her, wearing her token, making songs, jousting, sending her letters, tokens, brooches, rings. For a moment, Aeneas looks very much like the Squire in the General Prologue. This *exemplum* is both narrative and nonnarrative. Precisely when it all happened is left conveniently vague. Presumably after he had won her, but possibly some of it happened before. Placed within the *exclamatio*, the events are taken out of time. It does not matter. We have a sufficiently comprehensive picture of Aeneas playing the game of love when and as long as it pleased his fancy. What matters is that it was all false.

What pulls these charges of ingratitude and falseness together is an overall impression of Aeneas as a fellow who has fallen into a cushy spot and is enjoying it to the full:

He nevere beter at ese was in his lyve.
. . . .
This Eneas is come to paradys
Out of the swolow of helle, and thus in joye

Remembreth hym of his estat in Troye.

(1099, 1103–1105)

He takes his ease and his rest; he and his companions do as they please (1112–1113). When the news of his liaison with Dido spreads and her suitor Iarbus hears of it and is filled with woe, Aeneas laughs with self-contentment:

> But, as in love, alday it happeth so,
> That oon shal laughen at anothers wo.
> Now laugheth Eneas, and is in joye
> And more richesse than evere he was in Troye.

(1250–1253)

He seems thoroughly heartless and self-satisfied; he "hugs his kicky-wicky here at home, spending his manly marrow in her arms." That self-satisfied smile marks him for what he is. Once he tires of present pleasures he will move on. He will have no more sympathy for Dido than for Iarbas:

> This Eneas, that hath so depe yswore,
> Is wery of his craft withinne a throwe;
> The hote ernest is al overblowe.   (1285–1287)

He prepares to steal away by night. He is not even allowed his divine mission by Chaucer. In Aeneas' mouth, the urgings of Mercury and his father's ghost sound like so many grandiose prevarications, for he concludes by telling her his heart is breaking:

> Therwith his false teres out they sterte,
> And taketh hire withinne his armes two.

(1301–1302)

We never hear his response to Dido's final, frantic pleas:

> But al this thing avayleth hire ryght nought,
> For on a nyght, slepynge, he let hire lye,
> And stal awey unto his companye,
> And as a traytour forth he gan to sayle. . . .

(1325–1328)

He is a thorough rascal, treacherous in love, ungrateful,

and thoroughly pleased with himself. This last touch in-
dividualizes what otherwise might simply be a generic
portrait of a faithless man brilliantly done. He is identifiable in his faithlessness, and so completely self-devoted,
so immune to outside considerations, that he ends by being
almost fascinating. He never succeeds in being a hateful
villain. He is not allowed sufficient time upon the stage for
any reaction that intense. Even if he were given more
space, he could probably have been shown no further
swollen in malice. For outside of melodrama or sentimental tragedy, a man's betrayal of a woman's love cannot
be made a matter to shake the heavens. The betrayed
woman can win our sympathy and the betrayer can earn
our contempt. But the lady's misfortune cannot quite seem
high tragedy and the cad's actions cannot inspire horror.
These limitations on the tragic implications of unhappy
love are another reason why Dido does not quite succeed
as a tragic heroine. Death and suicide deepen the issue and
can be tragic. Her suicide carries Dido close to tragedy,
though Chaucer's flirtation with pathos slackens the tragic
tension. Aeneas, however, is of no assistance if the poem is
aiming for an exalted tragic mood. He is not truly evil. He
did not seek Dido's destruction; he was only after a good
time. No doubt some of the ladies in Chaucer's audience
hated him and wept at Dido's abandonment and betrayal,
but theirs was a sentimental reaction and it was not, I think,
Chaucer's. He saw what was always hovering on the edge
of the game of love — the comedy of human manners and
human limitations which it exemplified, even when being
played most seriously. The treatment of Aeneas laughing
and in joy is touched at moments with comedy; he is amusing to watch in his faithless quest, playing the old, old game.

> O sely wemen, ful of innocence,
> Ful of pite, of trouthe, and conscience,
> What maketh yow to men to truste so?
> Have ye swych routhe upon hyre feyned wo,
> And han swich olde ensaumples yow beforn?
> (1254-1258)

The poem is one of curious combinations: an almost tragic Dido, an almost comic Aeneas; a great concentration on objective narrative and description and a basic concern with states of feeling; a courtly world and a private, domestic situation; conventional, almost stock roles, and, within limits, believable characters. These combinations enable the poem to range further into human experience and the nature of love than its brevity would suggest was possible. And what is most remarkable, it does this while maintaining a steady narrative pace. The *Dido* is not Virgil, and Virgil would not have liked it, but he might have recognized the skill that went into the curious, complete, and, in its way successful, reworking of his story.

[VI]   Hypsipyle and Medea

Cleopatra, Thisbe, and *Dido* gave Chaucer experience with the three principal ways in which a narrative poet intent on brevity might treat his source materials: limited invention or improvisation where the source was inadequate; a reasonably close following of a source of appropriate length and kind; and abbreviation or cutting of a source too long or complex or containing material inappropriate for his purposes. The remaining legends have nothing very novel to offer him on this score. Having said this, I must immediately suggest that *Hypsipyle and Medea* does perhaps demonstrate still a fourth method, the piecing together of incident or detail from several sources. Essentially, however, this is a variation or combination of the methods used for *Cleopatra* and *Dido*: improvising or borrowing when his immediate source is thin; cutting where it is too long or is inappropriate. What is perceptible as one reads through the remainder of the legends is a continuing exercise of these methods.

It is not a story of uninterrupted progress toward their mastery. The reason for this erratic movement, for the mixture of successes and partial failures, is not exclusively the difficulties of fitting his sources to the demands of the short narrative. Chaucer was at the same time attempting to achieve a variety of effects with his legends, and some of his difficulties stem from problems on this score. It is, again, partly a problem of his material, the difficulty of achieving a particular effect with material not always easily adapted to the effect desired, and partly a problem of mastering the techniques needed to achieve such effects. If one attends to these variations in effect, the *Legend* emerges as not quite so uniform in theme and tone as it has been charged with being.

There are variations in tone in the first three legends. *Cleopatra* is not long enough or successful enough to achieve its own voice, but whatever tone is suggested, it is not that of *Thisbe*. Nor is the tone of *Dido* that of *Thisbe* or *Cleopatra*. What really differentiates the three legends, however, is theme. The concern for a specific tone and for variety in tone is much more apparent in the next three legends, and this accounts for some of their difficulties as well as for some of their attraction.

This consideration applies with special pertinence to *Hypsipyle*. The experience of reading this legend several times in succession is an odd one. I recommend it as an exercise in indecision. The first reading leaves one feeling there is nothing much there. (This feeling is perhaps heightened by its position. After the much richer *Dido* it seems sparse and bare, and the intense, emotional *Lucrece* which follows makes it seem somewhat inconsequential, rather milk-and-waterish. Even in isolation, however, it is a problem.) A second reading may arouse the suspicion that there is something here after all, but exactly what? The third reading is again discouraging; the fourth, perhaps, exciting. And so the poem goes, or so it does for me, oscillating between a sense of achievement and a sense of failure. It never quite comes into focus. A final judgment rests with this reaction: it is a blurred poem, certainly not first class, but certainly interesting.

The poem, of course, is not about Hypsipyle and Medea; it is about Jason. Herein is Chaucer's originality, and here also, I think, is the root of his difficulty. His interest in Jason is another instance of the masculine preoccupation so prevalent in the *Legend*, which R. M. Lumiansky noted,[1] though to do as Lumiansky does and accuse Chaucer of

1. R. M. Lumiansky, "Chaucer and the Idea of Unfaithful Men," *MLN*, 62 (1947), 560–562.

illogicality in using unfaithful men as a guiding device is
both to overstate the case (it is an occasional device, not an
invariable one) and to forget that part of Chaucer's charge
by Alceste is to

> telle of false men that hem bytraien,
> That al hir lyf ne do nat but assayen
> How many women they may doon a shame;
> For in youre world that is now holde a game.

$$(486-489)$$

The battle scene in *Cleopatra* and the fascination with
Aeneas in *Dido* are examples of the masculine emphasis.
Though at first glance this may seem as though a compiler
of saints' lives were in his heart of hearts a devil worshiper,
Alceste's charge reminds us that the masculine interest is
legitimate. The concentration on Jason here is not an arch
and awkward effort to be funny. It occurs, I believe, because Chaucer saw this as a way of unifying his narrative
materials and because Jason intrigued him.

His sources are the real villains.[2] There they were in the

2. For the sources of *Hypsipyle and Medea*, see M. Bech, "Quellen und Plan
der 'Legende of Goode Women' und ihr Verhältniss zur 'Confessio Amantis,' "
Anglia, 5 (1882), 324–331; W. W. Skeat, *The Complete Works of Geoffrey Chaucer* (Oxford, Eng., 1894), III, xxxviii–xxxix, 324–330; Edgar F. Shannon, *Chaucer
and the Roman Poets* (Cambridge, Mass., Harvard University Press, 1929), pp.
208–219, 340–355. Bech first noted that Chaucer's sources were Guido delle
Colonne, *Historia Destructionis Troiae*, and Ovid's *Heroides*, vi and xii ("Hypsipyle to Jason" and "Medea to Jason"). Skeat cites all these and suggests also
the *Argonauticon* of Valerius Flaccus; Ovid's *Metamorphoses*, vii; Book V of
Statius' *Thebaid* for lines 1457 and 1467; Hyginus, *Fabulae*, chaps. xiv and xv;
and Boccaccio's *De Claris Mulieribus*, chaps. xv and xvi, and *De Genealogia
Deorum*, XIII, chap. xxvi. Guido, he asserts, is by far the most important
source. His suggestions as to Statius, Hyginus, and Boccaccio may be disre-
garded. Shannon argues for *Metamorphoses*, vii, 1–158, and *Heroides*, xii, as the
source of Chaucer's presentation of Jason's great personal attractiveness. He
contends also that the *Argonauticon* (which Chaucer refers to: lines 1453–
1458) was the source for the list of heroes who accompanied Jason in the quest
for the Golden Fleece and for certain details in Hypsipyle's welcome and enter-
tainment of Jason, but the argument seems tenuous. He believes that Virgil's
account of Aeneas' visit to Dido also influenced the account of Jason's visit to
Hypsipyle, especially for the figure of the male messenger, who may derive from
Achates and his services to Aeneas. But Hypsipyle's welcome might derive
from the hostile welcome of Jason and Hercules by the messenger on the first

books for all to read, two women loved and betrayed by the same man. The accounts of Hypsipyle and Medea stand side by side in Boccaccio's *De Claris Mulieribus*, and for each of them Ovid creates a separate epistle in the *Heroides*. Guido delle Colonne, to be sure, ignores Hypsipyle completely in the *Historia Destructionis Troiae*, and Guido is Chaucer's principal guide in this legend. But Guido's treatment of Medea posed its problems for a writer committed to presenting womankind in the best possible light. Here was a chance to kill two birds with one stone, but the stone becomes more important than the birds.

Chaucer's tactic does seem the most sensible way to solve the problem: unify the two separate but connected stories of Hypsipyle and Medea by centering attention on Jason, the betrayer of both. If anyone doubts that Jason is Chaucer's central concern, let him look again and note how much of the legend is devoted to Jason, how much to the two women. The introductory address to Jason, which aims the narrative squarely at him, and the long exposition involving Jason, Pelleas, and the quest of the golden fleece occupy 94 of the poem's 312 lines. In the section devoted to the story of Jason and Hypsipyle (1462–1579), slightly more than half the lines are given to Jason,[3] and, what is even more important, many of the lines centering on Hypsipyle actually concern Jason.[4] The same is true of the Medea section, where we hear Medea more, but she is talking about Jason.[5]

---

visit to Troy and by the warm welcome of Oetes at Colchis; see Guido de Columpnis, *Historia Destructionis Troiae*, ed. Nathaniel E. Griffin, Mediaeval Academy of America Publication No. 26 (Cambridge, Mass., the Academy, 1936), pp. 11–12, 15. According to Sanford Brown Meech, lines 1673 and 1675 of Medea's final lament (1672–1677) are translated from Filippo's fourteenth-century Italian translation of the *Heroides*: "Chaucer and an Italian Translation of the *Heroides*," *PMLA*, 45 (1930), 115.

3. With as much exactness as seems possible in questions of this kind, I divide the lines as follows: Hypsipyle: 1466–1478, 1497–1523, 1564–1579, a total of 56; Jason: 1462–1463, 1479–1496, 1524–1563, a total of 60.

4. For example, 1504–1518 really make us as much aware of Jason and Hercules as of Hypsipyle.

5. Division is more difficult here. Jason is talked about or is talking in 1580–

This slighting of the women is most strikingly established by comparison with the sources. Medea's reactions to Jason, her struggle between love and shame, and her violent passions are recounted at length by Guido della Colonne.[6] All of this vanishes in Chaucer and is replaced by a perfunctory description of her beauty — "Medea, which that was so wis and fayr / That fayrer say there nevere man with ye . . ." (1599–1600) — and an even more perfunctory treatment of her falling in love — "And, as Fortune hire oughte a foul myschaunce, / She wex enamoured upon this man" (1609–1610). The lament and the pathetic mental agony of Hypsipyle and the ferocious remorse and recriminations of Medea in the epistles in the *Heroides* gave Chaucer two full-length studies in woman betrayed, but he would have none of it, or almost none. The epistle from Hypsipyle to Jason occupies the last twelve lines or so of her narrative (1564–1575); there are six lines from Medea's letter to Jason (1672–1677). The rejection of the women as objects of interest could hardly be more decisive.

Admittedly it is difficult to say to what degree this treatment was forced on Chaucer by his material. There is little narrative content in Ovid's epistle of Hypsipyle, and the *Historia*, we have already noted, omits her completely from Jason's story. If Chaucer knew Valerius Flaccus' *Argonauticon*, as he suggests,[7] he would have found a narrative, but one not too familiar and not too appropriate for a legendary of ladies: the story of the Lemnian women who murdered all the men of the island because they believed their husbands had been false to them. Hypsipyle, to be sure, saved her father, but this is hardly enough to rescue her whole sex. For Hypsipyle, Chaucer probably had too little story, or possibly an unsuitable one.

Matters were even worse for Medea. The Medea of the

1597, 1603–1608, 1620–1628; Medea is the focus in 1598–1602, 1609–1619. From 1629–1660 the two are together. The final lines, 1662–1677, are of course completely Medea's.

6. Guido, *Historia Destructionis Troiae*, ed. Griffin, pp. 17–25.

7. See Shannon, *Chaucer and the Roman Poets*, pp. 340–355.

Argonauticon is a hypersensitive, Richardsonian study of a woman's mind. If Chaucer read it, it left no mark on his portrait. The *Historia*, which he read and used, was an even odder handbook for his purposes. Guido's Medea is not so much a martyr as a monster of love. Though shame wrestles with desire within her, desire wins an overwhelming victory. Her falling in love is immediate and violent. Guido holds her up as an example of the weakness and duplicity of women and describes her wedding night in immodest terms. A little over a century later Lydgate, the good monk of Bury, in his poeticizing of the *Historia*, felt obliged to apologize to the ladies for Guido's harsh treatment of women. Influenced, perhaps, by Chaucer's treatment of her, he considerably softened her portrait.[8]

It is difficult not to think Chaucer had his tongue in his cheek as he scratched away at Medea's story. With not so much as a by-your-leave he applied to Jason Guido's lines on form and matter: "As mater apetiteth forme alwey, / And from forme into forme it passen may . . ." (1582–1583). In Guido, however, the remark is inspired by Medea's volcanic passion the moment she sees Jason; more especially, it is part of his comment on women in general.[9] Guido's lascivious sorceress had a later history that was well known but ill adapted for panegyric. Her slaughter of her (and Jason's) children Chaucer discreetly planted in Hypsipyle's final lament. But we must resist the temptation to assume that a skeptical attitude toward women and toward the idealization of women will explain everything in this legend or in the legends in general. Though it seems reasonable to posit an ironic consciousness of Medea's limitations in Chaucer, this is not what is most important in this poem. It is not a clumsy attempt at leg pulling. The limitations of his sources and a concern for narrative unity seem the major considerations that pushed Chaucer into

8. Lydgate, *Troy Book*, I, 2097–2135. For the wedding night scene, see I, 2938–2965.
9. Guido, *Historia Destructionis Troiae*, ed. Griffin, p. 17.

minimizing his heroines and making Jason the dominant figure.

In addition, Chaucer became interested in Jason. In his legend Jason is the figure of the false lover, and what is most significant about the false lover, Chaucer perceived, is not that he is false, but that he is successful. Being false, he is undeserving, and so he should fail. But the deserving fail, and the false succeed. Jason succeeds in love, and in everything else. He becomes, almost, the emblem of the lucky one, the magically successful man. His uncle the king plots against him, and Jason frustrates the scheme without even being aware of it. Friends flock around him. He lands on the strange shore of Lemnos and immediately a messenger is dispatched to ask if he needs anything – a pilot, perhaps, or food? His friend Hercules woos the first lady for him, and she falls into his arms. A second lady falls into them without any effort whatsoever and brings with her the secret for overcoming all his perils. The bulls are yoked, the dragon conquered, the golden fleece purloined. And from Medea's arms he drifts to a third lady – a king's daughter, naturally. What is the secret of his success? Chaucer does not pretend to explain. All of the graces and none of the virtues is perhaps the implied answer. There is no accounting for this kind of magical success; it is simply something to wonder at.

Chaucer condemns Jason, but he does so without moral indignation. There is, after all, something comic about such a phenomenon if seen from the proper perspective. The rascal is amusing; the archrascal is comic. The treatment of Jason is generally comic, but the comic attitude is not consistently maintained. This inconsistency accounts for some of the blurred effect of the poem. The opening lines introduce a comic view of Jason; the indignation Chaucer expresses is not deeply felt, but hovers between a moderate condemnation of the seducer and mock indignation. There is an extremity of language and an exaggeration in the attack which suggests posturing rather than genuine feeling. Coupled with this is a certain overfamiliarity in the treatment of Jason inappropriate for true seriousness: "Have at thee, Jason! now thyn horn is blowe!" (1383). Some of the language and imagery deflate whatever serious tone has developed, by associations with the vulgar rather than the courtly. There is anticlimax in the charge that the false lover is more successful "Than he that hath abought his love ful dere, / Or hadde in armes many a blody box" (1387–1388), an anticlimax heightened by the ambiguity of "in armes" — a blow in battle or a buffet from his lady? — and further heightened by the line and rhyme which follows:

> For evere as tendre a capoun et the fox,
> Thow he be fals and hath the foul betrayed,
> As shal the good-man that therfore hath payed.
>
> (1389–1391)

The image of the devouring fox and the tender capon picks up the image of Jason and his victims in the opening lines: "Thow sly devourere and confusioun / Of gentil wemen, tendre creatures" (1369–1370), and reduces any *O altitudo* effect of the opening to the music of the pratfall. Jason the devourer of women becomes a hungry, prowling fox, and the tender women become juicy capons. The courtly associations of the hawking images ("thy recleymyng and thy lures" [1371]) are similarly reduced by the fox-capon image to barnyard level. The possibility of tragedy is destroyed by equating Jason's falseness with the crime of chicken stealing, a reprehensible action, but comically, not tragically so.

Launched with these deflationary lines, Jason never completely loses this comic air. Pelleas' plotting against him has nothing ominous about it, in part because the dangers which Jason is sent to brave are so presented as to invite incredulity in the audience rather than terror: The ram with the golden fleece

> was kept alwey with a dragoun,
> And many other merveyles, up and doun,

And with two boles, maked al of bras,
That spitten fyr, and moche thyng there was.

(1430–1433)

Pelleas' challenge to Jason is too sly and colloquial for
real seriousness: "Lat sen now, darst thow take this viage?"
(1450). In various ways the adventure is denied any heroic
quality, mainly by ignoring it. His success is ascribed solely
to Medea's arts and is hurried over undramatically:

And doth his oth, and goth with hire to bedde;
And on the morwe upward he hym spedde,
For she hath taught hym how he shal nat fayle
The fles to wynne, and stynten his batayle;
And saved hym his lyf and his honour;
And gat hym a name ryght as a conquerour,
Ryght thourgh the sleyghte of hire enchauntement.

(1644–1650)

Indeed, undramatic is hardly the adequate word. Anti-
heroic is this bedroom warrior who masters the enemy
because his lady is such a mistress of arts: "And saved hym
his lyf and his honour." Since the first half of the line is
true, the second half must be false.

Most effectively comic is the portrait of Jason as the
meek, sly man who answers the messenger from Hypsipyle
"mekely and stylle" and who is represented by Hercules as

                                    agast
To love, and for to speke shamefast.
He hadde lever hymself to morder, and dye,
Than that men shulde a lovere hym espye.

(1534–1537)

And truly comic is his description, after he plots at nights
with Hercules to "bedote" the queen:

And Jason is as coy as is a mayde;
He loketh pitously, but nought he sayde,
But frely yaf he to hire conseyleres
Yiftes grete, and to hire officeres.   (1548–1551)

The first line suggests Nicholas of the *Miller's Tale*, and the method of objective, ironic juxtaposition of detail used here anticipates a primary method of that tale and others in the *Canterbury Tales* and of the General Prologue. Less successful but still effective is the glimpse of Jason sitting beside Medea:

> Now was Jason a semely man withalle,
> And lyk a lord, and hadde a gret renoun,
> And of his lok as real as a leoun,
> And goodly of his speche, and familer,
> And coude of love al the art and craft pleyner
> Withoute bok, with everych observaunce.
>
> (1603–1608)

His mealymouthed speech to Medea, in response to her offer of aid, concludes this portrait of the pseudomeek man:

> "My ryghte lady," quod this Jason tho,
> "That ye han of my deth or of my wo
> Any reward, and don me this honour,
> I wot wel that my myght ne my labour
> May nat disserve it in my lyves day.
> God thanke yow, there I ne can ne may!
> Youre man I am, and lowely yow beseche
> To ben my helpe, withoute more speche;
> But, certes, for my deth shal I nat spare."
>
> (1620–1628)

His incredible successes, considering his incredible falsity (as I have already suggested), possess comic implications. Such a character demands the method of irony. Irony is visible at moments, but hesitantly, which is almost worse than no irony at all. This hesitant irony can be observed in the poem's treatment of love, and it creates, again, uncertainty — uncertainty, as one reads the poem, about what Chaucer is doing. Is courtly love, or the exaltation of love implied by his theme, under attack? It is hard to say.

Jason has all the courtly graces: "of gentilesse, / Of fredom, and of strengthe and lustynesse" (1404–1405). He has a royal look and goodly speech, and he knows all the

art and craft of love. The virtues ascribed to him by Hercules are those which ought to win a maiden's heart. He
is "trewe . . . of love," "wis, hardy, secre, and ryche . . ."
(1526, 1528). Unfortunately Hercules' praise is both extreme and patently false. Hercules' role as Jason's go-be-
tween, extolling him to the skies by day and plotting the
next move with him by night, seems a parody of the *amis*
relationship. He is Pandarus twice removed, for he lacks
sincerity and subtlety. The one sample of his talk seems a
kind of bumbling nonsense, Bottom in the boudoir:

> As wolde almighty God that I hadde yive
> My blod and flesh, so that I myghte live,
> With the nones that he hadde owher a wif
> For hys estat; for swich a lusty lyf
> She shulde lede with this lusty knyght!
>
> (1538–1542)

His speech is indeed a "tangled chain, nothing impaired,
but all disordered," a jumble of exclamations that con-
tradict each other: "I would gladly die, if I could live." And
just before this speech he has indicated Jason is in love, but
here he expresses the unromantic wish that Jason should
have a wife appropriate for his rank,[10] a wife *anywhere!*
This oafish fellow is a fitting *amis* for the unscrupulous
hero. Certainly no man is dispatched more rapidly in and
out of bed than Jason. With Hypsipyle we are told, "And
upon hire begat he children two, / And drogh his sayl, and
saw hir nevere mo" (1562–1563). And with Medea,
"And doth his oth, and goth with hire to bedde; / And on
the morwe upward he hym spedde . . ." (1644–1645).[11]

But is it all parody? Is it all ironic? The most that one
can say is that the business of love is presented here too
realistically to qualify as courtly love. Where it parallels
courtly procedure, the parallel is somewhat disillusioning.

---

10. "estat" in this passage must mean "rank." See *MED*, s.v. *estat* (n.), 10a:
"A person's position in society, one's station; rank or degree in the social, political, or ecclesiastical hierarchy; social class."

11. Cf. the "bedde-spedde" rime in the *Miller's Tale* (*CT*, A 3649–3650).

But the intention does not seem to be to attack or satirize courtly love. Rather, Chaucer seems to have lost all interest in love of that kind and is taking a look at love from another perspective, which is the most interesting point of all. He has passed beyond the tolerantly ironic, sympathetic-objective attitude toward courtly love employed in the *Parliament of Birds* and *Troilus and Criseyde.* This is not the occasionally "realistic" treatment of "romantic" love discoverable in those poems, but something new — unromantic love viewed realistically. The story of Jason, for so it should be called, is located midway between *Troilus* and the *Miller's Tale.* The sporadic reminders or suggestions of courtly love seem not ironic here, as they are in the story of Nicholas and Alisoun, but accidental, details imposed by his materials or remnants of the familiar manner not yet discarded.

Here we hit at the root of the poem's failure, I believe. It lies in Chaucer's attempt to incorporate semicomic and unromantic scenes and characters (Jason, Hercules, perhaps Pelleas) within a poem whose predetermined theme and materials were fundamentally romantic. He tries manfully to make it work, in particular by making the women, so striking in his source, so shadowy here that we can have very little real involvement in their betrayal. But ultimately he must give us the scene of the betrayed, ever-loving Hypsipyle, and of the betrayed, ever-hating Medea. He cannot draw his story to an appropriate conclusion; his sources and his theme do not permit this.

Nor was there sufficient art, art of plot especially. Both parts of the narrative are too thin. For Hypsipyle, in all likelihood, his sources gave him almost no story to tell.[12] So he improvised, with some help from Guido, perhaps, a scene with the messenger and the meetings of Hercules and

12. There is literally no detail in the *Heroides.* The most interesting part of Hypsipyle's biography, of course, is her pious act in saving her father when the Lemnian women murdered all the men on the island. But this is not appropriate and it has nothing to do with Jason. Even if Chaucer knew Valerius Flaccus' *Argonauticon,* which is doubtful, he tells an entirely different story, one of his own devising.

Hypsipyle. But there is not narrative enough to realize the characters of Jason or Hercules or to project the kind of love which Jason and Hercules believed in. For Medea he had a story, but the wrong kind; thereupon he slashed his narrative so drastically that most of it was left on the cutting room floor. There is something admirable in this ruthlessness, this insistence on getting a story told quickly and on telling the kind of story, within limits, that he wished to tell, but it unfortunately left him without incidents or scenes. The truth is that Chaucer needed to have a narrative provided him. He was not a great inventor of plots. The one scene between Medea and Jason is not enough. Chaucer summarizes where we wish to see. Some sense of the false Jason has by now emerged, but the effect achieved with this fascinating philanderer is too easily undercut by the final scenes of the emotional, betrayed heroines. Yet these scenes are not strong enough to set their mark, finally, on the poem. It falls to pieces in the hand.

Though a good balance in length is maintained between the story of Hypsipyle and that of Medea, in one respect the narrative is badly proportioned. The exposition involving Pelleas' plot against Jason is too long for the tale of which it is a part. It gives us another false man, but it contributes almost nothing to either the theme of the false lover or the theme of woman betrayed.

There is, on the other hand, evidence of an imagination working actively in the poem. A recurrent night motif links the parts of the narrative. "The false fox wol have his part at nyght" (1393). Pelleas "in his wit, a-nyght, compassed he / How Jason myghte best distroyed be . . ." (1414–1415). As for the plot against Hypsipyle, "And al this was compassed on the nyght / Bytwixe hym Jason and this Ercules" (1543–1544). And Jason and Medea meet, she to betray her father, he to betray her honor, of course at night: "And hereupon at nyght they mette infeere . . ." (1643). Several animal images trail after Jason: the false fox of the introduction, a dragon, and a royal lion. He himself is in quest of a ram bearing a golden fleece and involved with dragons and brass bulls spitting fire when he is not in quest of and involved with women.

These images do not save the poem, though they help. What is most interesting in the poem is its concern with plotters and betrayers, with falseness as a way to success, and the curious tone that is created by an odd combination of the jaunty and the comic, with a dash of the bitter. It is a tone new to Chaucer. It is created by the spectacle of the successful traitor, Jason, going from easy conquest to easy conquest with never a care and never a scruple, leaving the rest of us wondering and, yes, envious, and aware that we are fair game for him. The creation of Jason, and, with him, of the poem's fresh, astringent tone, is not a negligible achievement. Chaucer forces him on our attention to the end, shrewdly restricting his excerpt from Ovid to words of Medea that focus on him:

> Whi lykede me thy yelwe her to se
> More than the boundes of myn honeste?
> Why lykede me thy youthe and thy fayrnesse,
> And of thy tonge, the infynyt graciousnesse?
> O, haddest thow in thy conquest ded ybe,
> Ful mikel untrouthe hadde ther deyd with the!
>
> (1672–1677)

[VII]   Lucrece

Lucrece achieves yet another tone, the pathetic. It is probably one of the earliest examples of the tale of pathos, a subgenre in Chaucer's canon that has received curiously little attention.[1] The category would include the *Man of Law's Tale*, the *Clerk's Tale*, the *Prioress's Tale*, the *Physician's Tale*, the story of Ugolino in the *Monk's Tale*, and *Philomela* from the *Legend*. There might be other candidates: *Thisbe* is a possibility, though it is not quite typical of Chaucerian pathos;[2] "Anelida and Arcite," especially in

1. See Charles Muscatine's perceptive, exploratory remarks on the "Chaucerian 'pathetic' style," which he locates "somewhere between realism and convention. . . ." It is composed, he says, "with simple characterization, plain diction, spare and humble setting, and reaching for great idealizing power." See his "*The Canterbury Tales*: Style of the Man and Style of the Work," in *Chaucer and Chaucerians: Critical Studies in Middle English Literature,* ed. D. S. Brewer (University, Alabama, University of Alabama Press, 1966), pp. 106–108.

2. For many readers in Chaucer's day and in the fifteenth century, *all* of the tales in the *Legend*, in varying degrees, may have seemed pathetic, and pathos was probably a good part of the *Legend's* appeal. (This is with some justice, of course. Almost invariably, the material from the *Heroides* works toward a pathetic tone.) Lydgate, after referring to Chaucer's telling of the tales of Lucrece and Dido, says:

> Eek othir stories which he wrot his lyue
> Ful notabli with eueri circumstaunce,
> And ther fatis dede pitousli descryue,
> Lik as thei fill put hem in remembraunce. . . .

(*Fall of Princes*, Part I, ed. Henry Bergen (London, Oxford University Press, 1924, reprinted 1967), EETS, ES 121: II, 988–991.) He is obviously glancing at the *Legend* primarily here, and the adverb, note, is "pitousli." Similarly, in the "Nine Worshipfullest Ladyes" or "Chronycle Made by Chaucer," a nine-stanza condensation or summary of all the tales in the *Legend* except those of Medea and Philomela, made not later than 1456, all the ladies emerge as pathetic heroines. See *Odd Texts of Chaucer's Minor Poems*, Part I, ed. F. J. Furnivall (London, 1871), Chaucer Society Publications, ser. I, Part 33, Appendix, p. vi.

the "Compleynt," seems to be reaching for the pathetic, without success. The chronology of these works, unfortunately, is confused. It is possible that *Lucrece* comes after the *Man of Law's Tale* and before the other pathetic tales in the *Canterbury Tales*, and it is even possible, if the list of works in the Prologue to the *Legend* is exhaustive, that it is the first fully developed tale of pathos he wrote. If, on the other hand, we assume that everything written in rhyme royal was composed before Chaucer began using the heroic couplet, which is not a very tenable assumption, *Lucrece* comes rather late in order of composition. I would put it early myself. What seems certain is that *Lucrece* is one of his first "published" tales of pathos and as such provided him with one of his first opportunities to test his audience's reaction to this kind of narrative and to test his success with it.

The roots of Chaucerian pathos have been largely unexplored. We do not know, because we have not asked, what his models were or where the impetus for this kind of narrative originated. The taste of his time, I suspect, was in some sense responsible or at least congenial. Religious emotionalism might well have been a major influence. Charles Muscatine's comment that Chaucer's pathetic heroines are all pretty much of a piece as to appearance and derive in part from the Virgin points in that direction.[3] The adulation of the Virgin and the emotionalism engendered by her image, particularly pictorial and literary representations of Mary and the infant Jesus and Mary swooning at the foot of the Cross accompanied by the weeping women, must have gone far to fix the pattern. The image of the in-

---

(On the dating of the manuscript in which the "Chronycle" appears, Ashmolean 59, one of the Shirley MSS., see Eleanor P. Hammond, "Lydgate and the Duchess of Gloucester," *Anglia*, 27 (1904), 397–398. The manuscript was written after the death of Humphrey, Duke of Gloucester (1447) and before Shirley's death (1456). See also E. P. Hammond, "Ashmole 59 and other Shirley Manuscripts," *Anglia*, 30 (1907), 320–348, specifically 325–326, 345–346.

3. Charles Muscatine, *Chaucer and the French Tradition* (Berkeley, University of California Press, 1957), p. 193. See also his "The Canterbury Tales," pp. 107–108.

nocent, helpless, suffering Christ may also be a contributing element.

On the secular side, the *romans courtois* undoubtedly encouraged the cultivation of sentiment and sentimentalism.[4] The literature of the "complaint" worked to produce much the same effect: its whole aim is the rendering and the arousing of intense emotion. The role of the lover in the courtly love ethic — reduced to impotence by his love and by the servility imposed by the code, "innocent" but cruelly treated, lamenting his agonies but helpless to relieve his own grief — may have reinforced the pathetic pattern though it can hardly have established it. The material Chaucer was working with here, Ovid's *Heroides*, is itself an exercise in pathos and must have educated him in the method and encouraged him in the practice. Perhaps here we have one of his models, though only one.

Whatever his models, Chaucer created a very characteristic pattern in his pathetic tales. Helplessness, innocence, suffering, and grief are the principal elements, above all innocence and helplessness. These elements are set off against a threatening violence, malevolent and overwhelming, leading to an assault on sensibility, usually physical as well as emotional, a laceration of flesh and feeling. Chaucer domesticates the action and the characters and their relationships, largely neutralizing the importance of class in the process. High birth or low birth becomes essentially irrelevant. The central figure in a Chaucerian tale of pathos is almost invariably a woman (Custance, Griselda, Virginia, Lucrece, Philomela) or a child, or both, and the important relationships are intimate and domestic: mother and child, father and child (Virginius and Virginia, Ugolino and his children), wife and husband.[5] The *Legend of Lucrece* moves

4. Lawrence Stone, *Sculpture in Britain in the Middle Ages*, The Pelican History of Art (Baltimore, Penguin Books, 1955), p. 157, refers to "a new moral outlook, resulting from the growth of sentiment, and even of sentimentality, both cause and effect of the popularity of such *romans* as that of Tristram and Iseult." (He is referring to the early fourteenth century.)

5. Pathos "associates itself in Chaucer with the themes of parent and child and of wronged innocence. . ." (Muscatine, "The Canterbury Tales," p. 106).

in this direction though not all the way: Lucrece is a wife betrayed by her husband's friend and kinsman.

We are, in fact, in attendance at the birth of a genre in English narrative. Northrop Frye's description of the pathetic is uncannily appropriate for what we find in Chaucer: "The best word for low mimetic or domestic tragedy is, perhaps, pathos. . . . Pathos presents its hero as isolated by a weakness which appeals to our sympathy because it is on our own level of experience. I speak of a hero, but the central figure of pathos is often a woman or child (or both, as in the death scenes of Little Eva and Little Nell), and we have a whole procession of pathetic female sacrifices in English low mimetic fiction from Clarissa Harlowe to Hardy's Tess and James's Daisy Miller." Frye also comments that "in contrast to high mimetic tragedy, pathos is increased by the inarticulateness of the victim." And he observes that "The exploiting of fear in the low mimetic is . . . sensational, and is a kind of pathos in reverse. The terrible figure in this tradition, exemplified by Heathcliff, Simon Legree, and the villains of Dickens, is normally a ruthless figure strongly contrasted with some kind of delicate virtue, generally a helpless victim in his power." [6] We shall find all of these elements in Chaucerian pathos. He seems to have created the mode full grown.

The helplessness of the central figure in a tale of pathos must be complete. It must be reinforced, furthermore, by a curious, almost catatonic passivity. The passivity seems rooted in the complete innocence of the character, which leads to a total trust in God or in virtue itself. (The religious associations established in many of these tales underlines the probable connections with religious emotionalism.) Resistance to the threatening evil is largely impossible and would apparently spoil the effect. Cecilia, in the *Second Nun's Tale,* is chaste and pure, and she is also exposed to and apparently defenseless against the evil which threatens her. But she is too vigorous and positive; she re-

6. Northrop Frye, *Anatomy of Criticism* (New York, Atheneum, 1966), pp. 38–39.

sists stubbornly, bravely, and even successfully. There is no passivity and there are very few tears, and so her tale cannot qualify. The effect is close to the heroic, never to the pathetic.

Lucrece observes the pathetic pattern completely. The final suicide may suggest the heroic, but it is after all a gesture of submission, not defiance. The tale even maintains the strong association between the pathetic and religion often found in Chaucer, although Lucrece was a pagan. He makes her a saint among her own people: "and she was holden there / A seynt, and ever hir day yhalwed dere / As in hir lawe . . ." (1870–1872). He begins her story by associating it with the name of Augustine and, presumably, the Christian saints legends: "Nat only that these payens hire comende, / But he that cleped is in oure legende / The grete Austyn, hath gret compassioun / Of this Lucresse . . ." (1688–1691).[7] With this introduction, Lucrece's story acquires a dignity it never loses. When her story is ended, he concludes by linking her kind of woman with Christ's praise of women (1879–1882).[8]

7. It has been assumed that Chaucer is referring to Augustine's *The City of God*, I, xix. But Lucrece's story is told (among many places) in the *Gesta Romanorum* (No. 135), and the version there begins: "Augustine relates, in his work *De Civitate Dei*, that Lucretia, a noble Roman lady," etc. (*Gesta Romanorum*, trans. Charles Swann, rev. and corrected by Wynnard Hooper, Bohn's Antiquarian Library [London, 1891], p. 239). Augustine is referred to as the source for several other tales in the *Gesta* (Nos. 22, 23, and 146; pp. 54, 55, 253). It seems possible, therefore, that Chaucer may have remembered Augustine's connection with Lucrece's story from the *Gesta Romanorum*, and his somewhat puzzling reference to "oure legende" might have resulted from his confusing in memory what he had seen in the *Gesta Romanorum* with the *Legenda Aurea*. Or, it might be a direct reference to the *Gesta* itself, to which the term "legende" would appropriately apply. See OED, *s.v. legend* (n.), 2.

8. Though the Church condemned suicide, and Augustine condemns Lucrece's suicide in *The City of God* (I, xix), Chaucer's treatment of Lucrece is totally sympathetic. Before he is condemned for heresy, or, worse yet, before *Lucrece* is transformed into a tale in which the heroine is condemned, we should remember that it was possible for the orthodox to praise Lucrece. Augustine, who is debating with the enemy here and defending Christian women for not committing suicide after rape, himself calls her a noble matron of ancient Rome ("matronam nobilem veteremque Romanam") and is obviously sympathetic toward her. Jerome praised her without qualification: "Ad Romanas feminas transeam; et primam ponam Lucretiam, quae violata pudicitiae nolens

To achieve the effect he wants, Chaucer, though he follows his source, Ovid's *Fasti*,[9] with considerable fidelity, cuts and alters with great skill. I therefore cannot agree with, nor can I understand, Norman Callan's comment that *Lucrece* "keeps so tediously close to the *Fasti* that, though it affords an admirable opportunity for comparing the Latin and the English (and incidentally for questioning Chaucer's Latinity again)[10] it affords little else." Chaucer worked,

---

supervivere, maculam corporis cruore delevit" (*Adversus Jovinianum*, I, xlvi [*PL*, XXIII, col. 287]). Jerome also praises other chaste virgins, widows, and wives in secular history who have committed suicide (cols. 282–288). Lucrece's story was told throughout the Middle Ages, notably by Jacques de Cessoles, in the *Solacium Ludi Schaccorum*, and by the Menagier de Paris. In the fourteenth century, Robert Holcot, who held the Dominican chair of theology at Oxford, listed Lucrece along with Penelope, Portia, and Dido as examples of faithful wives (from his commentary on *Wisdom*; see Beryl Smalley, *English Friars and Antiquity in the Early Fourteenth Century* [Oxford, Eng., Blackwell, 1960], pp. 155–156, 321). Lydgate cites Lucrece several times in catalogues of good women. See "On Gloucester's Approaching Marriage" (line 75), and "The Floure of Curtesye" (lines 201–202), in *The Minor Poems of John Lydgate*, ed. Henry Noble MacCracken, EETS, OS 192 (London, Oxford University Press, 1934, reprinted 1961), II, 604, 416; the *Temple of Glas*, ed. Josef Schick, EETS, ES 60 (London, 1891), lines 200–201 (see p. 76 for a list of references to Lucrece elsewhere in Lydgate). She is cited with Penelope as a kind of faithful wife no longer to be found in the *Roman de la rose* (8608–8650); Boccaccio tells her story in *De Claris Mulieribus* (chap. xlvi), and Gower, following Ovid and Livy, creates a sympathetic version in the *Confessio Amantis*, VII, 4754–5130. The list could go on.

9. Chaucer's source is clearly Ovid, as he himself indicates (*Fasti*, II, 685–852). The only question is whether he uses Livy (I, chaps. lvii–lix), whom he also mentions: "As seyth Ovyde and Titus Lyvius" (1683). See M. Bech, "Quellen und Plan der 'Legende of Goode Women' und ihr Verhältniss zur 'Confessio Amantis,' " *Anglia*, 5 (1882), 332–337, and W. W. Skeat, *The Complete Works of Geoffrey Chaucer* (Oxford, Eng., 1894), III, xxxix, 330–333. One or two details may come from Livy, including the name "Colatyn" (Collatinus), which is not in Ovid. But Chaucer could get this from Augustine (or the *Gesta Romanorum*, which has "Calatinus"). It seems unlikely that he used Livy or any source other than Ovid; see Edgar F. Shannon, *Chaucer and the Roman Poets* (Cambridge, Mass., Harvard University Press, 1929), pp. 220–228. He seems to have made no use of the versions in the *Roman de la rose* (8608–8650) or Boccaccio's *De Claris Mulieribus* (chap. xlvi).

10. He refers to W. W. Skeat's comment (*Oxford Chaucer*, III, 332) on line 1729: "That with a swerd it stingeth to myn herte," which Skeat saw as a misunderstanding of Ovid's "sed enim temerarius ille / est meus et stricto qualibet ense ruit" (751–752). Possibly, but this whole speech of Lucrece in Ovid is softened and much altered in Chaucer, and this change would be appropriate.

Callan thinks, with the *Fasti* in front of him; the effect of
Lucrece is "so dismally different from the 'Thisbe' that it is
hard to believe that one poet could have produced two so
dissimilar works when using the same method for both." [11]
Let us see.

Chaucer gets into his story and manages the particular
focus it needs with remarkable speed. That he should omit
the political background and the comments on the political
(and religious) significance of the event in Ovid is merely
common sense [12] and not especially meritorious. A few
characterizing details are added as the story opens: the
Romans "ful sterne were and stoute"; and Tarquin begins to jape, "for he was lyght of tonge" (1695, 1699). The
Romans, besieging Ardea, are bored by their inaction, and
Tarquin comments that "it was an ydel lyf; / No man
did there no more than his wif" (1700–1701). This last is
Chaucer's addition; it gets the story quickly and smoothly
into the topic of wives: "And lat us speke of wyves, that is
best; / Preyse every man his owene, as hym lest . . ."
(1702–1703).

Thereupon, in Ovid, each man lauds his wife, and, because of the wine, the dispute grows hot. In Chaucer, Tarquin's suggestion is followed immediately by Colatyn's
praise of Lucrece. The effect is not only more dramatic, but
the issue of Lucrece's goodness is stated at once and we can
move all the more quickly to the essential scenes. There is
no contestant for honors, as in Ovid; Lucrece stands alone.
Chaucer can therefore omit the visit to the royal palace and
the scene with the king's daughters-in-law, their necks
draped with garlands, keeping their vigils over the wine.

There is also a concentration of references to "heart" and "sword" in the poem,
frequently found together (see n. 19, below). Line 1729 fits this pattern. I
suspect it is deliberate.

11. "Thyn Owne Book; A Note on Chaucer, Gower, and Ovid," *RES*, 22
(1946), 272.

12. Chaucer cuts the beginning of Ovid's narrative, which relates certain
events connected with Tarquin, Ovid's account after Lucrece's suicide of the
political events which followed her death, and Ovid's comment after the ravish-
ing of Lucrece (811–812).

The strategy focuses our eyes on Lucrece and Tarquin (and Colatyn) alone. The other knights neither talk of their wives nor come to Rome; there are no rivals for our attention. In Ovid, we are told merely that the men gallop to Colatyn's house and find Lucrece spinning. Chaucer expands this slightly but most effectively. Later he will alter his original by making Tarquin's return to Lucrece a secret and stealthy one, not the open return of a kinsman who is given hospitality for the night. Here he shows in some detail the two men making their way to the chamber of Lucrece:

> The husbonde knew the estris wel and fyn,
> And prively into the hous they gon,
> Nor at the yate porter nas there non,
> And at the chambre-dore they abyde.
>
> (1715–1718)

The function of this addition is in part expository: it makes credible Tarquin's ability later to find Lucrece's room stealthily at night. In Ovid, also, there is no porter at the gate, but it is the gate of the royal palace that the men first visit. Shifted to the house of Colatyn, the detail introduces the possibility of secret access to Lucrece and suggests her defenselessness.

More important, the passage contributes to the story's structure and to its atmosphere. It is a private, surprise visit which anticipates and parallels the second private, unexpected visit of Tarquin alone. This first visit is innocent and legitimate: "The *husbonde* knew the estris wel and fyn." Its effect is to heighten the impact of Tarquin's second, criminal visit to the unguarded Lucrece. It contributes both to the tightness of the narrative and to the intensity of mood, which characterize this tale.

Chaucer has altered the portrait of Lucrece to make of her a truly pathetic heroine. He has made her a trifle softer and slightly more the devoted wife than she is in Ovid. He begins by cutting and changing her speech which Tarquin and Colatyn overhear. Her challenge to the city her husband is defending — "postmodo victa cades: melioribus, Ardea, restas" (*Fasti*, II, 749) — becomes the less vengeful, "God wolde the walles were falle adoun!" (1726). In Ovid she speaks of her husband as rash, rushing anywhere in battle with his sword drawn. Chaucer drops this. These changes, and a detail he adds of Lucrece sitting by her bedside, "Dischevele, for no malyce she ne thoughte" (1720),[13] make her a little less the Roman matron, a little more a soft, vulnerable, devoted woman whose only thought is of her husband. This, too, is the effect of the direct comment on her which follows. Chaucer's text is very close to Ovid here, but his presentation is slightly more rhetorical and, therefore, more emotional. The line about wifely chastity is his own:

> And therwithal ful tenderly she wep,
> And of hire werk she tok no more kep,
> And mekely she let hyre eyen falle;
> And thilke semblaunt sat hire wel withalle.
> And eek hire teres, ful of honeste,
> Embelished hire wifly chastite. . . .   (1732–1737)[14]

What is apparent is that Chaucer had a very clear image of Lucrece and of the effect he wished to create with her. She is the pure, innocent, devoted creature, and, what is usually though not necessarily a concomitant condition, she is defenseless. This defenselessness, which has already been suggested by Chaucer's changes, is further suggested by the line in which her husband Colatyn, "Or she of him was war, com stertynge in, / And seyde, 'Drede the nat, for I am here!' "

13. "Dischevele" is repeated when she *has* learned of "malyce" — when she summons her relatives after the rape: "And al dischevele, with hire heres cleere . . ." (1829). This comes from Ovid: "passis sedet illa capillis . . ." (813). Tarquin, in remembering Lucretia, mentions her hair lying carelessly on her neck: "neglectae collo sic iacuere comae" (772), which may have suggested the first "dischevele" to Chaucer. But the effect he gets from it, and from the repetition, is all his own.

14. There is only a comma after "chastite" in Robinson. Heavier pointing — a semicolon or period — seems called for.

The innocence of Lucrece, so essential for pathos in Chaucer, is strengthened by several changes in his material. The detail in Ovid repeated in, for example, the versions of Jacques de Cessoles and the Menagier de Paris, that of Tarquin's hand pressing on Lucretia's breast,[15] is omitted. The rape itself comes, not after Lucrece's submission before the threat of undeserved infamy, but after fear and shame cause her to swoon:

> . . . What for fer of sclaunder and drede of deth,
> She loste bothe at ones wit and breth,
> And in a swogh she lay, and wex so ded,
> Men myghte smyten of hire arm or hed;
> She feleth no thyng, neyther foul ne fayr.
>
> (1814–1818)

The intention of Chaucer's change seems quite clearly to intensify the emotional effect by conveying a sense of Lucrece's suffering and especially to make her an even more innocent (and passive), because unconscious, victim, than in Ovid.[16]

Lucrece's devotion is also stressed more than in Ovid. In fact, her chaste devotion to her husband becomes the central issue of the poem. In the opening lines we hear of her as "The verray wif, the verray trewe Lucresse" and of "hyre wifhod and hire stedefastnesse" (1686, 1687). The addition already commented on in her first appearance, the reference to "hire wifly chastite," sounds the note again, though at this point in the narrative chastity is not yet the issue; Chaucer's comment, however, makes it an issue in anticipation of events to come. In the conclusion, he once more sounds the theme: Even people with hearts of stone, he says,

---

15. "Positis urgentur pectora palmis, / tunc primum externa pectora tacta manu" (803–804).

16. In Gower's telling of the Lucrece story (Confessio Amantis, VII, 4754–5130), she is also unconscious (4986–4987). Gower's version, which lacks the economy and intensity of Chaucer's narrative, makes some effort to create a pathetic tone. The question of priority has not been settled or even much discussed. Many years ago Robert K. Root, in "Chaucer's Legend of Medea," PMLA, 24 (1909), 124–153, argued the priority of Gower's version (pp. 146–148), but he himself agreed it was a weak case.

would have pitied her, "Hir herte was so wyfly and so trewe" (1843). It is, in fact, the moral of his story, broadened, somewhat curiously, to make her the emblem of all women true in love:

> I telle hyt, for she was of love so trewe,
> Ne in hir wille she chaunged for no newe;
> And for the stable herte, sadde and kynde,
> That in these wymmen men may alday fynde.
> Ther as they kaste hir herte, there it dwelleth.
>
> (1874–1878)[17]

If the moral does not seem to do full justice to the story, let it pass. It will do as well as any sentiment, any moral. It springs from a rush of feeling, not a rational judgment, and is, therefore, appropriate. No simple intellectualized utterance would be adequate, and we have not been invited, at any moment in the poem, to intellectualize.

There is another quality in this poem, working with the pathetic mood, a quality rare in Chaucer, which gives the poem peculiar power. It is a sense of horror.[18] The horror is of course in the narrative itself, and Chaucer felt it and responded to it. The response does not take the form of overt comment, though he summarizes the story which Lucrece tells her assembled family as "This rewful cas and al thys thing horryble" (1838). His response is evident rather in his handling of the events in which the quality of horror inheres so as to underline this effect. The cutting and streamlining of the story, though possibly done for other considerations, contribute to this result. The swift, uninterrupted flow of action intensifies the nightmare.

The treatment of character, especially Tarquin's, plays its part. The two main figures, Tarquin and Lucrece, are of a kind to make for safety in this world: the one a king's son and the husband's friend; the other a chaste and devoted

---

17. There can be no suspicion of irony in this uncritical generalization, for the next lines go on to speak of Christ's praise of the faithfulness of women.

18. Horror may also be an integral element in the complex of qualities in the Chaucerian pathos. One can find traces of the "horrible" in all the narratives which qualify for the genre.

wife. But the combination leads to violence; chastity opposed to power and privilege engenders rape:

> For wel thoghte he she wolde nat ben geten;
> And ay the more that he was in dispayr,
> The more he coveyteth and thoughte hire fayr.
> His blynde lust was al his coveytynge.   (1753–1756)

It is from Tarquin that the horrible events spring, and Chaucer, following Ovid closely here, makes Tarquin's obsession with Lucrece believable, not by analysis but by display. We are given several glimpses of his inner thoughts, we have the image of the waves still heaving after a great storm, and we see his resolution. The hackneyed tempest metaphor is used freshly, for the force of the emotion is suggested not by the storm itself but by the waves still tossing after the tempest has gone. Chaucer has cut Ovid's image just a trifle, but to advantage. In Ovid the waves continue to heave because of the wind, which has fallen: "sed tamen a vento, qui fuit, unda tumet" (776). In Chaucer, the waves go on heaving without the wind, as though to suggest even more strongly the deep inner source of Tarquin's tumult:

> And as the se, with tempest al toshake,
> That after, whan the storm is al ago,
> Yit wol the water quappe a day or two. . . .
>   (1765–1767)

Chaucer has isolated and localized Tarquin in a way that Ovid does not do, with interesting consequences. We can see Tarquin more clearly in his emotion and can sense his betrayal of his moral code. In Ovid the men return to camp as the bird of morning sings. What follows, namely Tarquin's passionate reaction to Lucrece and his decision to have her by force, occurs in no specific place and at no specific time. Not so in Chaucer:

> A-morwe, whan the brid began to synge,
> Unto the sege he cometh ful privily,

And by hymself he walketh soberly,
Th'ymage of hire recordynge alwey newe. . . .

(1757–1760)

Not only do we see Tarquin with considerable clarity, but
the bird and the morning have strong associations with
courtly or romantic love and evoke the code that Tarquin
violates by his thoughts here and later by his actions.

The code of chivalry is invoked more explicitly in the
rape scene:

Tarquinius, that art a kynges eyr,
And sholdest, as by lynage and by ryght,
Don as a lord and as a verray knyght,
Whi hastow don dispit to chivalrye?
Whi hastow don this lady vilanye?
Allas! of the this was a vileyns dede!   (1819–1824)

This passage, which serves (as in Ovid) to cover the scene
of the rape without describing it, offers an ethical norm. In
part, it is a substitute for the weighty political significance
of the rape in Ovid: the end of kingly rule for Rome which
it occasioned. The broken code cannot compare with the
destruction of a dynasty; indeed, even in fourteenth-century terms it might seem inadequate. One may wonder
why there was no appeal to a larger morality. The answer,
I suggest, is that for this private martyrdom a proper opposition is achieved. Tarquin is false to his knightly code of
chivalry; Lucrece is true to her code of modesty and "wifly
chastite." [19] Her truth to her code, as well as her general

19. This opposition may account for a curious concentration of references
to the heart on the one hand, and the sword on the other. The two details
are frequently found together and perhaps direct our imagination toward the
climactic moments, Tarquin threatening Lucrece with death and (less clearly)
her own suicide, where heart and sword are in actual and dramatic conjunction. One may perhaps find a phallic significance in the sword image as
well. But the two images may also be explained as symbols of the two principles referred to here, devotion (heart) and chivalry (sword). Here are the
references to each. Where the detail is also in Ovid, the line reference to
the Fasti is given in parentheses. Where the two details occur together in the
same line, the line reference is italicized (for the heart image alone, to avoid
repetition): heart: 1704 (cf. 732), 1729 (cf. 754? "pectora"), 1738 (758, "anima"),

character of a loving, defenseless woman, demands the protection of chivalry. At the moral level, the horror is produced by the rejection of this demand, the brutal violation of this code by the knightly Tarquin. The horror is conveyed most immediately, however, by the atmosphere created in the climactic scene:

> And al alone his wey than hath he nome
> Unto the hous of Colatyn ful ryght.
> Doun was the sonne, and day hath lost his lyght;
> And in he cometh into a prive halke,
> And in the nyght ful thefly gan he stalke,
> Whan every wight was to his reste brought,
> Ne no wight hadde of tresoun swich a thought.
> Were it by wyndow or by other gyn,
> With swerd ydrawe, shortly he com in
> There as she lay, this noble wif Lucresse.   (1777–1786)

The darkness, the stealth, the loneliness convey a sense of the loss of all illumination, physical and moral, expressed in "and day hath lost his lyght;" the secret, criminal locale ("prive halke") through which the secret, criminal Tarquin slips evokes a mood of anticipatory horror. It is essentially Chaucer's own creation. In Ovid, Tarquin returns openly, is received and entertained as a kinsman, and, when all are asleep, comes to Lucrece's room. The Ovidian Tarquin is all the more despicable for violating the laws of kinship and hospitality, considerations that would have had some force with Chaucer. But Chaucer sacrifices them for the more ominous atmosphere of the lone and stealthy ravisher.[20]

The horror comes to a climax in Lucrece's words (not in Ovid) when she becomes aware of Tarquin's presence:

> And as she wok, hire bed she felte presse.

1751, 1764 (769? "sensus"), 1793, 1795, 1803, 1841, 1843, 1876, 1878; sword: 1729, 1775, 1785, 1793, 1795, 1804.

20. Shannon, *Chaucer and the Roman Poets*, p. 224, suggests that Lucrece's "perfect chastity and innocence appear in stronger relief when Tarquin enters her house stealthily by night." This is true, but the more notable effect, I believe, is the sense of horror.

"What beste is that," quod she, "that weyeth thus?"
"I am the kynges son, Tarquinius,"
Quod he. . . .   (1787–1790)

She thinks some animal is on the bed, a dog or cat perhaps, but it is too heavy for that. She is, however, right. It is an animal, Tarquin. The irony of "What beste is that" would be too obvious if we were forced, or allowed, to pause here. (The animal image links up with the wolf-lamb metaphor from Ovid a few lines later.) It is too easy for intellectual satisfaction, and any emotional response would be sentimental. But we are forced on and caught up much more intensely by what follows: "that weyeth thus." The sense of heaviness, the imagery of weight on the bed introduce the male attack, the masculine weight and power and the physical act of rape itself. These are Lucrece's only words in the scene, but they convey vividly the physical sensation and the emotional horror of her experience.[21]

The details that follow concentrate on violence, though the actual rape is not pictured: Tarquin's threat to kill her, the hand on her throat, the sword at her heart, the image of the wolf and the lamb, the threat to kill a servant and slander Lucrece. The point of view in the scene is worth examining. From the moment Lucrece's words make us aware of Tarquin's weight upon the bed, the scene, though reported by the narrator, is seen and felt primarily as Lucrece experienced it. Differences between Ovid's and Chaucer's handling of the wolf-lamb image point this up. Ovid writes, "Sed tremit, ut quondam stabulis deprensa relictis / parva sub infesto cum iacet agna lupo" (799–800). ("She trembled, as when a little lamb that has left the fold is seized and lies under a ravaging wolf.") In Chaucer it becomes, "Ryght as a wolf that fynt a lomb alone, / To whom shal she compleyne, or make mone?" (1798–1799). Ovid's version at first may seem more sympathetic, its syntax focusing on the lamb, Lucrece. But it is a view of her posi-

---

21. Derek Pearsall finds the line ludicrous: "Gower's Narrative Art," *PMLA*, 81 (1966), 481. But the word "beste" does not have quite the same overtones it has today. See *MED, s.v. beste* (n.), 6.

tion as seen by an observer. In Chaucer, the image is first of the wolf; the syntax is violated, but the result is Tarquin as he appeared to Lucrece. Most of the objective details of the scene relate to him, his actions and speeches. These are what she saw, what she heard. The subjective narration is restricted to Lucrece. The observer largely reports through her experience and her sensations.

After the rape scene the tone shifts once more to the pathetic. Essentially, Chaucer merely follows Ovid: Lucrece, dressed in mourning, weeping, sitting alone and silent as her friends and family gather, unable to look at them in her shame until at last she can reveal the whole story. The swift violence of the climactic action, her suicide, reduces the pathos somewhat. She is not completely helpless, though, as I have said, it is an act of resignation more than defiance. As in Ovid, the narrative attains a harmonious resolution. The act of violence that destroyed Lucrece's world is balanced by an act of violence that restores it. The modesty and chastity that have been her way of life are reasserted as she dies:

> And as she fel adoun, she kaste hir lok,
> And of hir clothes yet she hede tok.
> For in hir fallynge yet she had a care,
> Lest that hir fet or suche thyng lay bare;
> So wel she loved clennesse and eke trouthe.
>
> (1856–1860)

The detail, which is in Ovid, borders on the sentimental or the grotesque and perhaps slips over that border for some, but it makes vivid one final time the sense of modesty and chastity that were assaulted in her rape and the agony of her experience.

Several subsidiary qualities of the tale deserve comment. The story is perceived with remarkable clarity. There is rarely any clouding over of the narrative by excess of any kind, whether of comment, of emotionalism, or of authorial involvement. The judicious cutting of Ovid, the quick movement of the action contribute to this sense of

clarity. It derives from Chaucer's own perception. He
knows the issues and how serious and solemn they are. He
knows what kind of people Tarquin and Lucrece are and
how to suggest their characters to us. He has understood
their emotions and the horror of Lucrece's experience. His
compassion (his own word, early in the tale [1690]) serves
him well here, for the story has elements that invite murki-
ness and overinvolvement. He has resisted these invita-
tions and maintained control, sympathetic and perceptive
though he may be. The consequence is that he, and we, see
all things clearly.

His control is particularly evident in the style. It has perhaps less range than in *Thisbe.* Its quality is, if the phrase
will not be misunderstood, almost matter-of-fact. This tone
seems to have been adopted because the events, honestly
told, will speak for themselves. The main concern of the
style is not to elevate but to communicate what happened.
This does not mean it is merely reportorial. There is enough
variety to prevent monotony. There are, for example, occasional rhetorical passages, as when Tarquin remembers
Lucrece's "beaute and hyre cheere, / Hire yelwe her, hire
shap, and hire manere, / Hire hew, hire wordes, that she
hath compleyned. . ." (1746–1748). Or, "Thus lay hire her,
and thus fresh was hyre hewe; / Thus sat, thus spak, thus
span; this was hire chere; / Thus fayr she was, and this was
hire manere" (1761–1763). The alliteration of the second
line and the line's remarkable condensation (more con-
densed than the Latin) communicate that sense of speed
which animates the poem, and in a rhetorically constructed
passage maintains a steady, forward movement. But the
plain style predominates. Sometimes the language is pro-
verbial in effect if not in fact. This is the entire speech in
which Tarquin makes his decision:

> "For, maugre hyre, she shal my leman be!
> Hap helpeth hardy man alday," quod he.
> "What ende that I make, it shal be so."
>
> (1772–1774)

Even Lucrece has a touch of this in her voice in her final
scene, when her friends tell her she is forgiven everything:

> "Be as be may," quod she, "of forgyvyng,
> I wol not have noo forgyft for nothing."
> But pryvely she kaughte forth a knyf,
> And therwithal she rafte hirself hir lyf. . . .
>
> (1852–1855)

"Hap helpeth hardy man," "Be as be may." Thus matter-
of-factly, thus quickly, decisions of life and death are made
and events of momentous consequence occur in this poem.
There is no ranting, no reviling of Tarquin, no complaint
from Lucrece, no authorial wringing of hands. It is a remarkable performance in its restraint. Yet because of the
force of the events narrated and the skill of the narrating,
the final effect is moving and emotional. The pathetic,
underlined by a sense of violence and horror, attains full
but never excessive expression. The combination, de-
ployed with great success in this poem, is never achieved
in quite this form again. With this poem Chaucer has
mastered the pathetic mode.

[VIII]   Ariadne

Nothing shows more clearly than *Ariadne* Chaucer's intense concern to achieve in the *Legend* a variety of tones and styles and an expanded range of subject matter. This intention provides the best explanation for the peculiar effect of *Ariadne* and for its peculiar failure, which I believe the final judgment on this narrative must be. In its failure, and in its odd effect, it is most reminiscent of another failure, *Hypsipyle and Medea* (and, like that poem, a fascinating piece). Certainly it is totally unlike *Lucrece*, which it follows, and the differences seem the result of design, not accident.

A deliberate decision to avoid repeating the tone of pathos achieved with such success in *Lucrece* is suggested by Chaucer's treatment of his sources. There is still argument on some details, but without being inflammatory one can say that Chaucer drew on Ovid's *Metamorphoses* and *Heroides*,[1] Filippo's fourteenth-century translation of the *Heroides*,[2] and the *Ovide moralisé*.[3] In addition he may have used

1. Ovid, *Metamorphoses*, VII, 456–458; VIII, 6–182, and *Heroides*, x; M. Bech, "Quellen und Plan der 'Legende of Goode Women' und ihr Verhältniss zur 'Confessio Amantis,' " *Anglia*, 5 (1882), 337–342; W. W. Skeat, *The Complete Works of Geoffrey Chaucer* (Oxford, Eng., 1894), III, xxxix, 333–340; Edgar F. Shannon, *Chaucer and the Roman Poets* (Cambridge, Mass., Harvard University Press, 1929), pp. 228–258.
2. Sanford Brown Meech, "Chaucer and an Italian Translation of the *Heroides*," *PMLA*, 45 (1930), 110–128. The "Filippo" of the translation was possibly Filippo Ceffi. For the text, Meech refers to *Epistole Eroiche di Ovidio Nasone Volgarizzata nel Buon Secolo della Lingua Seconda la Edizione di Sisto Riessinger del Secolo XV . . .* (Milan, 1842). (I have not seen this edition. My references to Filippo's translation are to the Florence edition of 1819. See

Boccaccio's *Teseide*,[4] and *De Genealogia Deorum*,[5] a Latin version of Plutarch's Life of Theseus, the *Aeneid*, the *Fabulae* of Hyginus,[6] and Machaut's *Le Jugement dou Roy de Navarre*.[7] This sounds worse than the reality itself: *Ariadne* is not quite the crazy quilt this roll call would imply. It is true that the sources are responsible for some of the poem's difficulties. We can see Chaucer improvising at moments and creating his action out of bits and pieces, but this seems to have been largely a matter of deliberate choice. The

Chapter II, n. 8, above.) Meech says Filippo's work was "pedestrian," a "faithful translation which afforded no new interpretation to any of the stories of the *Heroides*." Chaucer used it, he believes, as a "pony" for *Dido, Medea, Phyllis, Hypermnestra*, and *Ariadne*. He may have garnered a few details of fact from the prefatory note to Phyllis' Epistle and perhaps, in that, to the letters of Phaedra and Ariadne (128).

3. *Ovide moralisé*, VIII, 1–1583. John Livingstone Lowes first advanced the *Ovide moralisé* as a source for *Ariadne* in "Chaucer and the *Ovide Moralisé*," *PMLA*, 33 (1918), 303–319. Shannon argued against any but the slightest influence from the *Ovide* (*Chaucer and the Roman Poets*, pp. 228ff., esp. 247). Sanford Brown Meech, "Chaucer and the *Ovide Moralisé* — A Further Study," *PMLA*, 46 (1931), 182–204, supported Lowes and offered further evidence that Chaucer used the *Ovide* for *Ariadne* and *Philomela* (see esp. 182–183, 185–201). But he found no satisfactory evidence that Chaucer used the *Ovide* in the other legends or in other works before the *Legend of Good Women*. He may have used it for the Theseus-Ariadne passage in the *House of Fame*, 405–426, but not necessarily (pp. 183–185, 201–202).

4. John Livingston Lowes, "The Prologue to the *Legend of Good Women* Considered in Its Chronological Relations," *PMLA*, 20 (1905), 805–807ff.

5. *De Genealogia Deorum*, XI, chaps. xxvii, xxix, xxx; Skeat's suggestion (*Oxford Chaucer*, III, xxxix), though in the notes to Ariadne he makes no reference to Boccaccio (see p. 333). C. G. Child, "Chaucer's *Legend of Good Women* and Boccaccio's *De Genealogia Deorum*," *MLN*, 11 (1896), 482–487, argued the case for borrowing in some detail. Shannon, in rejecting Lowes's suggestion of the *Ovide*, strongly supported *De Genealogia* as an important source (*Chaucer and the Roman Poets*, pp. 229–247ff.). Meech reinforces Lowes's case for the *Ovide*, opposing Shannon, and says, "the instances of the impress of Boccaccio's mythology cited by Shannon appear uniformly weak" ("Chaucer and the *Ovide Moralisé*," p. 182).

6. Suggested by Skeat, *Oxford Chaucer*, III, xxxix, 333. He cited *Aeneid*, VI, 20–30, and Hyginus, *Fabulae*, chaps. xli–xliii.

7. Lowes suggested Machaut as a source ("Chaucer and the *Ovide Moralisé*," pp. 320–325); Shannon opposed this in arguing the case for *De Genealogia* (*Chaucer and the Roman Poets*, pp. 228–248). But Meech, though he finds the *Ovide* accounts for all the details in *Ariadne*, believes Machaut gave Chaucer the story for the *House of Fame* ("Chaucer and the *Ovide Moralisé*," pp. 182–185). The passage referred to in Machaut is *Navarre*, 2707–2769.

Metamorphoses gave him only a précis of the Ariadne-Theseus story; the *Heroides* gave him a cadenza and a few details of action; Filippo's translation gave him a few more such details. *Ariadne* is, however, one of the two legends for which Chaucer seems certainly to have used the *Ovide moralisé*, and this offered a narrative with attractive possibilities. Though not a completely integrated and developed narrative, it could be made such with little difficulty.[8] The *Ovide* version focuses on Ariadne throughout; it moves quickly from a speech or scene in which she is dominant to another where she is again in the spotlight. The mood is perhaps hyperemotional; the method, too dependent on passionate soliloquy or passionate monologue. Chaucer was not content merely to lower the pitch or trim the method. Not much more than this would have made what he found in the *Ovide* harmonize with the *Lucrece*. Chaucer would have none of it, neither mood nor method.

The method of *Lucrece* had been economy throughout, with a concentration on event, on action. The method of *Ariadne* is expansion, relying chiefly on talk. *Ariadne* is almost a conversation piece. Its general manner is slack, where *Lucrece* is intense.

Ariadne begins with a longish exposition. After an apostrophe to Minos and a denunciation of the false Theseus, the narrative explains Minos' enmity against Athens because of the murder of his son Androgeos, Minos' siege, Athens' betrayal by Nisus' daughter Scylla, and the tribute of a human sacrifice to the Minotaur exacted from Athens which leads, finally, to Theseus' choice by lot and his appearance as a fated victim in Crete. One can blame the sources here if one wishes. In the *Metamorphoses* and the *Ovide moralisé* one gets to Ariadne and Theseus by way of Minos' siege, Scylla's love for Minos, the unnatural love of

---

8. Gower's version of the Ariadne story in *Confessio Amantis*, V, 5231–5483, is a rather routine performance, but it is a straightforward, unified narrative and demonstrates that the material was easily susceptible to unified narrative treatment. Chaucer, trying to do much more than Gower, fails, but he creates a more interesting version.

Minos' wife Pasiphae for the bull, thereby coming to the Minotaur. Chaucer wisely drops all reference to the Pasiphae story, but he keeps, unnecessarily it would seem, the story of Scylla's love. By shamelessly tampering with the evidence to remove her betrayal of father and country and Minos' horrified rejection of her love, Chaucer creates, apparently, another abandoned lady for his collection. But was this worth the delay in reaching the main story? And was this really his intention?

The puzzle is complicated further when Chaucer continues this slackness in the middle section, which also lacks tension; or perhaps it would be more just to say it avoids tension. It is constructed almost entirely of a series of speeches (158 lines of the poem's 342) between Ariadne, Phaedra, and Theseus. The suggestion may have come from the *Ovide moralisé*, where Ariadne has a soliloquy of 100 lines, a speech of 22 lines to Theseus, and several shorter speeches.[9] Chaucer eliminates the soliloquy and allows Theseus, who, as Meech observes, in the *Ovide* is "laconic to the point of *gaucherie*," to talk at length. Phaedra, who says nothing in the *Ovide*, is given a long speech which was originally Ariadne's. This greater dramatization in Chaucer's version is an improvement on the original: there are three voices instead of one, and we have a more fully realized scene and more fully realized characters. The possibility exists for heightened drama as well, but the possibility is never exploited. The absence of tension is due to several features. The speeches are too long for dramatic interaction. More important, Chaucer has completely discarded the lyric, emotional quality of the speeches in the original; instead, he has made the dialogue curiously circumstantial and prosy. Further, the characters emerging in these speeches are inappropriate for the romantic situation in

9. The soliloquy: *Ovide moralisé*, VIII, 1144–1249; her speeches to Theseus: 1273–1295, 1298–1301, 1306–1320. Her final lament after Theseus abandons her is comparatively brief: 1349–1361. The text of Book VIII of the *Ovide moralisé* is that edited by C. De Boer in *Verhandelingen der Koninklijke Akademie van Weteschappen te Amsterdam*, New Ser., XXX (1931).

which they are cast. Finally, and most comprehensively, the tone of these speeches and of the whole middle section is wrong for our preconceptions.

The problem of tone is the central problem of the poem. It can be sharply illustrated by a single word: "foreyne," that is, outhouse, privy. It is a word outrageously inappropriate in a love narrative, and yet it is there:

> The tour, there as this Theseus is throwe
> Doun in the botom derk and wonder lowe,
> Was joynynge in the wal to a foreyne;
> And it was longynge to the doughtren tweyne
> Of Mynos, that in hire chaumbers grete
> Dwellten above, toward the mayster-strete
> Of Athenes, in joye and in solas.
>
> (1960–1966)

And this "foreyne" is apparently the channel by which Ariadne and Phaedra hear Theseus' complaint in prison:

> Noot I not how, it happede par cas,
> As Theseus compleynede hym by nyghte,
> The kynges doughter, Adryane that highte,
> And ek hire syster Phedra, herden al
> His compleynynge, as they stode on the wal. . . .
>
> (1967–1971)

The "foreyne" clearly seems intended to deny romantic possibilities to the relationship which follows. It is reminiscent, inevitably, of May's reading of Damian's letter in the *Merchant's Tale:*

> She feynede hire as that she moste gon
> Ther as ye woot that every wight moot neede;
> And whan she of this bille hath taken heede,
> She rente it al to cloutes atte laste,
> And in the pryvee softely it caste.
>
> (E 1950–1954)

The *Merchant's Tale* is, in fact, the poem of Chaucer's later years which *Ariadne* suggests, and *Ariadne* can perhaps best be understood as an initial and incomplete exploration of an attitude toward love which the *Merchant's Tale* explores completely and successfully. The intention of the detail here, and of similar detail in the story of January and May, is to explode "romantic" attitudes. The artistic intent is all the clearer if we accept the source suggested for the passage. The word worried Skeat, and he tried to make it mean something gentler than it does.[10] But Lowes faced up honestly to the word's meaning in the course of arguing that Boccaccio's *Teseide* lay behind this scene.[11] The evidence is not overwhelming, though the argument has not been seriously challenged.[12] According to

10. Skeat, *Oxford Chaucer*, III, 335 (note on l.1962). See *MED, s.v. forein* (n.), 3. The meaning of the term was put beyond any shadow of doubt by J. W. Draper, in "Chaucer's 'Wardrobe,' " *Englische Studien*, 60 (1926), 238–251. Draper says of the situation here: "Once granted that he (Theseus) is imprisoned in the bottom of the tower and that they (Ariadne and Phedra) live at the top, apparently with several floors between, the importance of a wardrobe-flue at once becomes evident as a sound-conductor for his voice. From this rather obvious condition, it seems to me a reasonable inference that Theseus was imprisoned in an oubliette that may have served also as the pit for the garderobe tower the upper part of which belonged to the princesses' suite" (p. 251). Draper argues that there is no humor in the passage in *Ariadne*: "The Middle Ages apparently looked upon plumbing conveniences as fit subjects for references in serious literature." His references, however, are to the *Rhymed Chronicle* and the *Parson's Tale*. The *MED* has citations from the *Northern Homily* and *Handlyng Synne;* the *Legend* (this passage) is the only "literary" reference. The issue, in any event, is not so much humor as the antiromantic effect of the detail, and about this there can be no question.

11. John Livingston Lowes, "The Prologue to the *Legend of Good Women* Considered in Its Chronological Relations," *PMLA*, 20 (1905), 804–810; on "foreyn," see p. 805.

12. The "prison" and Theseus' offer to become Ariadne's page are the two details Lowes thought Chaucer might have borrowed from Boccaccio. If Lowes is correct, certain interesting possibilities open up. In the Italian, "giardino" has as one of its (obsolete) meanings "latrine, closet." (See *The Cambridge Italian Dictionary* [Cambridge, Eng., Cambridge University Press, 1962], *s.v. giardin-o.)* Chaucer did not simply mistranslate. But this other meaning may have started his thoughts in this direction, though the choice was deliberate. Moreover, if the *Teseide* was in his mind here, Chaucer has turned both the situation and the mood upside down. For two young men and a lady in the *Teseide* we have two young ladies and a man, with the young ladies playing the more masculine role. The prison is high in the *Teseide;* it is low (in several senses) here. The respective attitudes of men and women are reversed, in fact. The servant's role is played genuinely by Arcite; it seems only a hypocritical gesture by Theseus. The jailer, drugged and dispensed with in the *Teseide,* here

Lowes, Chaucer took Boccaccio's account of Palamon and Arcite's "prigione / Allato allato al giardino amoroso" and transformed it into Theseus' tower "joynynge in the wal to a foreyne." Lowes found the change completely puzzling and could only hypothesize that it was "the crude working out of a suggestion from a story not yet made the poet's own." But it seems self-evident that a writer does not change a "giardino amoroso" into a privy by accident or by inept design; only when he wishes to make his source completely his own does he take such coarse liberties with it.

The antiromantic attitude implied here explains much in the poem that is otherwise baffling or irritating. One can make a few reasonable guesses as to why Chaucer might have chosen this approach to his materials. The context in which the Ariadne story appears, and certain aspects of the story itself, suggest an antiromantic attitude, particularly toward women in love. The story begins with Scylla's infatuation for Minos when he is besieging Athens. Chaucer makes of it a sad little tale: in return for ensuring Minos' success against Athens, Scylla is rewarded by Minos' letting her "drenche in sorwe and distresse . . ." (1919). This is not the attitude of Ovid or the author of the *Ovide moralisé*, who condemn her outright, with no expression of sympathy whatsoever; nor does she deserve one.[13] Her passion has led her to betray her father (by cutting off the talismanic

---

becomes a fellow conspirator who is to be rewarded and who joins their company as they escape; this makes again for a lowering of tone, even if the hint for the jailer (never named) comes from the figure of Daedalus in the original.

13. It is just possible that Chaucer's attitude is not as sympathetic toward Nissus' daughter as it at first appears:

She made Mynos wynnen thilke place,
So that the cite was al at his wille,
To saven whom hym leste, or elles spille.
But wikkedly he quitte hire kyndenesse. . . .

(1915–1918)

There may be an irony concealed in the "spille-kyndenesse" conjunction. So also there may be an irony earlier in the introduction (though it does not relate to Scylla) in the account of the death of Minos' son in Athens, who was "slayn, lernynge philosophie,/Ryght in that citee, nat but for envye" (1898–1899). The "philosophie-envye" rime is a strange and unphilosophical pairing.

lock of hair in Ovid, by beheading him in the *Ovide*) and to betray her country. Minos recoils in horror at her unnatural act and righteously spurns her.[14] The story of the inflamed traitress is succeeded by the story of Pasiphae's unnatural lust for the bull and its consummation, which is quietly omitted. Ariadne's story, which follows, is the most savory of the three, but here, too, is a woman in a passion who takes the initiative in an affair of the heart and does, in a sense, betray her father. (In the *Ovide*, moreover, though the narrative proper gives her feelings the center of the stage, the moralization hardly supplies a floral tribute, for Ariadne is interpreted as the Synagogue, Theseus as Christ, and Phaedra as the Gentiles.[15]) The context, then, in the *Ovide*, might well discourage a romantic attitude.

A possibly more potent reason, however, would be an interest in variation. Theseus, like Jason and Aeneas, is the hero rescued but ungrateful (in Gower, the Theseus-Ariadne story is told as an exemplum of ingratitude). In *Dido*, Chaucer had already exploited the theme of ingratitude fully. In *Hypsipyle and Medea*, where some play is made at inverting courtly conventions, the magical success of the ingrate is explored. Another story of ingratitude should, ideally, receive fresh treatment of some kind.

Ingratitude implies a failure to supply a *quid pro quo*. There is always, in romance, an expectation of this *quid pro quo*. It is not stated, it is hardly demanded (at least not crassly), but it is there. Indeed, the essence of much romance is that the *quid*, when it finally arrives, is so delightfully out of proportion to the *quo*. The enormous happiness after the honest love is one simple form. Another is the great return (a wife *both* young and beautiful *and* faithful) for the correct response to the question (giving the woman

14. See Ovid, *Metamorphoses*, VII, 95–100, especially such phrases as "heu facinus!" (85); "praedaque potita nefanda" (86); "scelerataque dextra" (94). And the *Ovide moralisé*, VIII, 216–237: "Si fu plus hardie a mal faire / La desloiaux de put' affaire" (203–204); "La desloiaux fille enragie" (212); and later, "Putain devint abandonee" (396).

15. *Ovide moralisé*, VIII, 1395–1583.

authority) as in the *Wife of Bath's Tale*. So often the reward is the king's daughter and great wealth to one of lower rank or unknown birth and no possessions after the performance of faithful service.

The pattern is seen in some of its most outrageous forms in the Middle English romances. In *Libeaus Desconus*, the hero of no name and unknown birth (Gawain's illegitimate son), after a series of incredible victories, transforms (involuntarily) a dragon into a beautiful lady whom he marries and thereby becomes possessed of "fifty and five" castles and great wealth. In the *Squire of Low Degree* the young man of low birth, whose love lament for the king's daughter is overheard by her, is granted her love and, after seven years of chivalric service abroad, marries her. (The poem concentrates on the princess' faithful devotion to the squire, whom she believes to have been killed; she is rewarded by what is for her a miraculous return from the dead.)

What Chaucer seems to be doing in *Ariadne* is exposing this expectation of reward implicit in so much romance. Love takes on a curiously calculating quality in the conversation between Ariadne and Phaedra, and between Ariadne and Theseus. Though the situation is potentially dramatic and emotional, emotion evaporates and is replaced by reason. Instead of a pledged word, a promise based on intense feeling, a spontaneous, impulsive generosity, we have a bargain struck.

There is remarkably little talk about love, almost none in fact. The intense passion aroused in Ariadne in the *Ovide* after she sees the prisoner is replaced by pity in Chaucer's tale. Ariadne and Phaedra, under the antiromantic circumstances already noted, overhear Theseus lamenting his fate, "And of his wo they hadde compassioun" (1974). Ariadne then speaks briefly:

> Phedra, leve syster dere,
> This woful lordes sone may ye nat here,
> How pitously compleyneth he his kyn,
> And ek his povre estat that he is in.
> And gilteles? Now, certes, it is routhe!

> And if ye wol assenten, by my trouthe,
> He shal ben holpen, how so that we do.
>
> (1978–1984)

Phaedra responds, somewhat mechanically, "Ywis, me is as wo / For hym as evere I was for any man," and promptly launches into forty lines of detailed advice on how to rescue him. Her speech is built up out of a few lines of Ariadne's soliloquy in the *Ovide* and one of her speeches to Theseus [16] — purged, of course, of all the emotion in the original. Phaedra is concerned with practical matters connected with the rescue of Theseus. The speech is much expanded and unduly circumstantial:

> For in the prysoun, ther he shal descende,
> Ye wote wel that the beste is in a place
> That nys nat derk, and hath roum eek and space
> To welde an ax, or swerd, or staf, or knyf;
> So that, me thynketh, he shulde save his lyf.
> If that he be a man, he shal do so.
>
> (1997–2002)

It is an eminently practical voice speaking, a calculating voice measuring the room in which to wield a weapon, and it is the voice of inventory: "an ax, or swerd, or staf, or knyf." It can tell us in detail how the Minotaur will be overcome:

> And we shul make hym balles ek also
> Of wex and tow, that whan he gapeth faste,
> Into the bestes throte he shal hem caste
> To slake his hunger and encombre his teth;
> And right anon, whan that Theseus seth
> The beste achoked, he shal on hym lepe
> To slen hym, or they comen more to-hepe.
>
> (2003–2009)

And so on with plans for solving the difficulties of the Dae-

---

16. *Ibid.*, VIII, 1220–1224, where Ariadne remarks on the impossibility of Theseus' escaping from the maze, even if he does kill the Minotaur; see also *ibid.*, 1308–1320. (The first two lines here are punctuated in De Boer's text as though they are not part of Ariadne's speech.)

dalian maze ("for the hous is krynkeled to and fro, / And hath so queynte weyes for to go").

This might be put down as a trick of exposition, and it is true that we foresee the action in such detail that the event itself, when it occurs, can be summarized in six lines (2144–2149). But the effect is not only to murder suspense but to deflate heroism. Actions plotted out in advance for a man, by a woman, cannot easily stir the blood. Theseus becomes at best a stunt man, following his script. There is no sharp edge to his actions, presented so prosily by a shrewd-minded lady: a ball of wax and tow, to stick in the monster's teeth. It might almost have come out of *Mrs. Beeton's Household Management*.[17]

Lest any overtones of heroism cling to Theseus, Phaedra herself expresses her doubts about him several times in her speech. One instance has already been quoted: "If that he be a man, he shal do so" (2002). She begins by striking this note:

> Lat us wel taste hym at his herte-rote,
> That if so be that he a wepen have,
> Wher that he dar, his lyf to kepe and save,
> Fyghten with the fend, and hym defende.
>
> (1993–1996)

And she ends on the same less than triumphant chord: "This is my red, if that he dar it take" (2024).[18]

Theseus, summoned with the jailer, says nothing to brighten his image. When the scheme has been proposed to him (a one-line summary suffices: "Whan these thynges ben acorded thus" [2027]), he plops down on one knee and vows eternal service to her, "as a wreche unknowe":

> And, as I seyde, ben of youre court a page,

17. In all fairness, it should be pointed out that Ariadne gives explicit details in the *Ovide*: "Un poleton compost li baille / De glus, de saijn et de cole" (1308–1309; see also 1310–1320). Here, after her inner turmoil, the details come as something of an anticlimax, but they seem at worst inappropriate. In Chaucer, the details are part of a portrait where they seem quite in character.

18. See the same undercutting of Jason's "heroism" in *Hypsipyle and Medea*, Chapter VI, above.

> If that ye vouche-sauf that in this place
> Ye graunte me to han so grete a grace
> That I may han nat but my mete and drynke.
> And for my sustenaunce yit wol I swynke. . . .
>
> (2037–2041)

He is certain he will remain undetected, since Minos has never seen him.

> Ne no man elles, shal me conne espye;
> So slyly and so wel I shal me gye,
> And me so wel disfigure and so lowe,
> That in this world ther shal no man me knowe,
> To han my lyf, and for to han presence
> Of yow, that don to me this excellence.
>
> (2044–2049)

He will send the jailer to his country, where his father will reward him — he is, after all, a king's son. If all four of them were in his country, they'd see whether or not he was lying. And once more he is promising service:

> And if I profre you in low manere
> To ben youre page and serven yow ryght here,
> But I yow serve as lowly in that place,
> I preye to Mars. . . .
>
> (2060–2063)

And he is off for nine lines of cursing himself and his friends resoundingly if he should prove faithless, ending finally, "And mercy, lady! I can nat elles seye" (2073).

A strange speech. It is not just that we know in advance that his promises are false and that he will be forsworn. (The announced purpose of the poem is "to clepe ageyn unto memorye / Of Theseus the grete untrouthe of love"). There is too much insistence on the lowliness of the role he is willing to play. If this is, as Lowes suggested, an echo of Arcite's return to Athens disguised, willing "to drugge and drawe," serving as Emelye's page a year or two, it is a mocking echo. It is one thing for a knight in a romance to abase himself to be near his lady; it is another thing to be eager for self-abase-

ment to save one's skin ("To han my lyf"). He also is something of a calculator,[19] and he seems anything but a hero.
It is difficult to know whether the lowliness of the role he offers to play is important in itself, to rob Theseus of heroism and dignity, or whether it is important only to reveal the extravagance of his protestations and the villainy of his betrayal. Ariadne rejects his offer to serve her in so lowly a capacity. It is unworthy of him, and of her. She remarks, with another swipe at the heroic image, "But what is that that man nyl don for drede?" (2095). She suggests marriage instead and bids him swear to marry her when they return to his country. He responds with enthusiasm:

> "Ye, lady myn," quod he, "or ellis torn
> Mote I be with the Mynotaur to-morwe! [20]
> And haveth hereof myn herte blod to borwe,
> If that ye wole; if I hadde knyf or spere,
> I wolde it laten out, and theron swere,
> For thanne at erst I wot ye wole me leve."
>
> (2103–2108)

And so on for another five lines. There is something swaggering and foolish about all this talk of swearing by blood, especially when we know he will be false. But his speech concludes with an even more surprising turn:

> For now, if that the sothe I shal yow say,
> I have yloved yow ful many a day,
> Thogh ye ne wiste it nat, in my cuntre,
> And aldermost desired yow to se
> Of any erthly livynge creature.

19. The speech, and Theseus' offer to be a "page," may have been suggested by his brief speech in the Ovide, when Ariadne asks what her recompense might be if she rescued him: "Franche riens, cors et cuer vous don/Et vostre liges hom devieng,/Se vous m'aidiez" (1296–1298). But this is no more than the language of the courtly romance, not the language of domestic servitude. Chaucer has made Theseus' speech out of whole cloth (and "burel cloth" at that).
20. Is there any ambiguity here? The lines surely mean, "Yes, I'll marry you when we get to my homeland, or may I be torn to pieces by the Minotaur tomorrow." But could it also mean, "Yes, I'll marry you, or otherwise I must be torn to pieces by the Minotaur tomorrow"? This would make him not only a practical minded but a somewhat reluctant lover.

> Upon my trouthe, I swere, and yow assure
> This sevene yer I have youre servaunt be.
> Now have I yow, and also have ye me,
> My dere herte, of Athenes duchesse!
>
> (2114–2122)

It is the first anyone has heard of this, and, if Chaucer had meant us to believe it, he would have prepared us for it. Loving the distant, unseen, unknown lady for seven years is a stock device of romance at its most simpleminded; [21] in Theseus' mouth it becomes a bald-faced lie. He has made it all up on the spur of the moment. The man will say and do anything to squeeze out of a tight place or to gain an advantage. He may even be a coward!

One might feel a certain sympathy with Ariadne for being taken in by Theseus' promises, except that only a fool could be blind to his obvious insincerity. Ariadne is being handled in this scene in a way that almost precludes sympathy. When she responds to Theseus' offer of service, we find that Chaucer has replaced her delicate considerations of honor and dignity in the *Ovide* with delicate considerations of gentility and personal advantage. She rejects his offer to serve her as a page as unbecoming:

> "A kynges sone, and ek a knyght," quod she,
> "To ben my servaunt in so low degre,
> God shilde it, for the shame of wemen alle,
> And lene me nevere swich a cas befalle!"
>
> (2080–2083)

She has a more sensible and more advantageous proposal:

> Yit were it betere that I were youre wyf,
> Syn that ye ben as gentil born as I,
> And have a reaume, nat but faste by,
> Than that I suffered, gilteles, yow sterve,
> Or that I let yow as a page serve.
> It nys no profre as unto youre kynrede. . . .
>
> (2089–2094)

21. On the satiric treatment of this motif in *Flamenca*, see Gordon M. Shedd, *"Flamenca*: A Medieval Satire On Courtly Love," *Chaucer Review*, 2 (1967), 47–48.

She suggests, since her sister is also involved, that Theseus give Phaedra his son in marriage when they return to his homeland and demands his word upon it: "Ye swere it here, upon al that may be sworn." We have seen how promptly Theseus provides his oaths, and suddenly discovers a seven-year love as well.

When he concludes by dangling before her the bait of a title — "My dere herte, of Athenes duchesse!" — her response is wonderful to see:

> This lady smyleth at his stedefastnesse,
> And at his hertely wordes, and his chere,
> And to hyre sister seyde in this manere,
> Al softely: "Now, syster myn," quod she,
> "Now be we duchesses, bothe I and ye,
> And sekered to the regals of Athenes,
> And bothe hereafter likly to ben quenes;
> And saved from his deth a kynges sone,
> As evere of gentil women is the wone
> To save a gentyl man, emforth hire myght,
> In honest cause, and namely in his ryght.
> Me thynketh no wight oughte herof us blame,
> Ne beren us therfore an evil name."
>
> (2123–2135)

Not only is Ariadne unlike her original, she is unlike any other proper romance heroine. She seems a combination of Dorigen and the Wife of Bath! [22] It would shame woman-kind if she let a king's son be a page or let him die guilty of no crime. What a waste! Much better that she should become his wife since considerations of birth (you are as gen-teelly born as I) and geographical convenience (your king-dom is close by) recommend it. She arranges a marriage for her sister as well, on grounds of expedience (no question of love here). And with the gentle voice of the romance hero-ine ("softely") she tries the sound of "duchess" on her tongue for her sister and herself and finds it good. They will

22. See Pat Trefzger Overbeck, "Chaucer's Good Woman," *Chaucer Review*, 2 (1967), 75–94, esp. 81–82, 82–94, for the argument that the Wife of Bath is the logical development of the women in the *Legend*.

be allied to the royal family of Athens, the title of "queen" beckons from the future, and all this while saving a king's son, the customary business of gentlewomen. Garrett was surely correct in finding the whole interchange between Theseus and Ariadne farcical.[23] And Paull Baum did not let Ariadne's whisper to Phaedra pass unnoticed: "her eye," he says, "was obviously on the main chance."[24]

Or is it calculation? Can it be that Ariadne has read or heard too many romances and is talking and acting as she thinks a romance heroine should? Whisk Catherine Morland out of Northanger Abbey into a fourteenth-century castle, and she might talk this way. At any rate somebody has been reading too many romances. For there hangs over this middle section a sense of parody, parody of romance gestures and actions, speeches and language, though nowhere so clearly defined as in *Sir Thopas*, nor so skillfully handled. There are elements of a romance situation present: the lament overheard, the young hero in peril, the gracious highborn lady. Favorite romance words or phrases are to be found: "hire syster fre" (1977, 2152), dwelling "in joye and in solas" (1966), "in my [his] cuntre" (2022, 2053, 2057, 2116, 2216), and an untypical inversion, "twenty yer and thre" (2075).[25] Theseus is given a favorite romance posture: "Adoun sit Theseus upon his kne" (2028),[26] and we have two heroines, Scylla (1908) and Ariadne (1971), becoming romantically involved while standing on walls, which may be part of Chaucer's reason for including Scylla.

23. Robert Max Garrett, " 'Cleopatra the Martyr' and Her Sisters," *JEGP*, 22 (1923), 70–71.

24. Paull Baum, "Chaucer's 'Glorious Legende,' " *MLN*, 60 (1945), 380.

25. Chaucer's usual form for numerals is "5 and 20," "4 and 20," etc. Incidentally, the carelessness of the romances, at times, about consistency, or the willingness to condone the improbable, explains, I would guess, what has bothered commentators: the fact that Theseus' age is given as twenty-three at line 2075 and that Ariadne is asking him at line 2099 to marry his son to Phaedra when they return to his country. Chaucer cannot possibly have nodded this hard here. The wild incongruity is meant to amuse us, I am certain.

26. Rare in Chaucer. The only other instances are *Canterbury Tales*, D 1588, 2120; *Troilus and Criseyde*, II, 1202; *Romance of the Rose*, 1980; *Legend of Good Women*, F 455, G 445.

Parody may explain that undue circumstantiality in Phaedra's and Theseus' speeches, and the inclusion of such irrelevant, puzzling details as, for example, the information that Ariadne and Phaedra "Dwellten above, *toward the mayster-strete*" (1965), information that comes to nothing; or the comment that Ariadne and Phaedra stood on the wall "And lokeden upon the bryghte mone. / *Hem leste nat to go to bedde so sone . . .*" (1972–1973), which again seems completely gratuitous, even witless (unless meant to suggest an overromantic nature, and even then —). These are reminiscent of those pointless or excessive details one finds in the Middle English romances, sometimes to make a rhyme or fill a line or pad a stanza: what Laura Hibbard (Loomis) referred to as the "unhappy genius for the concrete and trivial at the expense of the imaginative effect." [27]

There is, too, the obsessive preoccupation with birth and rank and family that we have seen running through the narrative and deflating any romantic atmosphere. This preoccupation, less obvious, is not uncommon in the romances where an unknown or concealed parentage raises constant speculation until it proves to be properly elevated and where the reward for courage and service or for truth to one's love is so often a title or wealth or both. The phrase "a kynges sone" and its variant "a lordes sone" runs as a motif through the tale.[28] Together with the interest in being duchesses and queens, it exposes the naïve hunger of the romance for high birth and generous reward that constitute the happy ending.

Calculation seems to win the day. The adventure with the Minotaur is carried through successfully in six lines and Theseus, Ariadne, Phaedra, and the jailer flee the country, but not before Theseus has lined his pockets: "And by the

27. Laura Hibbard (Loomis), *Mediaeval Romance in England: A Study of the Sources and Analogues of the Non-Cyclic Metrical Romances* (New York, Oxford University Press, 1924), p. 97. Italics in the passages quoted in the preceding paragraph are mine.

28. "Kynges sone," 1953, 1975, 2055, 2080, 2130; "lordes sone," 1979, 2023; allusion to his royal birth, 1944–1945. Another king's son, Minos' son, Androgeus, is alluded to at 1896, 1900–1901, 1938–1939.

gayler geten hath a barge, / And of his wyves tresor gan it charge . . ." (2150–2151). It will never do to forget the dowry! They land briefly, as if to give Chaucer a chance to summon forth the spirit of romance:

> There feste they, there daunce they and synge;
> And in his armes hath this Adryane,
> That of the beste hath kept hym from his bane. . . .
>   (2157–2159)

But Ariadne's happy ending is to last for but a moment. They land "in an yle, amyd the wilde se," and there Theseus abandons Ariadne while she sleeps, and "for that hire syster fayrer was than she," sails away with Phaedra. The narrative ends with the betrayed Ariadne's lament.

If the middle section leaves us uncertain whether to see Ariadne as naïve or calculating and leaves us uncertain whether the primary intention is to mock romantic attitudes or to parody romance elements, this is nothing compared to the uncertainty generated by this context for the final section. The middle section is comic, whatever the precise thrust of its comedy may be. How then are we to read the final section? Chaucer here turns to the *Heroides* and gives us Ariadne abandoned and overwhelmed with grief. Are we to forget the comedy of the middle section and shift moods abruptly? Or are we to continue the comic mood and somehow be amused, seeing her, perhaps, as a poor ninny whose romantic daydreams have suffered a proper shipwreck? The decision is made no easier by the opening and the closing of the poem. Paull Baum pointed out that the poem begins with the undignified assault on Theseus: "Be red for shame!" (1893) and ends with a flippant curse: "But thus this false lovere can begyle / His trewe love, the devel quyte hym his while!" (2226–2227). Chaucer, he says, "has made a mock of poor little Ariadne; her story is put in a framework of levity." [29]

---

29. Baum, "Chaucer's 'Glorious Legende,' " p. 380. The same kind of flippant curse is used to dispatch Theseus when his part in the narrative has ended: "A twenty devel-wey the wynd hym dryve!" (2177).

I shall opt for the possibly more dangerous choice and read the last section seriously. The comic line of the middle section will not support an attempt to read it in a mood of mockery, however much the comic mood which has been generated may urge it. The worst that can be said of Ariadne is that she wanted to be a heroine of a romance, or that she wanted to be a duchess. There is nothing comic about Ariadne abandoned on a lonely isle, and it would be cruel to try to make her so.

Read sympathetically, the last section is a moving lyric scene. All of it comes from Ovid, but not word for word or line for line. Chaucer uses the first sixty-four lines of the *Heroides*, but uses them very selectively and with some re-arrangement of the original. Ariadne's first line in the Epistle, "Mitius inveni quam te genus omne ferarum" is shifted to the central section of the scene: "Meeker than ye fynde I the bestes wylde" (2198). Instead of the immediate emotional confrontation of Ariadne and Theseus, appropriate and even necessary for the epistle form, Chaucer presumably wished to begin by concentrating exclusively on Ariadne and her plight, and to draw Theseus into the line of vision only later. Again, Chaucer leaps some twenty lines beyond the sixty-fourth line for a passage in the epistle (83–87) in which Ariadne expresses her fear of the wild animals on the island. He places this in her first cry for Theseus: "And myghte thus with bestes ben yslayn!" (2192). Ovid is more elaborate and rhetorical, specifying wolves, lions, tigers, and seals. Chaucer simplifies, and by so doing achieves an effect of innocence and helplessness.[30]

The helplessness and innocence are communicated with great economy in Ariadne's first two speeches. (Chaucer

30. This can best be demonstrated by a line-for-line identification. References to the *Heroides*, x, will be in parentheses. Where a line in Chaucer has no identifiable source in Ovid, it will be omitted: 2185 (7–8); 2186 (9–10); 2188 (16); 2189 (20?); 2190 (21); 2192 (83–87); 2193 (22); 2194 (17–18); 2195 (25–28); 2196 (29–30); 2197 (31–32); 2198 (1); 2200–2201 (35–36); 2202–2205 (41–42); 2206 (43?); 2207 (43? "tum denique flevi" and 49? "in saxo frigida sedi"); 2208–2209 (53–54?); 2210–2213 (56–58); 2214–2217 (59, 63–64).

has broken up the monologue of the *Heroides* and presented
it dramatically as both speech and summarized action.)

> Ryght in the dawenyng awaketh she,
> And gropeth in the bed, and fond ryght nought.
> "Allas," quod she, "that evere that I was wrought!
> I am betrayed!" and hire her torente. . . .
>
> (2185–2188)

She runs barefoot to the strand: [31]

> "Theseus! myn herte swete!
> Where be ye, that I may nat with yow mete,
> And myghte thus with bestes ben yslayn?"
> The holwe rokkes answerde hire agayn.
> No man she saw, and yit shyned the mone. . . .
>
> (2190–2194)

Each of the last two lines has magic powers of evocation.
Each communicates an endless echoing of the sense of isolation.

Ariadne is seen now as the childish innocent, unable to
comprehend, to imagine, the monstrous action of which
she is the victim:

> She cryed, "O turn ageyn, for routhe and synne!
> Thy barge hath nat al his meyne inne!"
> Hire coverchef on a pole up steked she,
> Ascaunce that he shulde it wel yse,
> And hym remembre that she was behynde,
> And turne ageyn, and on the stronde hire fynde.
>
> (2200–2205)

Her belief in the happy ending has become something
pathetic. But why did Chaucer believe he could mix
comedy and pathos in the same poem and hope for success?
The answer seems to be that he wanted to, whatever the
cost. The effect to be achieved by a juxtaposition of tones

31. This touch seems original with Chaucer, based probably on Ovid's "alta
puellares tardat harena pedes" (20): "The deep sand stays my girlish feet." He
has pushed the implications of "girlish" toward something more pathetic:
"barefot" communicates the sense of a child and of the unprotected, the vulnerable.

seems to have preoccupied him in *Ariadne*. The solemn, Miltonic opening line, "Juge infernal, Mynos, of Crete kyng," is followed by the slangy, cheeky, "Now cometh thy lot, now comestow on the ryng." The reference to Theseus immediately thereafter returns to a more elevated tone: "Of Theseus the grete untrouthe of love; / For which the goddes of the heven above / Ben wrothe, and wreche han take for thy synne." But this Dantean voice is abruptly grounded: "Be red for shame! now I thy lyf begynne" (1886-1893). One can work through the whole first section and plot a zigzag alternate raising and lowering of tone. The incongruous allusion to "a foreyne," we should note, not only limits romantic possibilities for the middle section, which it introduces, but it also brings the pathetic voice used to describe the sacrifice of "children dere" and the plight of Theseus, "this woful yonge knyght," to an abrupt and almost ugly stop. The comic middle and the pathetic close (with the flippant coda) are only extensions of this technique of discordance.

In a sense the technique had been used before. The varying and conflicting attitudes toward love in the *Parliament of Birds* are one form; the range of attitudes from Troilus through Criseyde to Pandarus is another. There is not the disharmony there, however, that we have here. A philosophic position, an overarching sense of irony, holds the warring elements together in these poems, assisted by the pervasive presence of the code of love as the norm to which all the given attitudes refer in some fashion. The code is gone here. There is no sense, no pretense, that the range of experience looked at in the narrative — and this is the real source of the varying tones — relates any longer in any meaningful way to the code. With it has gone most of the unifying, comforting sense of irony. Such irony as the poem possesses is at best disunifying, perhaps even discomforting.

For *Ariadne* looks at a disquieting range of human experience: a young man killed studying philosophy, a city turned over to an enemy's sword by a young woman in love, revenge and human sacrifice, romantic young ladies in the moonlight, privies, a cynical, opportunistic antihero, betrayal, and isolation. What is most significant about the poem is not its failure but the fact that Chaucer wanted to look at so much and to look at it all outside the perspective of courtly love. There clung still to *Hypsipyle and Medea* some remnants, some of the furniture of the code. Here, there is none. There he left his feminine characters without substance in his pursuit of an antiromantic narrative. Here he gives them recognizable forms and voices to support his escape from romance. No ideal form of the romantic experience lies behind Ariadne's comic efforts to live the romantic pattern or behind her pathetic disappointment. The romantic pattern is viewed as simply artificial and irrelevant.

The parody of the romance form that I believe is also here is intended to reinforce that sense of artificiality and irrelevance. True, it is handled rather awkwardly. But it is not a bad first try, and the English romance will be mined from now on for much the same purpose, though more skillfully: to underline the artificiality of the Prioress, the gaucherie of Absolon, the animality of Alisoun, the posturing of Symkyn and his family, until finally the worst crudities of the romance form and romance attitudes will be laughed off the stage in *Sir Thopas*.

The parodying of romance here, however, suggests something more. The parody is played with and then discarded. Experience (garnered from old books) spills outside romance form and mocks it. The serpentine, one might say labyrinthine, movement of tones in the opening section, the clash between the romance postures of the characters and the calculation of their real motives revealed in their speeches and actions, and the violent wrench with which we move our heroine from the ridiculous to the pathetic suggests a dissatisfaction with conventional form, a refusal to be limited by it to saying only what it will properly permit being said. This is often evident in the *Legend of Good Women*, but most notably in *Ariadne*. The image of the labyrinth, conventionally a metaphor for art and its intricacy, is given short shrift in *Ariadne;* it is there the house "krynkeled to and fro," dismissed in a phrase. In *Ariadne* content flows outside available form. It is not art — at least not conventional, courtly, fourteenth-century forms of art — but experience that is labyrinthine here.

What is wrong with *Ariadne* is that it tries to include too much, too many attitudes, too much of experience. If Chaucer seems here to lack a unifying position, if he has not yet found solid ground to stand on to replace the abandoned courtly code, this is understandable. In the distant realm of legend, of faraway times and countries, anything could happen, and anything is a great deal more than the restricted possibilities of the world of the dream garden and of courtly love and courtly conduct. If the prospect is dizzying, and for the moment satisfying in itself though artistically inadequate, the enormous widening of the artist's vision is no small achievement. With the scheme of the *Canterbury Tales* the variety of experience will find a richly rewarding and pliant method to give it expression and a metaphor of pilgrimage to enfold, unify, and sustain it. But that is in the future. For the moment, the seeing is everything. "Bernard the monk ne saugh nat all, pardee!"

[IX] Philomela

That wild and quivering tale of Philomela in Ovid's *Metamorphoses* exists in several medieval versions. Chaucer's treatment of the story makes an instructive contrast with two other tellings, Chrétien de Troyes's *Philomena*,[1] which was incorporated in the *Ovide moralisé*,[2] and Gower's "Tale of Tereus" in the *Confessio Amantis*.[3] Each telling, though based on Ovid, achieves an individual emphasis and artistic structure, striking evidence both of the plasticity of the Ovidian material and the capacity for variation and invention within medieval forms.

Chrétien's version is a greatly amplified treatment of the original,[4] combining a curious interest in some of the details of the pagan world revealed in the myth, a kind of primitive anthropology,[5] with a perspective which trans-

1. Chrétien de Troyes, *Philomena: Conte raconté d'après Ovide*, ed. C. De Boer (Paris, P. Geuthner, 1909). On the authorship question, see pp. v–xiv. The poem consists of 1468 lines of octosyllabic verse.

2. *Ovide moralisé*, ed. C. De Boer, in *Verhandelingen der Koninklijke Akademie van Wetenschappen te Amsterdam*, New Ser., XV (1915).

3. Gower, *Confessio Amantis*, V, 5551–6047. Derek Pearsall contrasts Chaucer's treatment with Gower's, to Chaucer's complete disadvantage ("Gower's Narrative Art," *PMLA*, 81 [1966], 478–479).

4. See the interesting though not very sympathetic commentary on Chrétien's *Philomena* in Douglas Bush, *Mythology and the Renaissance Tradition in English Poetry* (Minneapolis, University of Minnesota Press, 1932), p. 13. Bush remarks that "the Old French poem is six times as long as Ovid's." See, for example, Chrétien's treatment of the evil omens at the wedding of Tereus and Progne (15–31), or the *descriptio* of Philomena (126–204).

5. See Chrétien's discussion of "pagan law" at 219–233, and Progne's sacrifices to the gods, 1010–1056. There may have been some intention to create an atmosphere of the strange and terrible by these discussions.

forms that world into a thoroughly medieval frame of reference.[6] The emotional possibilities attract Chrétien's deepest attention, and he elaborates upon these. He analyzes Tereus' intense passion when he meets Philomela (her entrance is spotlighted by a long *effictio* and *notatio*) and his duplicity. This last takes on special dramatic significance because of Pandion's dependence on his daughter Philomela in his old age; the scene becomes a struggle between the two for Philomela. Tereus' guilty passion is pitted against Pandion's pathetic emotional needs. The rape scene, though Philomela's innocence is skillfully underlined, is weakened by long speeches which distract attention from the dramatic and emotional situation of the characters. Most effective is the scene in which Tereus is fed the flesh of his own child. If one grants the initial heavy irony of Tereus' demand that his son attend the banquet,[7] the scene achieves a *grand guignol* effect of horror. The stratagem, developed from Ovid, whereby Tereus asks and asks again where his son is and is assured that he will be there, dramatizes the father's love for the child and doubles and redoubles the horror.[8] Throughout the narrative Chrétien stresses the ironies of misunderstanding in which characters consistently fail to read one another's intentions correctly. And since the concealed desires and motivations of Tereus are the mainspring of the story's action, he becomes the real center of interest.

Gower's treatment is less preoccupied with ironies and subterranean passions and more interested in the events leading to the climactic horrors. He transforms his material into a dramatic presentation of two strong-minded

6. The discussion of pagan law, for example, is followed by a more familiar sentiment: "Qui porroit Amors contrester/ Que trestot son voloir ne face?" (234–235). And see Philomena's interesting remark to Tereus in Athens: "Tel est la costume as François" (280).

7. The ironic request is in Ovid, but Chrétien elaborates and continues the irony (Ovid, *Metamorphoses,* VI, 650–656).

8. Bush is quite mistaken in his comment, "there is no emotion at all in the ambling little couplets of the French poem" (*Mythology and Renaissance Tradition,* p. 13).

women. Their determination in a world of male power and man-made terrors approaches the heroic. Perhaps a moment of pathos is created for Philomela:

> And sche began to crie and preie,
> "O fader, o mi moder diere,
> Nou help!" Bot thei ne mihte it hiere. . . .
>
> (V, 5634–5636)

After the rape, however, she boldly threatens to denounce his crime (the effect is boldness, though the speech is introduced by the comment, "with wofull herte thus sche saide" [5654]). She cannot speak after her tongue has been cut out "with a peire scheres," but we hear as interior monologue her prayer to Jupiter (5741–5752), which concludes with a cry for vengeance.

Progne's strength is first revealed when she receives the false news of Philomela's death: "sche fond non amendement / To syghen or to sobbe more . . ." (5728–5729).[9] She swoons on receiving Philomela's message, but recovers quickly:

> And eft sche takth the cloth on honde,
> Behield the lettres and thymages;
> Bot ate laste, "Of suche oultrages,"
> Sche seith, "wepinge is noght the bote. . . ."
>
> (5790–5793)

She is all prayers to Venus and Cupid and to Apollo, and vows of vengeance follow her tears when she sees the violated Philomela:

> With signes pleigneth Philomene,
> And Progne seith, "It schal be wreke,
> That al the world therof schal speke."
>
> (5868–5870)

The brutal and vengeful killing of her child is thus prepared for, as is her bitter denunciation of Tereus in the banquet

---

9. Developed perhaps from Progne's reaction in Ovid when she receives the message from Philomela: Ovid, *Metamorphoses*, VI, 583–586, "dolor ora repressit," etc.

scene.   The action comes to a fitting dramatic climax full of violence and noise:

> With that he sterte up fro the mete,
> And schof the bord unto the flor,
> And cauhte a swerd anon and suor
> That thei scholde of his handes dye.
> And thei unto the goddes crie
> Begunne with so loude a stevene,
> That thei were herd unto the hevene. . . .

(5928–5934)

Even their metamorphosis seems, in Gower, something they have wrested from the gods by their own strength.

The effect of Chaucer's version [10] is utterly different and seems almost pallid if contrasted with Gower or Chrétien. His story could hardly be like their tales because he quite changes the character of the Ovidian narrative, eliminating the killing of the child and the feeding of his flesh to Tereus (and, as always, eliminating the metamorphosis). In doing this he has denied himself a major part of the dramatic potential of his material. At first glance his motive for cutting seems obvious enough. The incident is not appropriate for a chronicle of good women. We have seen him

10. Chaucer's source was Ovid, *Metamorphoses*, VI, 424–674. See M. Bech, "Quellen und Plan der 'Legende of Goode Women' und ihr Verhältniss zur 'Confessio Amantis,' " *Anglia*, 5 (1882), 342–343; W. W. Skeat, *The Complete Works of Geoffrey Chaucer* (Oxford, Eng., 1894), III, xxxix, 340–344. Edgar F. Shannon provides a thorough comparison of Ovid and Chaucer (*Chaucer and the Roman Poets* [Cambridge, Mass., Harvard University Press, 1929], pp. 258–283). Chaucer may also have made some use of Chrétien's version as he found it in the *Ovid moralisé*; see John Livingston Lowes, "Chaucer and the *Ovide Moralisé*," *PMLA*, 33 (1918), 302–325, esp. 303–318. Shannon questioned many of the parallels with the *Ovide*. Sanford B. Meech, however, though he argues the case for Chaucer's use of the *Ovide* for *Ariadne*, simply asserts flatly that Chaucer's indebtedness in the *Philomela* to the *Ovide* for details not to be found in the *Metamorphoses* "was established" by Lowes (Meech, "Chaucer and the *Ovide Moralisé*: A Further Study," *PMLA*, 46 [1931], 182). Chaucer's use of the *Ovide* is largely a matter of details, if he did use it. Ovid was clearly his main source. According to Meech, "What . . . he does take over from the *Ovide moralisé* are the details that enhance the vividness and clarify the motivation of the narrative" (318). Vividness, then, and the "new turns given to the narrative" are what interest Chaucer. But these new turns are very slight matters, and I shall not comment on them.

shying away from the same kind of detail in the Medea story.   His general theme may have betrayed him here, but this explanation, though there may be some truth in it, does not resolve certain larger issues relating to the technique and intention of the *Philomela*.

The technique is curious. The poem as a whole suffers from overcutting. The Latin original occupies 250 lines; even after we eliminate the scenes portraying the slaying of Itys, the feast of flesh, and the transformations, there remain 175 lines of Latin verse which become a mere 150 lines of English pentameter (omitting 16 lines of invocation).[11] Chaucer has hacked away in every scene. Some omissions suggest a ready explanation. One suspects he discarded the scene of the Bacchic frenzies (during which Progne spirits away Philomela from her place of imprisonment disguised as a reveler) to avoid puzzling his medieval audience, who had no Bulfinch to guide them.[12] He condenses and transforms the scene thus:

> But feynede hire to gon on pilgrymage
> To Bacus temple; and in a litel stounde
> Hire dombe sister sittynge hath she founde,
> Wepynge in the castel, here alone.
>
> (2375–2378)

The effect of the change is worth noting. Chaucer has literally domesticated his original, for he has robbed it of the wildness, the violence and horror that run through not only the scene of Progne's rage and frenzy but the whole tale as Ovid tells it. The same shying away from violence may account for the dropping of the climactic scene, the banquet of flesh. It operates again in his handling of the tongue cutting. Here Chaucer comes as close to the matter-of-fact as is possible with such an action: "And with his swerd hire tonge of kerveth he . . ." (2334). Ovid, on the other hand, assaults the sensibilities to the point of nausea.

---

11. Gower's "Tale of Tereus" is 497 octosyllabic lines; if one omits the slaying of Itys, the banquet, and the transformation, Gower still uses 330 lines for Chaucer's 150.

12. Gower also omits the Bacchic rescue.

One might suspect a fundamental lack of sympathy with his material here. The feeling persists, certainly, that Chaucer took no relish in supping at a banquet of horrors and preferred to avoid such occasions. If he had no taste for the grisly and the gruesome in this story, then why did he choose to tell it? [13] All of his cutting cannot be attributed to a delicate sensibility. A case in point is his treatment of the longish passage between Tereus and Pandion. In Ovid the scene is fully developed. The passion of Tereus is vividly portrayed, Philomela pleads for permission to go, Tereus spends a sleepless night agitated by his desire for Philomela, and on the morning of the departure the weeping Pandion begs Tereus to return Philomela to him soon. Chaucer cuts it to the bone. The essentials remain, and as a summary of a scene it has its moments of brilliance. All of Tereus' lust flashes forth in a single line — "He caste his fyry herte upon hyre so" — but the dangers of condensation are revealed in the flatness of the next line — "That he wol have hir, how so that it go . . ." (2292–2293). The emotionalism, the irony, the violent passion threatening to spill forth are not completely gone, but they are presented so thinly that they lack impact.

Chaucer has learned almost too well the art of abbreviation. He can suggest an action and move his story with lightning swiftness: "The ores pullen forth the vessel faste, / And into Trace aryveth at the laste" (2308–2309). A whole scene of hypocrisy and false grief is conveyed in a phrase

13. One could manufacture a mystery for *Philomela* if one wished. It is the one story in the *Legend* whose heroine is not mentioned in the "Alceste" balade. Does this mean it was an afterthought? Does it suggest all the more a deliberate choice — or just the opposite? Again, it is not mentioned in the puzzling list provided in the "Introduction" to the *Man of Law's Tale* (B 60–76) — nor is the *Cleopatra*. And, oddly enough, there is no stanza for *Philomela* in the "Nine Worshipfullest Ladyes" (or the "Chronycle Made by Chaucer" as it is alternately known), the nine-stanza summary of the *Legend* which includes all the other heroines except Medea, though she is mentioned, and includes Alceste, a double error, since the stanza for her actually summarizes the story of Ceyx and Alcyone. See *Odd Texts of Chaucer's Minor Poems*, Part I, ed. F. J. Furnivall (London, 1871), Chaucer Society, Series I, Part 23. I can only suggest that the subject matter, rape, led to omission in some of these instances.

when Tereus returns after the rape to tell Progne that her sister is dead: "And in his armes hath his wif ynome, / And pitously he wep, and shok his hed . . ." (2343–2344). That "and shok his hed" is magnificent. This compression is splendid when a scene is not essential. As an example of how to produce a concise narrative, *Philomela* might serve as a model. As an example of how to produce a powerful narrative, it does not.

Is it solely a question of a technique gone awry? Or that plus a distaste for the hideous and the painful? Not completely. I suspect that behind Chaucer's cutting and paring was an attempt to make Ovid's story of pain and horror into a story of a different kind, a tale of the pathetic. Pathos would be in order after the largely comic or sardonic *Ariadne*. As Chaucer presents the story, Progne and Philomela possess the requisite qualities of helplessness and innocence. The effect of many of Chaucer's cuts has been to rob them of forceful action or even a sense of will. Gower's strong-minded women contrast vividly (as do Ovid's) with these passive, melting heroines who, once disaster smites, hardly act and never speak.[14] They are seen almost always in tears. When Philomela begs Pandion, it is "with salte teres eke . . ." (2284). When Progne is told her sister is dead, "This sely Progne hath swich wo / That nygh hire sorweful herte brak a-two. / And thus in terys lete I Progne dwelle . . ." (2346–2348). When Progne finds Philomela ("this woful lady" [2350]), she is weeping, and Progne weeps also:

> Allas! the wo, the compleynt, and the mone
> That Progne upon hire doumbe syster maketh!

14. Philomela's one "action" is the weaving of the tapestry. The story cannot happen without this, but even this hardly seems in character, except that it is given something of the air of a "genteel" accomplishment. The passage, which explains also what provision was made for her — that she could read and write but was not allowed to use a pen — is rather overdeveloped and flat. It is not dramatic, and neither is the scene with the messenger that follows. After the rape, the poem seems to go deliberately downhill to the tearful reunion of the two sisters, like a long drawn out sigh.

In armes everych of hem other taketh,
And thus I late hem in here sorwe dwelle.

(2379–2382)

That image of twofold, helpless, passive grief is the closing scene of the narrative. We are not even given any feeling that Progne "rescues" Philomela.

The innocence of the women is constantly stressed. Progne's urgings to Tereus to send for Philomela are done "with al humblesse of wifhod, word and chere" (2269). It is "O sely Philomene" (2339) and "this sely Progne." His final comment on Philomela restates her innocence: "Thus was she served, / That nevere harm agilte ne deserved / Unto this crewel man, that she of wiste" (2384–2386).

All of these elements come together in the most effective and most fully dramatized scene in the poem, the rape:

> And up into a forest he hire ledde,
> And to a cave pryvely hym spedde;
> And in this derke cave, yif hir leste,
> Or leste nat, he bad hire for to reste;
> For which hire herte agros, and seyde thus:
> "Where is my sister, brother Tereus?"
> And therwithal she wepte tenderly,
> And quok for fere, pale and pitously,
> Ryght as the lamb, that of the wolf is biten;
> Or as the culver, that of the egle is smiten,
> And is out of his clawes forth escaped,
> Yit it is afered and awhaped,
> Lest it be hent eft-sones; so sat she.
> But utterly, it may non other be.
> By force hath he, this traytour, don that dede.
> That he hath reft hire of hire maydenhede,
> Maugre hire hed, by strengthe and by his myght.
> Lo! here a dede of men, and that a ryght!
> She cryeth "syster!" with ful loud a stevene,
> And "fader dere!" and "help me, God in hevene!"
> Al helpeth nat. . . .   (2310–2330)

The fragmentary cries which end the scene express the innocence and helplessness and the sense of suffering and

violation characteristic of Chaucerian pathos. Furthermore, this scene has power. It communicates totally and
does so (except for the lamb-dove metaphor from Ovid) [15]
by an exclusively narrative means.

The evidence points unmistakably to a specific, contrived
effect. In perceiving an element of the pathetic in the Philomela story, Chaucer saw something that was unquestionably there.[16] Why, then, is his version not more satisfying?

15. Chaucer makes a slight but interesting change here, which Shannon has
noticed (Chaucer and the Roman Poets, p. 271), though his only explanation
is that it is "for better dramatic effect." In Ovid, the lamb-dove figure (527–
530) comes after the rape and expresses Philomela's state of mind at that moment, before she recovers and bursts out at Tereus. By placing the image before
the rape, Chaucer communicates her state of mind, her terror and pathetic
hope before the violation and heightens thereby the tension and horror. The
rape itself, in Chaucer, is more explicit, more moving, and more terrible than
in Ovid. He has rendered dramatically, for example, Ovid's "frustra clamato
saepe parente,/saepe soror sua, magnis super omnia divis" (525–526): "vainly
calling, often upon her father, often on her sister, but most of all upon the
great gods." Note the force achieved by his translation of "frustra" as "al
helpeth nat" and by shifting it from the beginning to the end of the passage.

16. A pathetic reaction to the story of Philomela and Progne and, within its
narrow limits, a pathetic treatment of it are found in the address to the night-
ingale in James I of Scotland's Kingis Quair, ed. John Norton-Smith (Oxford,
Eng., Clarendon Press, 1971), lines 379–392:

> And eke I pray, for all the paynes grete
> > That for the loue of Proigne, thy sister dere,
> Thou sufferit quhilom, quhen thy brestis wete
> > Were, with the teres of thyne eyen clere
> > All bludy ronne — that pitee was to here
> The crueltee of that vnknyghtly dede
> Quhare was fro thee bereft thy maidenhede —
>
> Lift vp thyne hert and sing with gude entent,
> > And in thy notis suete the tresoun telle
> That to thy sister trewe and innocent
> > Was kythit by hir husband false and fell;
> > For quhois gilt (as it is worthy wel)
> Chide thir husbandis that ar false, I say,
> And bid thame mend, in the twenty deuil way.

W. W. Skeat, in his edition for the Scottish Text Society (Edinburgh, 1884),
pp. 71–72, suggested that lines 382–383 might be reminiscent of Gower's version, V, 5692–5694. John Norton-Smith, in his edition, suggests the lines come
from Troilus and Criseyde, III, 1445. It is likely, however, that James knew
Chaucer's version. He seems also to have been reading Ariadne. Some references to the Philomela story are collected in John Lydgate, Temple of Glas,
ed. Josef Schick, EETS, ES 60 (London, 1891), p. 76.

I believe he overestimated the degree of the pathetic in the original — or, rather, he underestimated the cost to his material involved in an intensely pathetic treatment. Philomela, helpless victim in the rape scene, must be similarly helpless elsewhere, and, to reinforce this image, Progne must be, also. Therefore, the banquet scene must go, along with Philomela's speech of defiance and vengeance after the rape. This makes any elaboration of the tongue cutting unnecessary. Since the poem must concentrate on the pathetic objects, that is, the women, as much as possible, the scene between Pandion and Tereus must be pared down, though the pathos of Pandion's condition must have tempted Chaucer. He gives him a few lines, but, strictly speaking, Pandion's emotions are an irrelevance, and, quite correctly by his terms, Chaucer cuts away here, too.

Tereus is the most curious victim of the transformation. The villains in Chaucer's pathetic tales can rarely be very interesting; it is enough that they be pure evil. Their victims, not they, are the center of attention. Since the victims are helpless and offer no resistance, the villain is robbed of any chance to display a strong will or even impressive strength.[17] Chaucer props up Tereus by means of an apostrophe or invocation as the poem opens:

> Thow yevere of the formes, that hast wrought
> This fayre world, and bar it in thy thought
> Eternaly, er thow thy werk began,
> Why madest thow, unto the slaunder of man,
> Or, al be that it was nat thy doing,
> As for that fyn, to make swich a thyng,
> Whi sufferest thow that Tereus was bore,
> That is in love so fals and so forswore,

17. Walter in the *Clerk's Tale* manages to be more interesting than most of the "villains" because he is not all bad and because there is a struggle in this tale. The very quality which makes Griselda a pathetic heroine, her "patience" or acquiescence, is the object of Walter's attack. He struggles throughout the poem to test and destroy this patience, and he fails. By her patience she resists him. But the struggle makes him more human than most agents in such tales.

> That fro this world up to the firste hevene
> Corrumpeth, whan that folk his name nevene?
>
> $(2228-2237)^{18}$

This effort to give some philosophic weight and foundation to the poem tells us how to look at Tereus, but we are not given much chance to observe him, much less to understand or become involved with him. We cannot see him acted upon or reacting, as when Philomela threatens or when he is served the gruesome banquet. He is much more interesting in Ovid and Chrétien, and of more substance at least in Gower.

The general condemnation of men with which the poem ends, therefore, though it seems sincere and even intense, is not very moving:

> Ye may be war of men, if that yow liste.
> For al be it that he wol nat, for shame,
> Don as Tereus, to lese his name,
> Ne serve yow as a morderour or a knave,
> Ful lytel while shal ye trewe hym have —
> That wol I seyn, al were he now my brother —
> But it so be that he may have non other.
>
> (2387-2393)

It is difficult to know how to read the last line. Some lightening of tone there is, but how much? Very little, it seems to me. Since Tereus is not very real, however, and since there are few genuinely dramatic moments in the poem, it is difficult to share Chaucer's serious feeling.

The poem, read as a tale of pathos, is a competent narrative but nothing more. It remains insufficiently developed, not merely overcut. The cutting has been too severe, but this need not have been fatal. A few additional fully developed scenes, one or two more dramatized passages like the splendid rape scene, would have given the poem body.

---

18. On the first three lines and their Platonism, see Karl Young, "Chaucer's Appeal to the Platonic Deity," *Speculum*, 19 (1944), 1–13. Their source could be Boethius, the *Roman de la rose*, or, as Young thinks most probable, either the *Ovide moralisé*, I, 71–97, or "a medieval commentator's annotations upon the Latin text of the *Metamorphoses*" (p. 11).

It was perhaps symbolically appropriate to allow Philomela, after her mutilation, to sink into mute agony, but the poem suffers from a kind of total silence thereafter. *Ariadne* had too much talk. There is not enough here. Surely even muteness can be rendered dramatically effective. The story as Chaucer tells it is too thin to sustain even its slighter burden of tears. Ironically, if he had preserved the horrors of his original, he might have achieved more pathos, not less. As it stands, the poem's achievement is a haunting silver-gray tone and a sense of bewilderment at human cruelty.

[X] Phyllis

The story of Phyllis and Demophoon is so simple in both outline and substance that it might serve as the archetypal tale of betrayed love. Perhaps for that reason it was popular in the late Middle Ages.[1] Chaucer first alluded to it in the *Book of the Duchess*:

> And Phyllis also for Demophoun
> Heng hirself, so weylaway!
> For he had broke his terme-day
> To come to hir.   (728–731)

His acquaintance with the story here may have come from the *Roman de la rose* (13211–13214), and Jean de Meun may have had it from Ovid's *Remedia Amoris* (591–608), but by the time Chaucer summarized the history again in the *House of Fame*, he apparently had read *Heroides*, ii:[2]

> Loo, Demophon, duk of Athenys,
> How he forswor hym ful falsly,
> And traysed Phillis wikkidly,

1. See Lydgate, *Temple of Glas*, ed. Josef Schick, EETS, ES 60 (London, 1891), p. 75. In addition to a number of references in Lydgate, Schick cites Dante, *Paradiso*, ix, 100; Petrarch, *Trionfo d' Amore*, I, 127; Gottfried von Strassburg, *Tristan*, 17193, and others. Note also the *Roman de la rose*, referred to in Chapter VIII.

2. See George Lyman Kittredge, "Chaucer's *Medea* and the Date of the *Legend of Good Women*," *PMLA*, 24 (1909), 350. This was accepted by Robert K. Root, "The Date of Chaucer's *Medea*," *PMLA*, 25 (1910), 233. Root had argued earlier that the passage in the *House of Fame* also was based on the *Roman de la rose*: "Chaucer's Legend of Medea," *PMLA*, 24 (1909), 129–131, as did W. W. Skeat, *The Complete Works of Geoffrey Chaucer* (Oxford, Eng., 1894), III, 252.

That kynges doghtre was of Trace,
And falsly gan hys terme pace;
And when she wiste that he was fals,
She heng hirself ryght be the hals,
For he had doon hir such untrouthe.
Loo! was not this a woo and routhe?

(388–396)

Gower, who told the sad little story in the *Confessio Amantis* (IV, 731–878) as an example of forgetfulness, followed the familiar pattern and developed from the scanty materials of the *Heroides* a touching scene of Phyllis waiting all night for the return of Demophoon. A lantern burns in a tower to guide him till the morning star reveals that day is at hand and the sea empty of ships as far as eye can reach. Then, after a gentle lament, she twists a silken girdle about a green bough, and around her white throat, and so dies.

The orientation of sentiment in the tale would seem to have been firmly established. But Chaucer, rarely content to repeat himself or others, flips the story on its back. Instead of Phyllis, Demophoon holds the stage; from a sad tale, it becomes a mocking tale, light in tone rather than serious. This is a daring but understandable maneuver. Phyllis, a queen who helps a stranded warrior returning from Troy and gives herself to him only to be abandoned, is another Dido, though neither so romantic nor so glittering. There was no missing the parallel, for her story was paired with Dido's on occasion, notably by Ovid and Jean de Meun.[3]

3. Ovid, *Remedia Amoris*, 55–58; and, probably because of the pairing here, so also in the *Roman de la rose*, 13173–13214. Illustrations in several MSS show Dido and Phyllis together, Dido dying on a sword, Phyllis hanging from a tree: see Douce MS. 371, f.87r; Pierpont Morgan MS. 132, f.97r, and some of the early printed editions of the *Roman.* Cf. J. A. W. Bennett, *Chaucer's Book of Fame* (Oxford, Eng., Clarendon Press, 1968), p. 45n. The Morgan MS. illustration is reproduced in *The Romance of the Rose*, trans. Harry W. Robbins (New York, E. P. Dutton & Co., Inc., 1962), facing p. 274. As though to stress the parallel with Dido, Chaucer (and Gower) says Demophoon was coming from Troy, a detail not found in Ovid. This could have been taken from a gloss or *apparatus criticus* attached to the text or taken from the fourteenth-century translation of the *Heroides* by Filippo; see Sanford Brown Meech, "Chaucer and an Italian Translation of the *Heroides*," *PMLA*, 40 (1930), 110–128, esp. 119–120.

In *Ariadne* Chaucer had deftly avoided repeating a serious treatment of the theme of generous love repayed by ingratitude and betrayal. All the more reason to sidestep repetition in a story especially reminiscent of Dido's.[4] By avoiding one kind of repetition, however, he risked another. Aeneas, Jason, Theseus — Demophoon is only one of many faithless lovers. The problem will be to show him in some fresh light, to endow him with some distinction. Chaucer's solution is to capitalize on his difficulties, as it were. Since Demophoon is the son of a betrayer we have already met, namely Theseus, Chaucer stresses this (as did his source)[5] for all it is worth. Like father, like son. Philandering and betrayal are asserted to run in the blood. Nature, in the stockbreeder's sense, is invoked as the governing principle. Before he has finished, Chaucer has been able to suggest, through Demophoon, that betrayal is natural to

4. *Heroides*, ii, is unquestionably Chaucer's source for the story here, though he probably also knew the references to the story in Ovid's *Remedia Amoris*, 55–58 and 591–608. And, as we have seen, he knew the version in the *Roman de la rose*. For the *Heroides*, see M. Bech, "Quellen und Plan der 'Legende of Goode Women' und ihr Verhältniss zur 'Confessio Amantis,' " *Anglia*, 5 (1882), 343–346; W. W. Skeat, *The Complete Works of Geoffrey Chaucer* (Oxford, Eng., 1894), III, xxxix–xl, 344–346; and Edgar F. Shannon, *Chaucer and the Roman Poets* (Cambridge, Mass., Harvard University Press, 1929), pp. 283–291. Bech also suggested that the storm passage derived from Virgil, *Aeneid*, I, 81–147, and one line (2422) from *ibid.*, V, 822–826; Skeat and Shannon agree. Clarence G. Child, "Chaucer's *Legend of Good Women* and Boccaccio's *De Genealogia Deorum*," *MLN*, 11 (1896), 475ff., suggested Books X and XI of *De Genealogia Deorum* as the source of several details, and Shannon (p. 284) agrees. A suggestion by F. Holthausen that a gloss on Theodulus was the source of the story in the *Legend* has been largely ignored ("Chaucer und Theodulus," *Anglia*, 16 [1894], 264–266).

5. *Heroides*, ii, 75–78:

> de tanta rerum turba factisque parentis
> sedit in ingenio Cressa relicta tuo.
> quo solum excusat, solum miraris in illo;
> heredem patriae, perfide, fraudis agis.

("Of all the great deeds in the long career of your sire, nothing has made impress upon your nature but the leaving of his Cretan bride. The only deed that draws forth his excuse, that only you admire in him; you act the heir to your father's guile, perfidious one" [translation by Grant Showerman, in Ovid, *Heroides and Amores*, Loeb Classical Library (London, William Heinemann, 1921)]). This, Phyllis suggests, is what should be inscribed on Demophoon's statue in Athens. It is very freely rendered in Chaucer's *Phyllis*, 2541–2549.

men and a foolish susceptibility to betrayal is natural to women. Demophoon is a male master of the "olde daunce," and our laughter is aroused by the very oldness of that dance: the old ways of son, and father, and his father before him, all the way back to the "wiked tre," and the "subtyl fo," the devil in all men (except Chaucer!) whom most of the Eves find irresistible though his ways never change.

These, then, are Chaucer's tasks in the poem: to switch attention from Phyllis to Demophoon, to alter the tone radically by lightening it, and to create something fresh out of the very staleness of Demophoon's story. The opening lines make a brilliant start on all three:

> By preve as wel as by autorite,
> That wiked fruit cometh of a wiked tre,
> That may ye fynde, if that it like yow.
> But for this ende I speke this as now,
> To tellen yow of false Demophon.
> In love a falser herde I nevere non,
> But if it were his fader Theseus.
> "God, for his grace, fro swich oon kepe us!"
> Thus may these women preyen that it here.
> Now to the effect turne I of my matere.
>
> (2394–2403)

The tone, and the principles appealed to here, are established in one stroke by the exclamation of the women, which is, if not ribald, at least practical and certainly not pious. They speak in a voice which anticipates the Wife of Bath, as does also the talk in the first line of "preve" and "autorite."

The beginning of the narrative proper continues to rivet attention on Demophoon by describing his tempestuous voyage from Troy:

> Byhynde hym com a wynd and ek a reyn
> That shof so sore, his sayl ne myghte stonde;
> Hym were levere than al the world a-londe,
> So hunteth hym the tempest to and fro.

> So derk it was, he coude nowher go;
> And with a wawe brosten was his stere.
> His ship was rent so lowe, in swich manere,
> That carpenter ne coude it nat amende.
> The se, by nyghte, as any torche it brende
> For wod, and possith hym now up, now doun. . . .
>
> (2411–2420)

This is a splendid run of narrative-descriptive poetry; it is notable for its rapidity of movement, the quick accumulation of detail, and the creation of a desperate scene by a few touches. Though expository, it serves also, by its picture of a man hounded by the elements, weary and tempest tossed, to make vivid Demophoon's indebtedness to Phyllis. This is further stressed:

> Unnethe is Demophon to londe ywonne,
> Wayk, and ek wery, and his folk forpyned
> Of werynesse, and also enfamyned,
> That to the deth he almost was ydriven.
>
> (2427–2430)

And again:

> For syk he was, and almost at the deth;
> Unnethe myghte he speke or drawe his breth. . . .
>
> (2436–2437)

From such desperation, we are made to understand, Phyllis rescued him, and behold how the cad betrayed her!

It might be objected that the opening section of the narrative proper fails to maintain the mocking tone of the introduction, and there is some truth in this. The hero has already been introduced, however, as "false Demophon," and an ironic perspective therefore controls our view of the opening action. He is shown, furthermore, in no heroic role, but simply being knocked about, and the storm is hardly epic in effect with its talk of broken rudders and carpenters.

It is without strain, accordingly, that Demophoon, going to Phyllis' court for succor, can be spoken of in this anti-heroic vein: Like his father, he is duke of Athens,

> And lyk his fader of face and of stature,
> And fals of love; it com hym of nature.
> As doth the fox Renard, the foxes sone,
> Of kynde he coude his olde faders wone,
> Withoute lore, as can a drake swimme
> Whan it is caught and caryed to the brymme.
>
> (2446–2451)

The deflationary effect of this allusion to Renard the fox and swimming drakes and of rhymes like "swim-brim" undermines the solemn couplet that immediately follows:

> This honurable Phillis doth hym chere;
> Hire liketh wel his port and his manere.
>
> (2452–2453)

Her total failure to comprehend his nature (after all he is a man) becomes something comic. Appropriately, therefore, Chaucer raises his voice at this moment in mock despair:

> But, for I am agroted herebyforn
> To wryte of hem that ben in love forsworn,
> And ek to haste me in my legende,
> (Which to performe God me grace sende!)
> Therfore I passe shortly in this wyse.
>
> (2454–2458)

There are so many Demophoons in the world, and so many Phyllises! He will, therefore, take a shortcut. He has already described how Theseus betrayed Ariadne; well:

> At shorte wordes, ryght so Demophon
> The same wey, the same path hath gon,
> As dide his false fader Theseus.
> For unto Phillis hath he sworen thus,
> To wedden hire, and hire his trouthe plyghte,
> And piked of hire al the good he myghte,
> Whan he was hol and sound, and hadde his reste;
> And doth with Phillis what so that hym leste,
> As wel coude I, if that me leste so,
> Tellen al his doynge to and fro.   (2462–2471)

"The same wey, the same path" — the same old story. Promises to marry, oaths sworn, and Phyllis, when Demophoon has his strength back, plucked ("piked") of everything worth taking. The passage is thoroughly unromantic and antipathetic. Phyllis can hardly rouse our pity; she is too easy a mark for this purloiner of purses and maidenheads. It is a generic, not a personal weakness, as Chaucer's groan of satiety shows; she shares it with most of womankind.

Throughout, Chaucer is concerned to keep her from our sympathies. She is introduced almost curtly with a cliché from the romances: "Ligurges doughter, fayrer on to sene / Than is the flour ageyn the bryghte sonne" (2425-2426). Her honor ("this honurable Phillis") helps her not one whit in judging Demophoon, and she succumbs to the old line without, so far as we are permitted to see, a struggle. Chaucer will not even allow her a tearful parting from her lover. All we hear are Demophoon's excuses and false promises to be back in a month's time for the wedding (2472-2481). Inasmuch as the parting is one of the few genuine scenes provided in the *Heroides* (ii, 91-98), the flat, cursory treatment of this moment is final evidence of Chaucer's antipathetic intention.

There remains, however, a major technical difficulty. Since the *Heroides* is his source, the epistle of Phyllis must finally be included in some fashion. And since the epistle is pathetic and is by Phyllis, its inclusion threatens to reverse the tone and emphasis of Chaucer's poem. This difficulty is handled as successfully as seems possible. First, the modulation into the epistle maintains the mocking tone and prolongs the talk about Demophoon. Phyllis' sad fate is communicated as briskly as can be managed:

> Allas! that, as the storyes us recorde,
> She was hire owene deth ryght with a corde,
> Whan that she saw that Demophon hire trayed.
>
> (2484-2486)

But before she did that, says Chaucer, she wrote Demophoon begging him to come back, and I'll repeat some of her letter — though *him* I refuse to discuss any longer:

Me lyste nat vouche-sauf on hym to swynke,
Ne spende on hym a penne ful of ynke,
For fals in love was he, ryght as his syre.
The devil sette here soules bothe afyre!

(2490–2493)

Never was an *occupatio* put to more skillful use. The epistle is introduced with the sound of jeers still ringing in the air and with Demophoon still in the mind's eye. Though it is impossible to divest the epistle completely of pathetic echoes, Chaucer has chosen carefully some of the least pathetic sections and presented them with minimally emotional effect.[6] In large part he does this by continuing to concentrate on Demophoon. Phyllis talks not so much about herself and her feelings as about Demophoon — *his* promises, *his* false tears, *his* oaths to the gods. She provides, in fact, what amounts to a handbook for philanderers. Since the emphasis is largely on duplicity, the tone does not change so radically as it might. We see her not so much as sufferer, but as dupe:

"But I wot why ye come nat," quod she,
"For I was of my love to yow to fre.
. . . .
To moche trusted I, wel may I pleyne,
Upon youre lynage and youre fayre tonge,
And on youre teres falsly out yronge.
How coude ye wepe so by craft?" quod she.
"May there swiche teres feyned be?"

(2520–2521, 2525–2529)

Halfway through the epistle Chaucer interrupts, to break up the monologue and to indicate that he is cutting. The effect of the *occupatio*, however, is to reduce any emotion that may have been building up:

6. The first seventeen lines of Phyllis' letter (2496–2512) follow *Heroides*, ii, 1–8, very closely. After the five-line *occupatio*, 2513–2517, Chaucer begins again at line 26 of the *Heroides*. Thereafter he borrows as follows (lines from *Heroides* in parentheses): 2518–2521 (26–27); 2522–2524 (43–44); 2525–2529 (49–52); 2530–2532 (63–64); 2533–2535 (66); 2536–2537 (67–72); 2538–2549 (73–78); 2550–2554 (134–137).

But al hire letter wryten I ne may
By order, for it were to me a charge;
Hire letter was ryght long and therto large.
But here and ther in rym I have it layd,
There as me thoughte that she wel hath sayd.

(2513–2517)

The author's own language is not sympathetic. The joking
reference to his burden, to the penance he is performing,
and his objective attitude to her epistle as a lengthy docu-
ment from which he will select passages where she has expressed herself effectively keep us not too far from the styp-
tic tone of the early part of the poem.

Phyllis concludes by dwelling on Demophoon's lineage,
the topic with which the poem began. When your "olde
auncestres" come to be painted, she says, I hope you will be
painted with them. Then people can read how you betrayed
one who loved you truly,

But sothly, of oo poynt yit may they rede,
That ye ben lyk youre fader as in this,
For he begiled Adriane, ywis,
With swich an art and with swich subtilte
As thow thyselven hast begyled me.
As in that poynt, althogh it be nat fayr,
Thow folwest hym, certayn, and art his ayr.

(2543–2549)

The epistle, we can see, never escapes for too long the
poem's amusement at man's neural itch, its comic gene-
alogy of Casanovas and Lotharios. Phyllis seems to be
lamenting something as old as nature itself. Though in the
last lines she threatens that Demophoon may soon see her
body floating in the harbor at Athens and though we are reminded again that she hanged herself in despair (2550–
2558), her feelings have never been made to seem very real,
and such gestures are admittedly futile, as her last line
recognizes: "Ye ben harder than is any ston" (2254). The
image is trite because it is so true.

Appropriately, therefore, the poem ends on a note of

mockery. Chaucer poses as a man seeking, like all men, to gain an unfair advantage with women and proving himself untrustworthy by the very claim to distinction:

> Be war, ye wemen, of youre subtyl fo,
> Syn yit this day men may ensaumple se;
> And trusteth, as in love, no man but me.
>
> (2559–2561)

For this, the proper response seems that cry of knowing women heard in the opening lines: "God, for his grace, fro swich oon kepe us!" With most unpromising material, poor Phyllis' story, we have come close to the mood if not the matter of the fabliau.

[XI]   Hypermnestra

It seems mere accident, not design, that *Hypermnestra* is the last of the legends. Though unfinished, it is within a few lines of completion. There are no valedictory comments in the legend itself, and the evidence suggests that Chaucer, at the time he wrote it, intended not only to complete it but to continue with his larger plan.[1] What interrupted him we shall never know. It is all the more gratifying, therefore, that the last of the legends should be so accomplished a performance. Not that *Hypermnestra* is a magnificent work of art, or even that it is the best of the legends, though it is one of the best. It does not possess the power or effectiveness of *Thisbe* or *Dido* or *Lucrece*. It is hardly possible that it should. The material lacks the dramatic potentialities of these histories, nor does it give Chaucer, as they did, a fully developed narrative to work with. It is in the solving of problems posed by his material that the poem stands as a brilliant technical achievement. It tells a story that is complete and satisfying and that communicates the sense that it has fully realized its possibilities.[2]

This achievement is the more remarkable because he was

1. On this question, see the "Excursus," below.

2. Edgar F. Shannon (*Chaucer and the Roman Poets* [Cambridge, Mass., Harvard University Press, 1929], p. 297) is of the same opinion concerning the material but not the finished product: "The failure of this *Legend* to measure up to the standard of most of the others lies in the weakness of the story told by Ovid. With all his art Chaucer could not make it pulsate with genuine emotion. It appealed to him perhaps only because of the variation that it offered upon the general theme of his poem."

working again with the troublesome *Heroides*.[3] His problem is to transform an essentially lyric-dramatic monologue into narrative form, and he succeeds completely.[4] It is further proof, if proof be needed, of his versatility and of his developed sense of the proper means for achieving in a narrative the effects he wishes. *Hypermnestra* makes a striking contrast in its method (and its tone) with *Phyllis*. There we observed a studied avoidance of incident or scene (after the storm) in order to minimize the tragic and pathetic elements in his material; instead, by narrative summary and authorial comment, he was able to establish and maintain the mocking tone he desired. Here he seeks the strongest emotional impact possible, and so he chooses dramatized scenes with a minimum of authorial comment.

3. His source is *Heroides*, xiv, "Hypermnestra to Lynceus." See M. Bech, "Quellen und Plan der 'Legende of Goode Women' und ihr Verhältniss zur 'Confessio Amantis,' " *Anglia*, 5 (1882), 348–354; W. W. Skeat, *The Complete Works of Geoffrey Chaucer* (Oxford, Eng., 1894), III, xl, 346–351; Shannon, *Chaucer and the Roman Poets*, pp. 291–297. Skeat thought Chaucer also used Boccaccio, *De Genealogia Deorum*, II, chap. xxii, particularly for the form of the names, and Shannon supported his suggestion. Shannon contended that Boccaccio's statement that Danao (Egiste in Chaucer) was warned by an oracle that one of his nephews would kill him was the source of the statement in Chaucer that he had been warned in a dream (2658–2660). But Sanford Meech shows that in Filippo's fourteenth-century translation of the *Heroides* the "community of name-forms" is greater between the *Legend* and the translation than it is between the *Legend* and Boccaccio. And Filippo's preparatory note to this epistle stated that Danao had been warned by a dream that one of his nephews would kill him: "Danao avea veduto *in visione* che uno *nepote* suo il dovea uccidere, *ma no sapea quale* . . . " [Meech's italics]. Meech concludes that Ovid and Filippo's translation are his sources, not Boccaccio ("Chaucer and an Italian Translation of the *Heroides*," *PMLA*, 45 [1930], 123–128). Hyginus, *Fabulae*, chap. clxviii, tells the story, and Bech thought this was the source of Chaucer's reversal of the parents' names; see n. 5, below. Boccaccio also tells the story in *De Claris Mulieribus*, chap. xiii, with a long moral comment.

4. Though the tale is unfinished, Chaucer seems not to have planned to conclude with a lyrical coda from the *Heroides*, as he does in *Dido, Hypsipyle and Medea, Ariadne,* and *Phyllis*. The shift from the narrative proper to the direct translation in the conclusion of at least some few lines from the lyrical *Heroides* was, as we have seen, sometimes awkward. Chaucer seems to have freed himself here from the sense either that he *must* do some direct translation of the *Heroides* or that, where this material was available, this way of using it was rhetorically effective.

Narrative and dramatic considerations seem to take precedence throughout. Instead of fifty sons of Danaus (Aegyptus in the original — for some unexplained reason Chaucer reversed the names)[5] married to fifty daughters of Aegyptus (Egiste[s] in Chaucer), all of whom save Hypermnestra obey their father's command to slay their bridegrooms on their wedding night, there is in Chaucer only one marriage, that of Lyno and Hypermnestra. Thereby the tale gains in probability and in intensity.[6] The contrast between Hypermnestra's action and that of her forty-nine sisters is lost, but this loss is more than compensated for by the consequent sharp focus on Hypermnestra alone with her father and Hypermnestra alone under the injunction to murder her husband. We are not distracted by the actions or reactions of other persons; the poem is all hers.

More than in the other legends, Chaucer exploits here the narrative device of suspense. The "nativity" supplied for Hypermnestra upon her introduction hints in its concluding lines at a harsh fate but without supplying real information:

> That Ypermystra dar nat handle a knyf
> In malyce, thogh she shulde lese hire lyf.
> But natheles, as hevene gan tho turne,
> To badde aspectes hath she of Saturne,

5. Bech pointed out that, as Hyginus tells the story (*Fabulae*, chap. clxviii), there are two murder plots, one against Danaus by Aegyptus and one against Aegyptus by Danaus. He suggested that, because of this, Chaucer carelessly confused the two plots and changed the names by mistake ("Quellen und Plan," pp. 350–351). But if Chaucer was using Filippo closely, such confusion seems unlikely.

6. Meech ("Chaucer and the *Heroides*," p. 127) observed that Chaucer's change "leads to a fallacy. The elimination of this one son-in-law could not of course insure the king's safety and the plotted crime in Chaucer's version of the story loses its logical motive." So much the better, apparently, for Chaucer calls attention, not to the illogicality so much as to the general nature of Aegyptus' decision. Having told Hypermnestra that he has been warned in a dream that his nephew will kill him, he says, " But which I noot, wherfore I wol be siker" (2660). That is, I will not take any chances and so I will not spare this man, even though he is your husband. The effect of this is to make Aegyptus' action seem all the more arbitrary and monstrous, which is precisely the way Chaucer wanted us to feel about it.

That made hire for to deyen in prisoun,
As I shal after make mencioun.

(2594–2599)

In the scene with her father there is first the threat of death to Hypermnestra unless she performs an unnamed task; the plot is not revealed until Aegyptus replies dramatically to the trembling girl's hesitations by drawing a knife, thrusting it upon her, and commanding:

"Hyd this," quod he, "that it be nat ysene;
And, whan thyn husbonde is to bedde go,
Whil that he slepeth, kit his throte atwo."

(2655–2657)

The narrative construction of the tale is simple and expert. Out of the *Heroides* Chaucer has extracted a story of a tragic wedding day. In Ovid there are a command to kill, some references to the wedding celebration, and one scene, the moment, recalled by Hypermnestra, when she is alone with her sleeping bridegroom trying to decide, in terror, what action to take. Much of Ovid's dramatic detail in this scene, however, must be discarded: the references to the other brides, Hypermnestra's attempts as a dutiful daughter to carry out the command, and the motive of revenge (the bridegrooms have seized her father's land). Using what he can, inventing freely, and creating an ingenious technical device, Chaucer fabricates a story of his own.

We begin with the storyteller's "once upon a time" — "In Grece whilom weren brethren two. . . ." The exposition is brief. Aegyptus' dream that one of his nephews would kill him is saved (for greater suspense, I assume) until his scene with Hypermnestra (2658–2660). We are told of Danaus' many sons and Aegyptus' many daughters. Both Danaus and Aegyptus are labeled as false in love (2565, 2571), presumably to explain the many children [7] and to establish the two parents as unsympathetic characters,

7. Shannon makes this suggestion (*Chaucer and the Roman Poets*, p. 293).

especially Aegyptus. Since Chaucer has dropped the whole matter of fifty daughters ordered to kill fifty bridegrooms, he might have dropped completely the multitude of nephews and daughters. He keeps them, apparently, to create for the two young people a heightened importance that will intensify the drama of their situation. Of all the many sons, Lynceus is his father's favorite; of all Aegyptus' daughters, Hypermnestra is the youngest and legitimately born ("gat upon his ryghte wyf"). None of these details is in Chaucer's sources.[8]

To introduce Hypermnestra, Chaucer resorts to amplification and creates for her a horoscope, a "nativity."[9] By this device (there is no suggestion of it in Ovid) he provides her with a complete character:

> To alle thewes goode yborn was she,
> As likede to the goddes, er she was born,
> That of the shef she sholde be the corn.
> The Wirdes, that we clepen Destine,
> Hath shapen hire that she mot nedes be
> Pyëtous, sad, wis, and trewe as stel. . . .
>
> (2577–2582)

Venus, in the ascendant at her birth, endows her with

---

8. Since Meech says nothing on this point, I assume Filippo did not supply the details.

9. There is an astrological analysis of the nativity in Walter Clyde Curry, *Chaucer and the Mediaeval Sciences* (New York, Oxford University Press, 1926), pp. 164–171. The function of the nativity in *Hypermnestra*, which he describes as "apparently something in the nature of an experiment," is, according to Curry, "to explain to his audience the action of a ready-made story and to rationalize a given character by the process of referring them to astral influences. . . ." The interrupted nativity seems "to govern and direct the prescribed action" (p. 164). This, however, makes the nativity a much more direct and deterministic influence than in fact it is in *Hypermnestra*. William Spencer has recently argued that Chaucer used astrology, specifically the pattern of the zodiac and its ruling planets, as a guide for his procession of human types and characters in the General Prologue to the *Canterbury Tales*: "Are Chaucer's Pilgrims Keyed to the Zodiac?" *Chaucer Review*, 4 (1969), 147–170. Though the date of composition is unknown, *Hypermnestra* may have been a pioneer use of astrological materials for characterization. Chauncey Wood discusses the passage briefly in *Chaucer and the Country of the Stars* (Princeton, New Jersey, Princeton University Press, 1970), p. 112.

beauty, and, since Venus was compounded with Jupiter, the result for Hypermnestra is

> That conscience, trouthe, and drede of shame,
> And of hyre wifhod for to kepe hire name,
> This, thoughte hire, was felycite as here.
>
> (2586–2588)

Mars, however, is feeble, oppressed by Venus, so that, as we have seen, she dare not handle a knife. Because of the bad aspects of Saturn, she is, however, fated to die in prison. It is a brilliant stratagem. By means of the "nativity" Hypermnestra's later actions in the narrative are motivated. In receiving this attention she becomes at once the emotional and narrative pivot of the whole poem, and the account of her goodness and her fate wins for her the immediate sympathy of the reader. The references to the Fates and Venus and Jupiter communicate the sense that she is an exalted person. Though the nativity delays slightly the action of the poem, this is a small price to pay. It creates suspense, and it is functional within the poem. The sense of fullness, weight, and completeness which the poem achieves for its brevity is in part a consequence of this *amplificatio*. With it, Chaucer has hit on a method for handling characterization in the short narrative that he will exploit to great advantage in the *Canterbury Tales*.

The arranging of the marriage and the description of the wedding, merely preliminary to the main action, are handled swiftly and easily. We are told of the two brothers that

> It lykede hem to make a maryage
> Bytwixen Ypermystre and hym Lyno,
> And casten swich a day it shal be so,
> And ful acorded was it utterly;
> The aray is wrought, the tyme is faste by.
>
> (2603–2607)

The wedding itself is sketched in with a few details from Ovid and a few details of his own:

> The torches brennen, and the laumpes bryghte;

> The sacryfices ben ful redy dighte;
> Th'encens out of the fyre reketh sote;
> The flour, the lef is rent up by the rote
> To maken garlondes and crounes hye.
> Ful is the place of soun of minstralsye,
> Of songes amorous of maryage. . . .
>
> (2610–2616)

This is the art of summary mastered to perfection. Though it does not advance the action appreciably, except to show the wedding "happening," it does more than set the scene — if that phrase would have meant anything to Chaucer. The passage has a touch of exoticism — sacrifices, incense — but this is accompanied by more familiar touches, such as the sound of minstrelsy, so that the exoticism seems necessary because of the material but otherwise incidental. What the passage does do is to create a sense of normal expectation: this is a wedding, what is happening — the joy, the celebration — is what should be happening, and the expectation is that all will continue normally:

> And thus the day they dryve to an ende;
> The frendes taken leve, and hom they wende;
> The nyght is come, the bryd shal go to bedde.
>
> (2620–2622)

The effect of the father's command and the cruel reversal of fortune for Hypermnestra are thereby made all the more dramatic, all the more shattering.

Quite obviously it is a shock effect that Chaucer wants, for he builds the scene between Hypermnestra and her father to this end. The scene is entirely his own creation, without any hint in Ovid to build on (except, of course, that, for the events described to have taken place, some such scene between father and daughters must have occurred). As something imagined *in toto* by Chaucer, it is fascinating to study.

The pattern of normal expectation is continued at the beginning of the scene with tender words from Aegyptus:

> My ryghte doughter, tresor of myn herte,

Syn fyrst that day that shapen was my sherte,
Or by the fatal systren had my dom,
So nygh myn herte nevere thyng ne com
As thow, myn Ypermystre, doughter dere.
Take hed what I, thy fader, seye the here,
And werk after thy wiser evere mo.
For alderfirst, doughter, I love the so
That al the world to me nis half so lef;
Ne I nolde rede the to thy myschef
For al the good under the colde mone.
And what I mene, it shal be seyd right sone,
With protestacioun, as in this wyse,
That, but thow do as I shal the devyse,
Thow shalt be ded, by hym that al hath wrought!

(2628–2642)

It is a masterly speech,[10] supremely parental, invoking
mortality, love, parental authority and concern, and the
wisdom of an elder. Its conclusion is, therefore, an intensely dramatic reversal, bringing to sudden realization the
first faint note of menace contained in "under the colde
mone."

Hypermnestra's reaction is calculated to be dramatic in
itself and to heighten the drama of her situation in the next
scene. This is done by expressing her shock, terror, and
maidenly virtue. She casts down her eyes, trembles "as doth
the lef of aspe grene," and replies,

Lord and fader, al youre wille,
After my myght, God wot, I shal fulfille,
So it to me be no confusioun.

(2650–2652)

Aegyptus' response reveals the sheer force and cruelty of
what she must oppose:

"I nele," quod he, "have non excepcioun";
And out he caught a knyf, as rasour kene.

(2653–2654)

10. One flaw the speech does have. It goes on longer than necessary and re-
peats, for emphasis presumably, the threat of death; the second threat is no
more forceful or vivid than the first, however.

The command to slay her husband is accompanied by a warning grimly understated: "If thow sey ney, we two shul have a biker. . . ."
The transition to the second and final scene is deft; it returns effortlessly to the earlier pattern of normality, which now must be viewed ironically:

> Out cometh the bryd, and with ful sobre cheere,
> As is of maydens ofte the manere,
> To chaumbre is brought with revel and with song.
>
> (2672–2674)

The second scene is a solo piece, Hypermnestra alone with the sleeping Lyno. The pitfalls that beset such scenes are obvious — melodramatics, hysterical passion, tangled involutions of reflection. Chaucer is proof against them all. A single-souled, tender, simple girl, Hypermnestra is not one for elaborate reflection. The scene must preserve that tenderness and simplicity in a terrible situation. Chaucer maintains a delicate balance between objective and subjective presentation. Throughout she remains in character, not for the sake of consistency but because this kind of character will create a maximum dramatic effect of strength in tenderness, of feminine fearfulness and feminine steadfastness, those qualities already established for her in her "nativity."
She is first fixed for us by an image (from Ovid) of trembling and of cold, while a detail reveals her isolation:

> She rist hire up, and dredfully she quaketh,
> As doth the braunche that Zepherus shaketh,
> And hust were alle in Argon that cite.
> As cold as any frost now waxeth she. . . .
>
> (2680–2683)

The image of trembling, used already in the previous scene, here reveals both her fear and her fragility (something the softest breeze could shake). The image of cold leaps forward to her state of numbness and pale terror. The action is then presented directly:

> thryes doun she fyl in swich a were.
> She rist yit up, and stakereth her and there,
> And on hire hondes faste loketh she.
>
> (2686–2688)

This hovers on the verge of cliché and melodrama because
of the three swoons, but it is redeemed from both by the
"stakereth her and there," which seems too immediately
visualized not to be a true reporting of her dazed condition. It is a vivid revelation of her confusion and shock before a decision which must mean death either for herself
or her bridegroom. The gazing at her hands, a brilliant detail, seems a prelude to some more melodramatic gesture,
but it is followed by speech. The action is cut before it
goes too far. And to give Chaucer further credit, we should
note that Ovid *is* melodramatic:

> Thought of my violent father's mandates struck away my fear.
> I rise, and clutch with trembling hand the steel. I will not
> tell you aught untrue: thrice did my hand raise high the
> piercing blade, and thrice, having raised it, fell again.
> I brought it to your throat — let me confess to you the truth!
> — I brought my father's weapon to your throat; but fear and
> tenderness kept me from daring the cruel stroke, and my
> chaste right hand refused the task enjoined. Rending the
> purple robes I wore, rending my hair, I spoke with scant
> sound. . . .[11]

Chaucer has chosen to remain more faithful to what he
found a few lines later in Ovid: "A woman am I, and a
maid, gentle in nature and in years; my tender hands ill

11. Translation by Grant Showerman, in Ovid, *Heroides and Amores*, Loeb
Classical Library (London, William Heinemann, 1921), p. 175:

> Excussere metum violenti iussa parentis;
>   erigor et capio tela tremente manu.
> non ego falsa loquar: ter acutum sustulit ensem,
>   ter male sublato reccidit ense manus.
> admovi iugulo — sine me tibi vera fateri! —
>   admovi iugulo tela paterna tuo;
> sed timor et pietas crudelibus obstitit ausis,
>   castaque mandatum dextra refugit opus.
> purpureos laniata sinus, laniata capillos
>   exiguo dixi talia verba sono. . . .   (43–52)

suit fierce weapons." [12] This is used for Hypermnestra's speech as she gazes at her hands.

The speech maintains the sense of her innocence and fragility by the childlike quality of her reaction to the horrible task assigned her: "Allas! and shal myne hondes blody be? . . . Myne handes ben nat shapen for a knyf. . . . What devel have I with the knyf to do?" (2689, 2692, 2694); and by her childlike view of death: "And shal I have my throte korve a-two? / Thanne shal I blede, allas! and me beshende!" (2695–2696). Her final decision arises from her devotion and the steadfastness of her nature:

> "Or he or I mot nedes lese oure lyf.
> Now certes," quod she, "syn I am his wif,
> And hath my feyth, yit is it bet for me
> For to be ded in wifly honeste
> Than ben a traytour lyvynge in my shame.
> Be as be may, for ernest or for game,
> He shal awake, and ryse, and gon his way,
> Out at this goter, or that it be day —"
>
> (2698–2705)

The decision comes, finally, not so much as a consequence of rational conclusion but as a movement arising from instinct and feeling; it is a decision arrived at by a kind of inner necessity: "Be as be may, for ernest or for game. . . ."

The final action wastes neither time nor words:

> And wep ful tenderly upon his face,
> And in hyre armes gan hym to enbrace,
> And hym she roggeth and awaketh softe.
> And at a wyndow lep he fro the lofte,
> Whan she hath warned hym, and don hym bote.
>
> (2706–2710)

Hypermnestra, note, remains in character to the end; she woke him *softly*. And one must marvel at the control which

12. *Ibid.*, lines 55–56: "femina sum et virgo, natura mitis et annis;/non faciunt molles ad fera tela manus." Also lines 65–66: "quid mihi cum ferro? quo bellica tela puellae?/aptior est digitis lana colusque meis." ("What have swords to do with me? What has a girl to do with the weapons of war? More suited to my hands are the distaff and the wool.")

outdoes Ovid's restraint (75–78). Lyno, whom we have seen
not at all, nor do we need to, disappears with a leap, without
dramatic explanations or tender (or hypocritical) speeches.
The story has said everything it needs to say for its own
particular purposes, and it ends.

Hypermnestra should perhaps be classified as a tale of
pathos. The heroine has the proper qualifications of innocence and helplessness and tears:

> This sely woman is so weik, allas!
> And helples so, that, or that she fer wente,
> Hire crewel fader dide hire for to hente.

$$(2713–2715)$$

If it is a tale of pathos, it is so with a difference. There is the
quality of strength and steadfastness ("trewe as stel"), side
by side with physical frailty. Hypermnestra acts, and acts
courageously. Her suffering is not the sole substance of her
being. The restraint that characterizes the tale in general
also limits the pathetic simulacra — the tears are not insisted on, nor is the innocence. Melodramatic speech and
gesture are largely avoided.

Another quality of the narrative works against excessive
pathetic emotion. A sense of reality accompanies the action
and never disappears. Some of the language of the poem
contributes to this sense: "stakereth," "roggeth," "costret"
(flask), "as rasour kene," "goter." This language comes from
the real world, not a world of unbridled emotion. Details
which might seem strange are explained as practices of another age: the marriage of first cousins, for example ("For
thilke tyme was spared no lynage" [2602]), or some of the
features of the marriage celebration ("As thylke tyme was
the pleyne usage" [2617]). We are given the illusion that
this is something that happened, a real occasion, if you
wish, in which considerations of reality operate. It is not
a monstrous world in which passions are out of control or
where miracles of virtue are performed.

The pattern of normal expectation established by the
wedding scene which has been commented on, though it

heightens the impact of the dramatic reversal, also contributes to the sense of a normal world which acts as a brake upon our reactions. In the father-daughter scene, again, a sense of probability is retained, granted the melodramatic command. Hypermnestra agreed to her father's order, we are told, "for to passen harmles of that place, / . . . ther is non other grace" (2664–2665). Aegyptus gives her potions to drug Lyno — note his practical adjustment to the considerations of the moment: "And go thy wey, lest that him thynke longe" (2671). Hypermnestra's "ful sobre cheere" as she leaves her father's chamber, we have seen, seemed natural for a maiden on her bridal night (2672–2673). Lyno can escape "out at this goter." Even Hypermnestra's final moment seems to be given us with one eye on the limits of the possible:

> For, whan she saw that gon awey was he,
> And that she myghte nat so faste go,
> Ne folwen hym, she sat hire doun ryght tho,
> Til she was caught and fetered in prysoun.
>
> (2719–2722)

(This is where the "bad aspects" of Saturn indicated she would end.) This concern for probabilities maintains a balance, a sense of control within the tale. Our emotions, our sympathies, are not invited to run wild. They are engaged, but that is something different.

Hypermnestra emerges as a relatively pure story. It is an account of an action in which the central character operates within certain simply established probabilities and demonstrates in the circumstances of the narrative a reversal which is simply that same character further revealed. What made Hypermnestra a devoted daughter makes her a devoted wife who will not obey her father's command; tenderness and steadfastness make her choose, if there must be a choice, death for herself rather than death for her husband. The story fulfills its own conditions and demonstrates its own nature. The skill, finally, is everything, the skill of the masterly narrator.

[XII]   The Lessons Learned

The individual legends, as this examination may have suggested, are in various ways and to various degrees themselves an achievement. To ignore them completely or to condescend to them, as scholarship has done for many years, is to do them and to do Chaucer an injustice. They reward an observant and a sympathetic eye. There yet remains the question of the significance of the *Legend* in Chaucer's career. There is of course one difficulty in making a final assessment. We know that Chaucer began the *Legend of Good Women* before he began the *Canterbury Tales*, but we do not know that he had not begun the *Tales* before he had written all of the legends that we have. The *Canterbury Tales* project was probably not well under way much before the last legend, *Hypermnestra*. A growing preoccupation with the pilgrimage tales would explain the breaking off of the *Legend* at this point. It seems reasonably safe to hypothesize that Chaucer had written at least the first five or six tales, *Lucrece*, and probably *Ariadne*, before he began working on the narratives for the *Tales*. It will simplify matters to talk here as though all of the *Legend* as we have it was written before the *Canterbury Tales*, but the judgments expressed about the *Legend* hold, by and large, for what had been done and learned by the time Chaucer had completed *Lucrece*.

What, then, does the *Legend of Good Women* signify in Chaucer's history? Certainly there is a breaking away into new subject matter, the discovery and conquest of a new world, as the Prologue implied. The *Legend* shows him

moving, hesitantly at first but with growing confidence
(the progress from *Cleopatra* to, say, *Lucrece* would be our
evidence), into a new body of material and demonstrating
his ability to use this new matter effectively. We may imagine a sense of excitement and joy: his judgment had been
correct in deciding to abandon the old; his powers were
ample for mastering the new. The *Troilus* had been a bold
innovation, to be sure, and a triumph, but with familiar
themes, and a triumph, moreover, that was a culmination
and not a beginning. Before the *Legend* was completed, a
whole world of narrative material had become accessible to
his hungry genius. It is still a long step from the aristocratic
world of Jason or Theseus to the villein's world of Robin
Miller, but Jason and Theseus and Ariadne move outside
the garden wall of idealized love, and outside the wall
Robin's world is near at hand and he can be met there, as he
never could have been inside.

The accessibility of a new range of narrative matter and
its exploitation were, however, dependent on the mastery
of brevity. We must not underestimate what Chaucer
learned on this score from the *Legend*. The indecent haste
of *Cleopatra*, the indecision of *Hypsipyle and Medea*, the
truncation of feeling in *Philomela* show the pain and price
of this lesson. But the variety and amplitude of the *Canterbury Tales* might not have been possible within the ex-
pansionist method of *Troilus*. The narrative skill and the
comfortable control and mastery of the short verse tale
in the *Canterbury Tales* owe much to what was learned in
creating the legends.

There was first the willingness to be brief, a mastery of
the art of silence: refusing to amplify when opportunity
knocked and a fertile imagination beckoned, or deciding to
cut however attractive the material. It shows artistic tact
to recognize that no more or nothing need be said for the
purposes of the moment or of the tale as a whole: no passionate speech from Lucrece after Tarquin's terrible
threats, only "She axeth grace, and seyth al that she can."

The art of the brief narrative demands, of course, more

than silence. It must aim at rapid forward movement at appropriate moments in the narrative, and for this at least two techniques are indispensable. One is the art of quick summary of action. Chaucer learned this well: we remember the swift and secret journey of Tarquin to the house of Colatyn (1779–1786), the easy triumph of Theseus over the Minotaur (2140–2149), Philomela's message to Progne (2356–2375). A second technique is the art of the quick effect, the rapid brushstroke, whereby the tone of a scene is set, a character is established, a line of action is moved in a particular direction. The magnificent sea battle in *Cleopatra* is an example of this quick effect not really put to proper use. Lucrece alone with her servants, the hypocritical Tereus with his wife in his arms, Ariadne rolling the word "duchess" on her tongue, the storm at sea which drives Demophoon ashore are successful because they are functional instances.

The crucial art of selection in the short tale involves selecting what to treat more fully or emphasize, as much as determining what to omit or condense. Chaucer had difficulties here. *Cleopatra* suffers because the proper choices are not made. Very little in fact is given full treatment. We never see Antony and Cleopatra together, and so their passion has not much reality for us. The sea battle, given the proportions of the tale, is relatively extraneous and is the wrong scene to dramatize. The single correct choice, an inevitable one, is Cleopatra's preparations for death, together with her final declaration of faithful love. The emphases in *Thisbe* are perfect because he follows Ovid so closely. *Dido* has one curious moment, the full scene between Aeneas and Venus before his involvement with Dido. Otherwise the emphases are appropriate. *Hypsipyle and Medea* stumbles about badly in the early sections. Too much attention is paid to the Pelleus story, and Pelleus has one of the few speeches in the tale. In the Hypsipyle incident, Jason's one speech is to the messenger on the shore (1491–1495), not a dramatic moment, and nothing important is said. After these curious bulges, the story smooths out and one has no further sense that the wrong moment is being stressed. Thereafter Chaucer makes the proper selections. *Lucrece* seems flawless. If the speeches in the middle section of *Ariadne* seem curiously long, Chaucer appears to be working for a special effect by this means. If *Philomela* lacks some scenes we should like, the emphases are nevertheless right for his purposes — though one might wonder at the weight given the scene with Pandion (2270–2307). *Phyllis* is skillful in its calculated avoidance of dramatization, and *Hypermnestra* is a beautifully balanced production.

The difficulties in achieving a proper emphasis probably contribute heavily to the feeling that the heft of a legend, its weight in the hand so to speak, is not quite right. The legends frequently seem too brief, but some of the fault here may be attributed to modern taste and experience, or the lack of it. Brief poetic narrative is largely outside our range of familiar literary sensation. We need a carefully considered awareness of what a brief poetic narrative aims to do before we can make proper judgments about it. Parenthetically, our difficulties with the form are compounded because we so often find it in collections or clusters. We do a medieval series of tales like the *Confessio Amantis* or the *Legend of Good Women* or the *Monk's Tale* an injustice if we read them one after another after another. They may have been so read or heard, though not endlessly, in the fourteenth century. Examples of an unfamiliar form, however, seem all alike, and this sense of uniformity and monotony is magnified when the items of a series are read in rapid succession. Gower's reputation has suffered, I believe, because, when readers try him at all, they try to digest too many tales at one sitting. The tales not only seem much of a piece; they also seem disappointingly simple and flat. Our expectations from a "long read" are oriented toward the epic, for sweep or for progressive complexity. A series of tales in a medieval collection makes no such claims. We would do better, at least until we become adjusted to the form, to read one or two at a time.

First we must understand what a particular writer sets

out to do with the form. Chaucer's interest in the short poetic narrative is unmistakable, not only here but in the *Canterbury Tales* as a whole and in another particular example, the *Monk's Tale.* This last gives us one extreme, with narratives ranging in length from 8 lines (a single stanza) to 128 (16 stanzas), the median being 40 lines (5 stanzas). The primary intention of the Monk's narratives seems close to that of the *exemplum,* to point a moral by means of an interesting or entertaining short tale; in this instance, a moral (with varying emphases) about Fortune. Even here, however, the nature of the material chosen suggests an equal interest in presenting and transmitting important "historical" material, in fulfilling the valuable preservative function of writing and of literary art. At the same time, the method of presentation and, in at least one clear instance, the selection of material (the Ugelino of Pisa episode) reveal a concern to create by means of the narrative a specific emotional impact, pathos with "Ugelino" and horror with "Antiochus," to cite two examples. In the *Legend of Good Women,* though art's function as a key of remembrance is invoked, Chaucer's freedom in cutting and changing his material reveals other purposes as well. The moral intention of the brief *exemplum,* legend, or saint's life is of some importance, insofar as this relates to a (sometimes mocking) praise of woman's faithfulness in love and an (also sometimes mocking) indictment of man's fickleness. A more general "moral" intention is Chaucer's interest in making a series of observations about love and its workings in people, observations outside the familiar observations codified in the conventional love poetry of the time. But Chaucer's cuts and changes and shapings of his material reveal, above all else, a concern to create a specific effect (often a fresh or surprising one) by means of his brief narrative. The effect is usually emotional, but in a few instances it is ironic. It is relatively pure and concentrated.

If this description suggests the lyric, the analogy is not necessarily harmful. Chaucer's experience with the lyric and with the lyric-narrative does not evaporate when he shifts to the more purely narrative form. The legends have already been described as "narrative of sentiment." It is not only that the feeling of the principal character or characters is central to the narrative; a specific emotional effect is the narrative's goal. This strong element of feeling in the *Legend* accounted for much of its popularity in the nineteenth century — and the fifteenth. Since the dramatic lyrics of the *Heroides* lie behind many of the legends, the concentration on feeling is not surprising. Nor is it surprising in a transitional work. By retaining a lyric dimension Chaucer holds fast to something familiar and is assisted in making the difficult move to a more narrative poetry. The lyric intention provides a unifying element, a key to control his selection of materials and his development of the narrative line; it enables him to reject that other key to narrative control, both more conventional and more readily accessible, moralization.

Indeed, feeling or sentiment largely displaces the moral intention. It frequently usurps the classic position for moralizing statement, the concluding lines of a narrative, which are assigned to verses from the *Heroides* and become the most lyric moment of the legend. The action and the characters are shaped to contribute to this overall "feeling." The result is a more comprehensive kind of statement than is possible in the pure exemplum, since feeling is at once more complex and more ambiguous than moralization, which normally oversimplifies an action and narrowly limits the range of reaction. An audience can only accept or, less customarily, reject a moral. Feeling, however, does not disengage us from the human actions which created it, and it evokes reactions from a wider and subtler range of human experience. If we remember Chaucer's interest in an emotional effect as we read the legends, we shall come closer to understanding and judging them aright.

This lyric intention may explain the relative brevity of the legends, at least in part. One may, nonetheless, argue, and legitimately, that, compared to the *Pardoner's Tale* or the *Miller's Tale*, a legend seems of insufficient length.

Chaucer's relative inexperience with the short narrative may be another explanation. There is also the fact that the legends are to a considerable extent narrative improvisations on suggestions in the *Heroides*, whereas in the *Canterbury Tales* Chaucer used ready-made narratives as the basis of his fictions. At the very least they gave him a crude model to work with. And having learned to identify or to abstract the essential skeleton of a narrative ("the grete": *Legend*, F 574), he was freer to amplify once more — outside the structure as with the *Pardoner's Tale*, inside as with the *Nun's Priest's Tale* or the *Merchant's*, or both outside and inside as with the Wife of Bath's Prologue and tale — and to amplify for precisely calculated effects. But the sense of ease and mastery in working with a brief narrative goes back to the apprenticeship with the legends. And some of these have also their proper magnitude — *Thisbe, Lucrece, Hypermnestra*, and, yes, *Dido*.

Throughout the *Legend* Chaucer is using his new verse unit, the decasyllabic couplet. The decasyllabic line is nothing new to him, of course, and one might also argue that he has already had ample experience writing decasyllabic couplets. Not only is there the *Knight's Tale* ("Palamon and Arcite"), but the last four lines of a rhyme royal stanza — the *bbcc* section of the *ababbcc* pattern — are decasyllabic couplets if isolated in the stanza. They are obviously not so isolated in practice, and that makes all the difference. The possibilities opened up by the decasyllabic couplet as opposed to the rhyme royal stanza stem from several freedoms: freedom from the third *b* rhyme, for one; freedom to move forward with no necessity to fill out the seven lines of a rhyme royal stanza, for another. Although one rarely has any sense in reading Chaucer's rhyme royal that in his final lines he is padding out a stanza, one must simply accept the fact that a rhymed couplet allows more easily for rapid forward movement. A danger goes with this ease, naturally: either a choppy, spasmodic movement if the sense is broken too mechanically, purposelessly, at the end of every second line; or, conversely, a slackness or prolixity arising from the undisciplined running on of the verse in a form so loosely bridled. We see this last at times in Chaucer's early octosyllabic couplets. But his years of discipline with the rhyme royal stanza stood Chaucer in good stead. From the first he seems in complete control of the new form. I can perceive no movement from awkwardness to mastery in the course of the *Legend*; perhaps my ear is not sharp enough. All that can be claimed is that his experience with the *Legend* apparently confirmed Chaucer in his judgment that this new form was the right one for most narrative poetry.

As we read through the legends I believe we can, however, see development in another area: an awareness of the problem of "characterization" and a move to meet this problem. Just what "characterization" might mean, if anything, to a late medieval writer is difficult to say. We do not know much about the subject. Two observations about characterizations in Chaucer before the *Legend* are suggestive. If we look at *Troilus and Criseyde*, generally regarded as Chaucer's richest "psychological" creation, and observe how the characters are introduced, we are struck by the suddenness of their appearance on the stage. Of Criseyde we are told that she was Calkas' daughter, a widow without (powerful) friends, frightened at what might become of her because of her father's treachery, and, above all, beautiful. We have already been told that she will forsake Troilus (I, 56). Concerning her nature, however, nothing is really said. The most particularizing detail is that she is Calkas' daughter and a widow alone; this seems important for the plot (her separation from Troy and Troilus by petition and decree), but not for character. Troilus' introduction is completely abrupt: "This Troilus, as he was wont to gide / His yonge knyghtes" is how he appears. In the invocation, to be sure, we have been told that he is King Priam's son and that he will love and be unhappy, but that is all. In a moment we learn that he is scornful of love and lovers. But this relates to immediate situation and to ironic perspective — only minimally to characterization. Pandarus, who is ultimately the most sharply drawn of the three, appears with the least fanfare of all: "A frend of his, that called was Pandare" (I, 548). Minor characters are similarly pushed without preparation onto the stage: Antigone, Deiphebus, Diomede. Their relationship to a main character is all we need to know about the first two. We need to know a little more about Diomede, but it emerges a piece at a time as the action develops, the same method that provides our understanding of Troilus, Criseyde, and Pandarus.

In comparison with the introductory descriptions in the *Miller's Tale* this may appear to be a relatively sophisticated technique of dramatizing character, of "showing" rather than of "telling," but it is not. It arises, rather, from a somewhat simplistic view of the place of character in a narrative. Troilus, Criseyde, Pandarus need no introductions and no explanations because their fundamental role as agents in the action is pre-established by the kind of action in which they appear, a courtly love story: lover, lady love, friend. The concept of "role" is of supreme importance in medieval society, in medieval historiography, and in medieval literature. Such complexities and depths as may develop in the presentation of a character develop within the role and develop in considerable part either by accident of plot, where a character, because of the story, performs actions contradictory or unexpected and so may take on, willy-nilly, an appearance of complexity; or by the accident of vision, where the artist's perception and communication of subtleties of character are incorporated within the role. We can see both of these "accidents" occurring in some of the portraits of the Sins in *Piers Plowman* (for example, Ire). They are what we see in *Troilus and Criseyde*.

This attitude toward character explains the puzzling location of the "portraits" of Diomede, Criseyde, and Troilus in Book Five, when the action is almost ended. The placing would be impossible for a writer who saw specific configurations of character as a prerequisite for specific actions. It is not a belated effort to "explain" the three main actors in Book V, to "characterize" them. The portraits relate to action, not character; they are primarily visual, not psychological. They provide an artificial confrontation so that we shall "see" the three characters clearly as the betrayal occurs and the action comes to its unhappy end. This ironic conjunction underlines the fact that partial and imperfect choices must be made, and its purpose is to aid us in seeing what is happening, not why it is happening. It is hardly a bow to characterization.

This is not to deny Chaucer's sharp eye for the shape of a personality or his extraordinary gift for conveying that shape — warts, tricks of speech, and all. It is to deny that it is likely he thought primarily in terms of characterization, especially in his early poetry. He thought in terms of role. And in his early poetry his great gift for what we can call characterization was largely frustrated by the limited number of roles possible in the aristocratic, courtly genres in which he worked. I draw my conclusions on this point from a second observation.

It is curious that in Chaucer's earliest poems the most original characters are birds: the eagle in the *House of Fame,* the ducks and geese and cuckoos in the *Parliament of Birds.* This suggests that only when freed completely from the restrictions imposed upon the customary "human" roles in courtly poetry, set in manner and few in number, could his gift for characterization break forth with a leap and a whoop. The Man in Black, because of role (bereaved lover in a love elegy, great aristocrat in the real world), must be handled with strict attention to convention. The same is true for the Good Fair White. Aeneas and Dido in the *House of Fame* are featureless, Dido playing (very woodenly) the role of "lamenting, betrayed queen." The contradictory decisions the Goddess Fame must deliver give some sense of a lively, interesting character, and, though at moments she has her own voice, she is a variation on the goddess Fortuna, nothing more. Scipio Africanus in the *Parliament of Birds* is a summarized voice except when he shoves Chaucer through the gate, and it is really the dreamer we see at this moment, not Scipio. The sense of personality which, by contrast, we feel when the eagle is prosing or the duck is quacking is attainable in the early poetry only by escaping the human world completely. Is it sheer coincidence that pictorial realism in English painting erupts, in some of its earliest manifestations, on the margins of manuscripts in the form of sharply observed species of birds and of birds and animals acting out in mockery the crimes and follies of the real world? Suffice it to say that, inasmuch as a rigid iconography controlled the representation of both religious subjects and the aristocracy, it is not surprising that another sphere completely divorced from the human, the animal world, should be the area to locate observation that was fresh and free.

In *Troilus*, with the advantage of historical and geographical distance and the greater advantage of artistic maturity, Chaucer could enrich the central roles themselves with details of speech and action to make them vivid and lifelike. He drives toward the deepest realization of the potentialities of each role. Pandarus is the complete *amis*, including certain darker implications inherent in the role perhaps hitherto unnoticed. Criseyde is the "daungerous" lady *par excellence*; Troilus, the lover's cry of "Pitee!" personified. What follows in the *Knight's Tale*, however, is a complete reversal. For here Palamon and Arcite and Emelye are three roles — two lovers and the lady — and nothing more, completely drained of all content. This may or may not be further evidence of how near exhaustion the vein of courtly love was for Chaucer. It *is* evidence of how central, how crucial "role" was, how essentially irrelevant and at most secondary, or even tertiary, characterization still was in his art. Preoccupied with other purposes, he is content to throw the roles on the stage and let them run through their conventional paces, indeed, to exploit their emptiness. The example should warn us not to talk too glibly about Chaucer's concern for characterization before the *Legend*.

When he came to write the *Legend*, however, he faced a new problem. With these stories the conventional roles of the courtly love narrative would not work. Though most of the actors are aristocrats, they are from another world and another time, and they are performing actions imagined long before Froissart and Chrétien and Andreas Capellanus. With some changes, they might have been forced into contemporary and familiar molds, even as the thirteenth-century Anglo-Norman adapter filled the mouths of Pyramus and Thisbe with speeches in the best tradition of *fins amors*. But Chaucer is seeking to escape from this convention into freedom. Freedom there is, then, but a somewhat worrisome freedom. His faltering treatment of Antony and of Cleopatra reveal the difficulty. Chaucer assigns to Cleopatra the conventional "lovely loved lady" role, but she does not fit there very well. Antony fits even more awkwardly as "royal lover." They love, to be sure, but their significant actions have little relation to the usual lover-lady roles of fourteenth-century poetry into which they are cast. We have roles of one kind and actions of another.

With *Thisbe*, as we have seen, he follows Ovid closely, in the treatment of character as in other matters. He simply tells their story, and, since the role of ardent young lovers is a familiar one and since their story is well known, there are no difficulties. Dido is also well known, but Chaucer gives the story an original emphasis in making Aeneas so thorough a cad. The inadequacy of his customary approach to character for these materials is again revealed. In the first half of the tale he focuses our attention on Dido by means of two descriptive passages. Both dwell on her beauty at length and also on her "gentillesse," "fredom," "goodnesse, / And womanhod, and trouthe, and semelynesse" (1004–1014, 1035–1042). Dido is not being forced out of her customary role, but the descriptions do give her special prominence and firmly engage our sympathies for her. She is, as it were, "established." Since Aeneas is to emerge with his character blackened to an unusual degree, it is his character that needs establishing, but, aside from informing us in the opening lines that we will learn "How Eneas to Dido was forsworn" (927), Chaucer makes no move toward this end until the tale is almost three-quarters completed, when, in the cave scene, he is called a "fals lovere" (1236). Finally, in the apostrophe "O sely wemen" he is placed in the category of untrustworthy men: "This Troyan . . . / That feyneth hym so trewe and obeysynge, / So gentil, and so privy of his doinge," the master false seducer of women (1254ff.). It reveals a curious indifference to the problem of making a possibly unexpected role clear early in the action. Presumably Chaucer was still relying on his audience's general familiarity with the story.

With the next legend, however, he changes his practice and begins to "establish" the role of the central character and to experiment with devices for doing so. It is the role of the false lover that especially requires his attention. In *Hypsipyle and Medea*, before the narrative proper gets under way he provides an apostrophe to Jason that draws an unmistakable portrait: "Thow rote of false lovers, Duc Jasoun, / Thow sly devourere and confusioun / Of gentil wemen," and so on for twenty-eight lines (1368–1395). In the next tale he provides Lucrece, a more familiar figure, with a briefer introduction, but introduction it is: "The verray wif, the verray trewe Lucresse, / That, for hyre wifhod and hire stedefastnesse . . ." (six lines in all, 1686–1691). The stress on "wif" and "wifhod" is original and important. Tarquin, to be sure, is first introduced merely as "the yonge," and if we do not know the tale we get no sense of the role he will play until after he has seen Lucrece, when we watch his reactions and his "blynde lust" (1745–1774). Perhaps this is soon enough, though he is not specifically identified for us; we must know him from his thought and actions. In *Ariadne* we have another false lover, Theseus, established quickly in four lines of condemnation (1890–1893). If he is the sly opportunist I think him to be, however, this must be learned from his speech and actions, and there is no identifying word for him until he is called "Traytour" as he steals away. If Ariadne and Phaedra are something more than conventional heroines, they require definition. Perhaps this is being provided in the amusing, rather puzzling lines which describe how they heard Theseus lamenting

> as they stode on the wal,
> And lokeden upon the bryghte mone.
> Hem leste nat to go to bedde so sone;
> And of his wo they hadde compassioun.
> A kynges sone to ben in swich prysoun,
> And ben devoured, thoughte hem gret pite.

(1971–1976)

One side of their (or Ariadne's) nature seems to be revealed by the lines, namely a self-conscious "romanticism." Another side, a naïve "practicality," must emerge from several conversations. Our uncertainty, and the sense of awkwardness in this legend, may be evidence of Chaucer's difficulties: how do you handle several unfamiliar kinds of character in a short narrative?

In *Philomela* a variation on the apostrophe used for Jason is employed, a philosophical apostrophe addressed to "Thow yevere of the formes": why has "Deus dator formarum" created Tereus, "That is in love so fals and so forswore . . ." (2228–2243)? The device establishes Tereus' role as well as the tone, and this serves the story well for most of its action, though it leaves Philomela and Progne undefined. *Phyllis*, in which Chaucer seeks an unexpected mocking tone for a familiar sad story, opens with a *sentence* — "By preve as wel as by autorite, / That wiked fruit cometh of a wiked tre" — which introduces us to

> false Demophon.
> In love a falser herde I never non,
> But if it were his fader Theseus.

(2398–2400)

After his shipwreck, before the narrative proper, such as it is, has begun, Demophoon is again identified as false like his father Theseus: "it com hym of nature. / As doth the fox Renard, the foxes sone. . . ." (2446–2451). Tone and role are being established simultaneously. Finally, in *Hy-*

permnestra, as we have seen, he uses a horoscope, a new device, which functions in part at least to make us thoroughly
familiar with the nature of Hypermnestra before the action
begins.

By this time, of course, he may have been at work on some
of the short narratives of the *Canterbury Tales,* and he may
be profiting in *Hypermnestra* from further lessons learned
in creating those tales. It does, however, appear that, in the
course of working on the legends, Chaucer perceived the
virtue and the necessity of establishing at the beginning of
a narrative the role of a principal character where the character was not to operate within a conventional or familiar
role. The relative brevity of the narratives, as well as the
novelty of the role, urges such a practice. An extended
sequence of speeches and actions cannot be used to establish the precise dimensions of a character, as with Pandarus
and Criseyde. The explicit introduction of a character may
be profitably used in a short narrative even when the role
is not especially unconventional, as with Hypermnestra.

This technique will be employed with great effectiveness
in a variety of ways throughout the *Canterbury Tales.* The
portraits which open the *Miller's Tale* and the *Reeve's* are
perhaps the most brilliant examples, though not the only
ones. What is more, the technique leads directly to the
portraits of the General Prologue, whereby every narrator
is defined for us before the pilgrimage begins so that he may
tell his tale, interrupt a teller, or become involved in the
roadside drama with his role ("degree" and "condicioun")
clearly before our eye.

If this technique seems somewhat mechanical, if it seems
a regression from the more dramatistic method of the *Troilus,* this is only because of the distortions created by later
literary history. The method of *Troilus* is probably much
less sophisticated than it seems; we confuse it with a later,
highly self-conscious objective technique. Chaucer was
simply relying on his audience's familiarity with the roles.
The unfamiliar role, however, must be identified; indeed,
in the short narrative, it may be useful to identify the main

roles even when they are relatively familiar. In the *Legend*, it appears, Chaucer came to recognize this necessity and devised effective techniques for handling the problem. This is to say, further, that he achieved here a greater awareness than hitherto of the function of character in narrative.

The variety of characters treated in the *Legend* is impressive: Dido pouring out gifts like a personification of largesse, and the frantic and hysterical Dido; the awkward Hercules and the sham-shy Jason; Tarquin hopelessly obsessed with a fatal passion; Lucrece faithful and vulnerable; Theseus the adroit hypocrite; Ariadne the easy mark; the gentle, fearful, courageous Hypermnestra — the catalogue is instructive. The great charge against the *Legend* is that it lacks variety — not so. The charge relates primarily to theme, of course, but this is to take the announced theme, the faithfulness of women, too literally, too simplemindedly. The *Golden Legend* is about holiness and the *Metamorphoses* is about transformations, but that is only the beginning of their story. In the *Legend of Good Women* there were themes, not a single theme. Though both Dido and Lucrece were faithful women, the theme of *Dido* is not the theme of *Lucrece*.

Nor are the themes to be subsumed under some general scheme of moralization. The opportunity was there, but Chaucer quite clearly avoided it. His consistent practice with the *Metamorphoses*, the source for *Thisbe, Hypsipyle and Medea, Ariadne*, and *Philomela*, is relevant to this question. Except for noting that Bacchus out of pity placed Ariadne's crown among the stars, Chaucer omitted all the metamorphoses from these tales, yet this was particularly where Ovid's morality was seen to lie. Neither does Chaucer make any use whatever of the moralizations of the tales provided by the *Ovide moralisé* or follow the practice of this work and supply his own. This deliberate avoidance of metamorphosis and moralization would indicate that Chaucer was not being the explicitly moral poet here and that his aims were secular. His intention seems to be to entertain, to throw open a new treasury of tales, to pass on and make fresh and accessible notable stories found in notable authors of the past, to move to tears, to terror, to sympathy, or to laughter. In this respect, the *Legend* goes beyond Gower's *Confessio Amantis* in freeing narrative from the necessity of a restricted moral application. It opens the whole world of story, classical and traditional, to unapologetic adaptation.

The great achievement of the *Legend*, finally, is its amazing, its unexpected dedication to story, to narrative as such, to the simple "and then, and then" of E. M. Forster's simple narrative. Read for story alone, even *Cleopatra* captures the imagination. The variety and extent of narrative in the *Legend* are remarkable in themselves and doubly remarkable in a writer who had hitherto moved most often slowly and deliberately, devoted to elaboration of a situation rather than multiplication of incident. In the *Legend* princes woo and war, kingdoms are lost, heroes flee Troy, meet goddesses, become invisible, are miraculously rejoined with their men, are pursued by storms, kill bulls of brass and minotaurs, woo, win, betray, and depart; queens or faithful ladies talk earnestly with false go-betweens or false lovers, suffer betrayal, rape, suicide, wander desolate on island shores, weave messages in tapestries, hide from lions. Chaucer's submission to the simplicity of story was an act of great courage and great imagination. His was a subtle, complicated mind, fertile and inventive, quick to see ironies and comic qualifications of life's deepest experiences, profoundly involved in a vision of the ambiguities of human desire and human achievement in a universe governed by values absolute and eternal. For such an intelligence to turn toward the telling of story as story, concentrating on essentials and committed for the moment to avoid the elaboration of situation and point of view so long and so successfully practiced, was an act of great faith and great insight.

The tales he told were some of the enduring myths of the Western world. As he told them they were read and praised for many generations. But in his own history this dedication to story appears as a kind of rebirth, a turning by the artist to the simplicities of a new form, a pilgrimage to the well-spring of narrative. In our passion for complexity we blind ourselves to the truths of Chaucer's history if we do not see story as the root of his final achievement. And story is what the *Legend* attends to as Chaucer had never done before. Once he has submitted to it and in the process mastered it as he does in the *Legend*, he is ready for the *Canterbury Tales*, not before.

This concentrated attention to narrative, while it may not seem uncongenial to his talent, might appear to be a denial of his full powers, as though he were working with one hand tied behind his back. This special exercise, how-ever, gave him a strength and skill he put to marvelous use. Though he revives the arts of amplification in the *Canterbury Tales*, with brilliant results, the amplification is tightly controlled within the limits of a relatively simple and brief narrative in the tales of the Miller, the Merchant, the Nun's Priest, the Pardoner; action is never submerged or domi-nated by the catalogue, the apostrophe, the description, the digression. The rapid culmination and swift moving con-clusion of these tales reminds us that action is finally the crucial element of his art both for final form and final com-mentary. Indeed, the narrative as a whole has become the agent of his subtlest commentary: *this* tale against *this* tale; *this* action and what it implies about the truth of the human pilgrimage as opposed to *this* action and what it implies. It is a device that begins in the *Legend*.

If therefore for a time he limited his powers to acquire a strength and a skill new to him, we must applaud his cour-age and his wisdom. Unfinished though it is, the *Canter-bury Tales* is a more complex vision of experience than the *Troilus*. And, yes, unfinished though it is, so is the *Legend*. Its vertical range, its penetration, has nothing like the depth of the *Troilus*; its vision, nothing like the elevation. Nor does it possess the polished artistry. But it looks at aspects of human passion and experience not encompassed in the *Troilus* or earlier poems. Its psychology and its drama are more inclusive and fresher. The varieties of human experience become Chaucer's preoccupation, and the *Legend* opens up those varieties. By its devotion to action it goes to the heart of narrative power, and to the heart of another matter, too: people are what they do. To tell stories is to talk about the world.

[Excursus]   The Legend of Chaucer's Boredom

For many years a view widely held by scholars was that
Chaucer found the writing of the *Legend of Good Women*
boring and tedious. The thesis, based on a misunderstanding of comments within the legend, dates from the late
nineteenth century.

None of the several references to the *Legend* in the generations immediately succeeding Chaucer's death contain
any hint that he found the work an irksome task. There
was probably some awareness that the *Legend* was not completed, but only Lydgate supplied an explanation. In the
Prologue to the *Fall of Princes*, his translation of Boccaccio's
De Casibus Virorum Illustrium, Lydgate provided a list of
Chaucer's writings, among them the *Legend of Good
Women*:

> This poete wrot, at request off the queen,
> A legende off parfit hoolynesse,
> Off Goode Women to fynde out nynteen
> That dede excelle in bounte and fairnesse;
> But for his labour and [his] bisynesse
> Was inportable his wittis to encoumbre,
> In al this world to fynde so gret a noumbre.[1]

There is no need to take seriously Lydgate's explanation
that Chaucer found the task of unearthing nineteen good
women unbearable.[2] It is, of course, simply a joking re-

1. Lydgate, Prologue to the *Fall of Princes*, ed. Henry Bergen, EETS, ES 121
(London, Oxford University Press, 1924, reprinted 1967), ll. 330–336.
2. Chaucer promised no specific number. Lydgate's "nynteen" seems to be
based on Chaucer's reference to "ladyes nyntene,/In real habit" following the

mark from the antifeminist tradition, the same tradition that hovers behind the curtains throughout the whole performance of the *Legend*, ready to pop out at a moment's notice. Lydgate is invoking it here for the sake of an assured laugh, nothing more.[3] If Chaucer found the project boring, neither Lydgate nor anyone else in the period seems aware of the fact.

References to the *Legend* in the fifteenth and early sixteenth century suggest that, far from boring their readers, the legends delighted them. Indeed, in this period the *Legend of Good Women* seems to have been one of Chaucer's most popular creations, for it is alluded to and imitated a number of times.[4] It obviously was in the main stream of literary tradition throughout the fifteenth century.

Readers of Chaucer in the nineteenth century, for rather different reasons, seem also to have esteemed the *Legend of Good Women* highly.[5] In fact, an edition of the *Legend* in

---

God of Love (F 283–284; not in G). Eighteen "good women" (excluding, naturally, Absolon and Jonathas) are named in the *balade* within the Prologue, nineteen if we count "My lady" (F) or Alceste (G) in the refrain. The "Retractation" at the end of the *Parson's Tale* (I 1086) merely confuses the issue. The *Legend* is referred to there as "the book of the . . . Ladies," the number being variously given as "25," "xxv," "fyve and twenti," "xix," "Twenty," and "xv." The majority of MSS and the "best" MSS read 25 (in various forms), and this is the reading in Robinson and in Manly and Rickert. Skeat adopted 19 as the reading, presumably because of the reference in F 283. See the discussion in Eleanor Hammond, "Chaucer's 'Book of the Twenty-five Ladies,' " *MLN*, 48 (1933), 514–516; and in John Matthews Manly and Edith Rickert, *The Text of the Canterbury Tales* (Chicago, University of Chicago Press, 1940), II, 471–473; IV, 476–477; VIII, 546–547.

3. See *Fall of Princes*, I, 1809–1813, where Lydgate makes the same kind of joking remark again:

> Yit in my writyng it greueth me sore,
> Touchyng off women off feith or stabilnesse, —
> Blessid be God, — I fynde noon excesse;
> And for ther been so fewe, as thynkith me,
> The goode sholde been had in mor deynte.

4. For early references to the *Legend*, see Caroline Spurgeon, *Five Hundred Years of Chaucer Criticism and Allusion: 1357–1900*, Parts I and IV, Chaucer Soc., 2nd Ser., Nos. 48 and 53 (London, K. Paul, Trench, Trübner & Co., Ltd., 1914, 1922), pp. 15–68, and Appendix A, pp. 4–5, 9. Spurgeon's list of references is incomplete.

5. Evidence of the popularity of the *Legend* in the nineteenth century may be

1864 was one of the first efforts to make Chaucer's text available for students and "to furnish an easy text-book for beginners in the study of early English literature."[6] In 1889 W. W. Skeat produced the first genuinely scholarly edition of the *Legend*, and, with Skeat, so far as I can determine, the charge that Chaucer wearied of the project begins. In his preface Skeat argued for "the conjectural date of the spring of 1385" for both forms of the Prologue and continued, "and I suppose that Chaucer went on with one tale of the series after another during the summer and latter part of the same year till he grew tired of the task, and at last gave it up in the middle of a sentence. The expression of doubt as to the completion of the task already appears in l. 2457."[7] He glossed line 2456 with the comment, "This is a hint that Chaucer was already getting tired of his task." He repeated this statement and the gloss, word for word, in his *Oxford Chaucer* a few years later, in 1894.[8]

Skeat's observation seems to have been based on his reading of the text, particularly lines 2456–2457, and on the deduction he drew from the unfinished state of *Hypsipyle* and the project as a whole. The recording of the judgment in the authoritative Oxford edition would have been enough to ensure its dissemination, but a more extended and forceful expression of opinion on the subject of the *Legend* had appeared in 1892 with Thomas R. Lounsbury's

---

found in the selections from the *Legend*, translations, and comments in the following: Charles Cowden Clark, *The Riches of Chaucer*, 2 vols. (London, 1835), I, 32; II, 166–194; *The Poems of Geoffrey Chaucer Modernized*, ed. Richard Hengist Horne (London, 1841); Elizabeth Barrett Browning, *The Greek Christian Poets and the English Poets* (London, 1863), pp. 105–193, originally articles (an extended review) in the *Athenaeum* (June 4, 11, 25; August 6, 13, 1842); the Aldine Edition of the British Poets, 6 vols. (London, 1845), IV; Alfred Tennyson, "A Dream of Fair Women"; Annotated Edition of the English Poets, *Poetical Works of Geoffrey Chaucer*, 8 vols., ed. Robert Bell (London, 1856), VIII, 42–43 *et passim*.

6. *Chaucer's Legende of Goode Women*, ed. Hiram Corson (Philadelphia, 1864). The text is that of Bell's edition; see p. xxxvii.

7. *The Legend of Good Women*, ed. W. W. Skeat (Oxford, Eng., 1889), p. xiv.

8. W. W. Skeat, *The Complete Works of Geoffrey Chaucer* (Oxford, Eng., 1894), III, xxii.

Studies in Chaucer.[9] Lounsbury's conclusion was based on premises about Chaucer's literary development rather than on a reading of the text alone. Lounsbury stated his major premise succinctly: "The story of [Chaucer's] literary life is . . . a story of steady growth, in which he gradually rose superior to the taste of his time" (p. 296). He traced this growth in Chaucer particularly in his criticism and rejection of such genres as the medieval "gestes" (in *Sir Thopas*) and medieval tragedy (in the *Monk's Tale*). The *Legend* became Lounsbury's most telling example. We can go back, he said, to "a period in which [Chaucer] was still swayed by the taste he came in time to censure. We can even go back to the very work written under its influence, and observe during the process of its composition the change that was gradually coming over his opinions. It is in the 'Legend of Good Women' that we can trace the alteration in his point of view" (p. 335). Lounsbury accepted the thesis that the work was undertaken at the command or request of someone in high place, probably Queen Anne. Chaucer began the work with great enthusiasm, Lounsbury believed, and meant it to be his crowning achievement, to extend over a long period of his life (quoting F 481–485). But his attitude soon changed:

> There is nothing more peculiar in the "Legend of Good Women" than the steadily growing dissatisfaction of the author with his subject which marks its progress. It was not long before Chaucer began to see the folly of what he had set out to accomplish. His keen artistic sense could not fail to recognize the insufficiency of a plan which permitted him to deal only with the variations of a single theme. He was hampered still further by the limitations imposed by the legendary stories he was versifying. The necessity of adhering to their details prevented him from giving any wide play to his imagination. He knew at the beginning of every one precisely what he had to do, just as his reader would know in the same case that it was a dismal ending which he was to

9. Thomas R. Lounsbury, *Studies in Chaucer*, 3 vols. (London, 1892), III, 283–446.

expect. It is therefore not at all strange that the inevitable monotony wore upon him speedily. It made him at last careless and indifferent in the choice of these stories [p. 337].

He began to work carelessly. "At times he was prompted to relieve its monotony by the introduction of a humorous element," in support of which Lounsbury cites F 1383 (p. 338). In the eighth story (*Phyllis*) "he makes no pretence of concealing the disgust he has felt, and is continuing to feel, with his subject, and his desire to be done with it as soon as possible" (Lounsbury cites F 2454–2458). The conclusion of this tale, with its mock advice to trust no man but him, "is ample proof that the element of seriousness was departing rapidly from the work. Nothing of that nature could well be imputed to a professedly tragic poem . . ." (pp. 338–339).

So Chaucer abandoned the project: "The taste which made collections of stories of this kind popular came to be recognized by Chaucer as essentially vicious in art, and therefore transitory. It shows how thoroughly developed was the critical side of his intellectual nature that he should have reached such a conclusion while this style of composition was not only in full fashion, but had before it centuries in which to exist and flourish" (p. 339).

I have given Lounsbury's views at such length because he is, I believe, the wellspring of the judgment that Chaucer wearied unto nausea of the *Legend* and because he makes the main charges against the *Legend* as a literary failure on which that judgment is based. Some of the weaknesses of his argument are immediately apparent. Aside from his sweeping assumptions about Chaucer's material and his methods in the *Legend*, several statements reveal a literary position which most scholars would find unacceptable today. That the literary taste of his time was "vicious" and that Chaucer's history is essentially a history of his rejection of this taste are not currently held views. We no longer see Chaucer as an artist throwing off the literary conventions of his day and ceasing to be a medieval writer. We understand more adequately than did Lounsbury's generation the role of convention in art, and we do not stigmatize the particular conventions of Chaucer's age as inevitably crippling and destructive. We recognize the taste of his time as more sophisticated than Lounsbury allows, and we feel our knowledge about taste in that age is too incomplete, too uncertain, to permit such dogmatic assertions about its character.

It is not, in fact, completely clear what Lounsbury meant by "the taste of the time." The age, he felt, provided Chaucer with inadequate models, and he singled out prolixity as a particular medieval sin of which Chaucer blessedly purged himself.[10] He does not present Chaucer as an artist moving from artificiality to realism, the pattern so dear to Chaucerian criticism until recent years, though one senses, perhaps unfairly, that pattern hovering in the air. It is clear that Lounsbury's main premise must be rejected today, and, when we throw that out, we certainly damage his argument.

At the time he wrote, however, there was no disposition to challenge his premise: it was in harmony with the attitudes toward Chaucer then in vogue, and Lounsbury's influence is evident in subsequent criticism of the poem. In a study of the *Legend* published in 1902, J. B. Bilderbeck described the work as "no grateful task" and said, "it may be urged that the scheme of the Legend, as a whole, was one which could hardly have commended itself to the author's artistic temperament, and which it is improbable he would have voluntarily undertaken, in view of the burdensome monotony incidental to the treatment of such a subject."[11] Robert K. Root in his influential *The Poetry of Chaucer* (1906) cited Lounsbury, summarized his argu-

10. *Ibid.*, pp. 326–327. Ironically, the *Legend* is the work in which Chaucer labors most vigorously to avoid prolixity; it is Chaucer's "abbreviations" which in large part misled Lounsbury. See below.

11. *Chaucer's Legend of Good Women . . .* , ed. J. B. Bilderbeck (London, Hazell, Watson & Viney, Ltd., 1902), pp. 88–89. See also John Livingston Lowes, "The Prologue to the *Legend of Good Women* Considered in its Chronological Relations," *PMLA*, 20 (1905), 817, 862.

ment, and found new textual support: "Even as [Chaucer] wrote the last lines of the Prologue," said Root, "he began to be oppressed with the magnitude of his undertaking" (citing F 570–577, not in G).[12] He found "a similar note" in *Cleopatra*, 616–623, and in a footnote listed a number of other references to lines in the poem as evidence of Chaucer's weariness.[13] The next year J. S. P. Tatlock made much the same charge: "Chaucer expresses far more sense of haste and weariness than in any other of his works. At the end of Prologue F, 570–577, Love tells him to be brief, which is certainly more likely to be the poet's excuse than the record of a command by his patron; so even at first he felt the task to be a large one."[14] And he also cited a number of references, repeating Root's list with two omissions and three additions.[15] Thereafter the case appears to be closed. There is no further buttressing of the argument, and there is no real challenging of it. From this time forward, the expected remark to make about the *Legend of Good Women* is that Chaucer very early grew bored with the project, plodded ahead for a time because he was in some way obliged to, and finally abandoned it in utter weariness.[16]

What case can be made against the thesis? Lounsbury's "aesthetic" premise I have already discarded. There remain the textual references cited by Skeat, Lounsbury, Root, and

12. Robert K. Root, *The Poetry of Chaucer* (London, 1906), pp. 145–146.

13. *Cleopatra*, lines 1002–1003, 1552–1553, 1565, 1679, 1692–1693, 1921, 2257–2258, 2470–2471, 2490–2491, 2513–2515.

14. J. S. P. Tatlock, *The Development and Chronology of Chaucer's Works*, Chaucer Soc., 2nd Ser., No. 37 (London, 1907), pp. 112–113.

15. Tatlock omitted Root's citation of 1002–1003 and 2470–2471; he added 996–997, 2383, 2675, and extended 2513–2515 to 2517.

16. See, for example, Aage Brusendorff, *The Chaucer Tradition* (London, Humphrey Milford, Oxford University Press [1925]), p. 446; John Livingston Lowes, *Geoffrey Chaucer* (Oxford, Eng., Clarendon Press, 1934), pp. 131–132; Douglas Bush, *Mythology and the Renaissance Tradition in English Poetry* (Minneapolis, University of Minnesota Press, 1932), p. 21; Paull Baum, "Chaucer's 'Glorious Legende,' " *MLN*, 60 (1945), 380, 381; H. S. Bennett, *Chaucer and the Fifteenth Century* (Oxford, Eng., Clarendon Press, 1948), p. 63ff. By contrast, F. N. Robinson's statement in *The Complete Works of Geoffrey Chaucer*, 2nd ed. (Boston, Houghton Mifflin Co., 1957), pp. 481, 482, is commendably cautious.

Tatlock, and the interpretation of those references. The majority are interpreted as expressions more or less explicit by Chaucer that his task bored him; several passages of a mocking, humorous tone are also taken as evidence that Chaucer was bored. (Lounsbury explained them as prompted by a wish to relieve the monotony of his task, as proof that "the element of seriousness was departing rapidly from the work.") In conjunction with the passages interpreted as expressions of boredom, the fact that the scheme is incomplete and the final tale which we have is unfinished becomes further evidence that Chaucer grew weary: we know the project had grown wearisome and he didn't complete it; therefore, he didn't complete it because he was too bored to continue. This is circular, to be sure, but effective. Finally, there is the fact that the *Legend* is a mystery begging for some kind of explanation. It is a mystery because it comes between two triumphs, the *Troilus* and the *Canterbury Tales*. Less successful than either, and different from both, it remains a puzzle (and here the fact that it is unfinished contributes to the mystery). If one regards it as an outright failure, the mystery deepens. Why did it happen? The thesis that the task was an essentially uncongenial one, possibly imposed from outside,[17] pursued without enthusiasm and dropped in despair, provides an explanation that has the advantage of being also rather comforting. What we do not particularly like he did not like either, and we can go on to the *Canterbury Tales* with restored confidence and a sunny conscience.

To begin the case against the thesis, we must consider the evidence which suggests that the material and theme of the *Legend* were something Chaucer had been interested in for several years. Ovid, Virgil, Guido delle Colonne were his principal sources for the legends we have. His respect

17. The theory that the *Legend* was an assignment and not a willing choice derives from the fiction in the Prologue of the *Legend* that writing the legends was imposed as an act of penance, and from the tradition going back to Lydgate (see the passage quoted above) that Chaucer wrote the poem at the request of Queen Anne. This evidence is of course shaky, and it seems unreasonable to draw invidious conclusions from it.

for these writers need not be argued. The poet he draws most heavily upon is, of course, his beloved Ovid; as early as the *Book of the Duchess* he had tried his hand at retelling a story from the *Metamorphoses*, his "owne bok." The theme of the *Legend*, the heroines or martyrs of love, he had played with repeatedly. As early again as the *Book of the Duchess* he referred to Jason and Medea, Phyllis and Demophoon, Dido and Aeneas, Echo and Narcissus, and Samson and Delilah as examples of violent, tormented love, and to Penelope and Lucrece as examples of feminine goodness (731–739, 1080–1084). In the *House of Fame* he told in capsule form the story of Dido and Aeneas, and in a long complaint on the theme of lovers betrayed he invoked the names of Demophoon and Phyllis, Jason and Hypsipyle and Medea, Theseus and Ariadne and Phaedra, all of whom were to appear in the *Legend* (239–382, 388–426). In the *Parliament of Birds*, the wall of Venus' temple is painted with the loves of Semiramis, Candace, Hercules, Byblis, Dido, Thisbe, Pyramus, Tristram, Isolde, Paris, Achilles, Helen, Cleopatra, Troilus, Scylla, and the mother of Romulus, "and in what plyt they dyde" (288–294). Finally, as Tatlock himself observed, Alceste seems to have been lurking in Chaucer's imagination as he brought the *Troilus* to a conclusion — Alceste and Penelope and, Lowes noted, betrayed womankind in general: [18]

> Bysechyng every lady bright of hewe,
> And every gentil womman, what she be,
> That al be that Criseyde was untrewe,
> That for that gilt she be nat wroth with me.
> Ye may hire giltes in other bokes se;
> And gladlier I wol write, yif yow leste,
> Penelopeës trouthe and good Alceste.
>
> N'y sey nat this al oonly for thise men,
> But moost for wommen that bitraised be

18. Tatlock, *Chronology*, p. 107n; John Livingston Lowes, "The Prologue to the *Legend of Good Women* Considered in Its Chronological Relations," *PMLA*, 20 (1905), 820–821.

Thorugh false folk; God yeve hem sorwe, amen!
That with hire grete wit and subtilte
Bytraise yow! And this commeveth me
To speke, and in effect yow alle I preye,
Beth war of men, and herkneth what I seye! — [19]

We have here the theme, the first hint of the device, and much of the tone of the *Legend* established before the *Troilus* had quite finished flowing from his pen.

There are two other pieces of evidence to be noted: Chaucer was interested enough in the Prologue to rewrite it, and he was sufficiently interested in the *Legend* to refer to it by name in the introduction to the *Man of Law's Tale* ("his large volume . . . Cleped the Seintes Legende of Cupide") and to review what is in part a genuine table of contents and what is in part either a spurious table or an indication of some of the other stories he was considering for the *Legend* (*CT*, B 53ff.).

In view of these facts, the suggestion by Root and Tatlock that Chaucer began to weary of his project before he had even finished with the Prologue will not stand up. The suggestion, moreover, is inherently ridiculous. A writer does not go on with a project if he tires of it before he begins, he abandons it. If he is under unavoidable external pressure to carry it out, then presumably he keeps silent and finishes it. Chaucer did neither. Considering the interest Chaucer had shown for some time in the area which the *Legend* works, and his commitment to this area, his reworking of the Prologue, and his allusion to the work as something still of moment to him at some time after it had been begun, these scholars have him flagging much too early in the game. The passage they cited demands no such interpretation — indeed, it will not bear it:

I wot wel that thou maist nat al yt ryme,
That swiche lovers diden in hire tyme;
It were to long to reden and to here.
Suffiseth me thou make in this manere,

19. *Troilus*, V, 1772–1785.

That thou reherce of al hir lyf the grete,
After thise olde auctours lysten for to trete.
For whoso shal so many a storye telle,
Sey shortly, or he shal to longe dwelle.

(F 570–577)[20]

The passage merely stresses, before Chaucer begins, what is to be the essential method of handling his sources here: to "reherce of al hir lyf the grete." The relative brevity is required by the project's nature: "whoso shal so many a storye telle, / Sey shortly, or he shal to longe dwelle." The tone is businesslike. There is no weariness at all.

I have perhaps disposed of one passage. What of the others? Many of them, all of them I believe, have been misunderstood. A major rhetorical technique in the *Legend*, dictated in part at least by the great bulk of material Chaucer was intending to quarry from, is *abbreviatio*. It is this technique which Chaucer is announcing, in effect, in the concluding lines of the F Prologue quoted above. *Abbreviatio*, the shortening or cutting of one's material, is the counterpart to *amplificatio* or *expolitio*, the expansion of the writer's original idea or source. A frequent tactic of *abbreviatio* is *occupatio*, the refusal to describe or narrate while referring briefly to a subject or scene;[21] *occupatio* often takes the form of explaining that to do full justice to a subject or scene would be too long, even wearisome. "I saw to Goddes mak the Sacrifice, / Quhairof the ordour and maner to deuise / War ouir prolixt," says Gavin Douglas.[22] Frequently, *occupatio* fulfills other tactical functions in

20. What, given Root's and Tatlock's interpretation of this passage, we are to make of the fact that G omits the passage, I do not know. If G is later, then presumably he was no longer weary. If F is later, then apparently he hadn't tired at this point the first time through.

21. J. W. H. Atkins, *English Literary Criticism: The Medieval Phase* (London, Methuen & Co., Ltd., 1952), pp. 200, 202. Cf. Ernst Robert Curtius, "Brevity as an Ideal of Style," Excursus XIII, *European Literature and the Latin Middle Ages*, trans. Willard R. Trask, Bollingen Series, 36 (New York, Pantheon Books, 1953), pp. 487–494.

22. The "Palice of Honour," *The Shorter Poems of Gavin Douglas*, ed. Priscilla J. Bawcutt, Scottish Text Society, Series 4, No. 3 (Edinburgh, William Blackwood & Sons, Ltd., 1967), 1648–1650 (Edinburgh Text); see also 925–927.

addition to abbreviating. This double function is illustrated in an *occupatio* from Christine de Pisan's *L'Epistre au Dieu d'Amours* (1399):

> Penelope la feme Ulixes,
> Qui raconter vouldroit tout le proces
> De la dame trop trouveroit a dire
> De sa bonte ou il n'ot que redire;
> Tres belle fu require et bien amee,
> Noble, sage, vaillant et renommee.
> D'aultres [that is, loyal ladies] pluseurs, et tant que
>   c'est sanz nombre,
> Furent et sont et seront en ce nombre;
> Mais je me tais ades d'en plus compter,
> Car long proces seroit a raconter.[23]

[One who wished to tell the whole story of Penelope, Ulysses' wife, would find he had much to say about the lady, if only to recount her goodness; she was distinguished as most beautiful, and well loved, noble, wise, courageous, celebrated. Many other [loyal ladies], so many that they are without number, were, and are, and will be in this account, but I silence myself forever from counting more of them, for it would be a long story to tell.] This particular use of *occupatio*, while abbreviating, suggests the richness of the material available; *occupatio* of this kind often serves the ends of panegyric.[24] Christine de Pisan here avoids prolixity and at the same time suggests how many virtues Penelope possessed and how many loyal ladies there were. This latter effect seems as important for her purposes as the abbreviation itself. Intensification is only one of the possible supplementary functions of *occupatio*; others will be noted later.

Chaucer himself used *occupatio* throughout his poetry. An example, similar to several passages in the *Legend*, appears in an irreproachable context in *Troilus and Criseyde*. Chaucer is describing Troilus' agonies after Criseyde

23. *Oeuvres poétiques*, ed. Maurice Roy, SATF (Paris, 1891), II, lines 461–470.
24. Cf. Curtius, "Brevity," p. 488.

has departed for the Greek camp. After considerable detail, he concludes the scene thus:

> Who koude telle aright or ful discryve
> His wo, his pleynt, his langour, and his pyne?
> Naught alle the men that han or ben on lyve.
> Thow, redere, maist thiself ful wel devyne
> That swich a wo my wit kan nat diffyne.
> On ydel for to write it sholde I swynke,
> Whan that my wit is wery it to thynke.
>
> (V, 267–273)

Here the device is used to reinforce the sense of Troilus' intense suffering and to bring the scene to a conclusion. No one, fortunately, has yet suggested that we are to take the last line literally and to conclude that Chaucer had grown weary of *Troilus and Criseyde*.

The passages cited by Root and Tatlock from the *Legend of Good Women* as evidences of Chaucer's weariness are in fact passages of *occupatio*. Chaucer uses the device to abbreviate, to indicate he is cutting his material, to intensify, to conclude a scene, and to serve other rhetorical purposes. The passage in *Cleopatra* (616–623) both reaffirms the ambitious nature of this project [25] and suggests the elaborateness of the wedding feast without being obliged to describe it.[26] In *Thisbe* Root and Tatlock found no signs of weariness or

25. For an almost exactly parallel announcement that he is cutting his source because he is undertaking a narrative project of some length, see the *Knight's Tale* (*CT*, A 875, 885–888). There is considerable abbreviation in this tale, and, consequently, much use of *occupatio*: 875–888, 994–1000, 1201, 1380, 1417, 1459–1461, 1463–1464, 1480, 1485, 1487, 1782, 1872, 1895, 1953–1954, 2039–2040, 2052, 2073–2074, 2197–2207, 2264, 2366, 2820–2821, 2919–2960, 2963–2966.

26. *Occupatio* is used so often by medieval narrators as a kind of shorthand for feasts and celebrations that it appears to be a stock device or *topos*; I would suggest calling it the "feasting" *occupatio*. For other examples in Chaucer, see *CT*, A 2197–2207, F 61–75; *Legend of Good Women*, 1098. See also *Sir Gawain and the Green Knight*, 1007–1009; *Kyng Alisaunder*, ed. G. V. Smithers, I (Text), EETS, OS 227 (London, Oxford University Press, 1952), 539–542; "Fabula Duorum Mercatorum," 160–161, 167–168, in *The Minor Poems of John Lydgate*, Vol. II, ed. Henry Noble MacCracken, EETS, OS 192 (London, Oxford University Press, 1934, reprinted 1961); *The Ile of Ladies*, ed. Jane B. Sherzer (Berlin, Mayer and Müller, 1903), 2129–2134; *Eneas*, 2 vols., ed. J. Salverda de Grave, CFMA (Paris, É. Champion, 1925–1929), lines 828–833.

haste. The reason is that *Thisbe* is almost a word-for-word translation of Ovid's version in the *Metamorphoses*, with no abbreviation to speak of. *Dido*, as one might imagine, involved extensive cutting, and so we have an *occupatio: 994–997, 1002–1003.*[27] *Hypsipyle and Medea* contains what might be called a "false" *occupatio: 1552–1560.* It suggests an elaborate wooing of Hypsipyle by Jason although Chaucer will not report it in detail, and so it serves to intensify; in suggesting that the reader go to the original for the whole story, it implies a fully developed scene where there is in fact none. Chaucer is improvising from the sketchy outline of a story in the lyrical *Heroides*, but he claims the authority of a "source," much as Malory does with his "French book" when he improvises or improves upon his original. It also serves to conclude a stage in the narrative.[28] Chaucer resorts to *occupatio* so that Hypsipyle's final lament from the *Heroides*, and later Medea's, can be presented in a few lines, thus avoiding repetition of narrative already told (1564–1565, 1678–1679). The *occupatio* at the beginning of *Lucrece* (1692–1693) cuts the irrelevant historical material from Ovid's *Fasti*; that in *Ariadne* (1921) cuts away several irrelevant narratives in the *Metamorphoses* with which Ariadne's story is entwined.

Coming to the end of *Philomela*, Chaucer says, "The remenaunt is no charge for to telle" (2383). The remark seems unobjectionable; it is the storyteller's announcement that his tale is almost finished, whereby Chaucer also quietly drops the whole hideous scene of Tereus dining on the flesh of his child. In *Phyllis* Chaucer uses *occupatio* in virtuoso fashion. There are three instances of "false" *occupatio*, for *Phyllis*, like *Hypsipyle*, is constructed of hints and suggestions from the *Heroides* and, like that legend, at-

27. See the similar comment in the *House of Fame* (445–450) where the Dido story is used. There are several other instances of *occupatio* in *Dido* which neither Root nor Tatlock mention: 953–957, 1098, 1184–1185, 1366.

28. Curtius, "Brevity," p. 487, notes that the brevity formula was used in the Middle Ages as a pretext for ending a poem — or, I would add, a scene. (In this legend Root and Tatlock missed one further instance of *occupatio*, 1456–1458, and possibly another, 1634: the "shortly" formula.)

tempts an unexpected, comic tone. The most important of the three will be discussed separately below. One (2469–2471) ends a stage in the action and possibly avoids indelicacy in declining to present the seduction of Phyllis in detail. The other (2490–2493), a mock indignant refusal to waste more ink on the false Demophoon, skillfully points up an attitude toward a character and contributes to a semi-comic tone. There is one genuine *occupatio*. To end this legend, Chaucer makes direct use of Phyllis' epistle in the *Heroides*, but he abbreviates extensively, and his announcement of this intention breaks up what would otherwise be an overlong monologue and prevents an undesirable seriousness of tone from developing.[29] Tatlock found only one sign of weariness in *Hypermnestra*, where presumably weariness overcame Chaucer: "And shortly, lest this tale be to long . . ." (2675). This is not a true *occupatio*, only a brevity formula, a storyteller's phrase.[30] Chaucer uses it here to move quickly from one developed scene to another.[31]

The two passages which give strongest support to the thesis that Chaucer was bored with the *Legend* require special consideration. The first occurs early in *Philomela* and describes the wedding of Tereus and Progne:

> This revel, ful of song and ek of daunce,
> Laste a fortenyght, or lytel lasse.
> But, shortly of this story for to passe,
> For I am wery of hym for to telle,
> Fyve yer his wife and he togeder dwelle,
> Til on a day she gan so sore longe. . . .
>
> (2255–2260)

As the *occupatio* already quoted from *Troilus and Criseyde* would suggest, such a statement — "For I am wery of hym for to telle" — need not, in fact should not, be taken literally.

---

29. See Chapter X, n. 6.

30. "Shortly" is a recurrent word in Chaucer. For the whole phrase, compare the Franklin's "What sholde I made a lenger tale of this?" (*CT*, F 1165).

31. I have reviewed these passages at greater length in "The Legend of the *Legend of Good Women*," *Chaucer Review*, I (1966), 110–133.

Chaucer has used the same language elsewhere for the same purpose. Near the end of the *Man of Law's Tale* we find this:

> Long was the sobbyng and the bitter peyne,
> Er that hir woful hertes myghte cesse;
> Greet was the pitee for to heere hem pleyne,
> Thurgh whiche pleintes gan hir wo encresse.
> I pray yow alle my labour to relesse;
> I may nat telle hir wo until to-morwe,
> I am so wery for to speke of sorwe.
>
> (B 1065–71)

And the same language is used in the *Canon's Yeoman's Tale:*

> Al to symple is my tonge to pronounce,
> As ministre of my wit, the doublenesse
> Of this chanoun, roote of alle cursednesse!
> He semed freendly to hem that knewe hym noght,
> But he was feendly bothe in werk and thoght.
> It weerieth me to telle of his falsnesse,
> And nathelees yet wol I it expresse,
> To th'entente that men may be war therby,
> And for noon oother cause, trewely.
>
> (G 1299–1307)

In the *Philomela* passage Chaucer is omitting a few lines of Ovid's *Metamorphoses*, or a good many lines if his source is the *Ovide moralisé*,[32] but the primary function of the device is to cover the leap in time of five years which he found in his source. The expression of weariness seems to be a Chau-

---

32. The wedding and events at Trace before Progne expresses a desire to see her sister occupy 48 lines in Chrétien de Troyes's *Philomena*, which is incorporated *in toto* into the *Ovide moralisé*: see *Philomena: Conte raconté d'apres Ovide*, ed. C. De Boer (Paris, P. Geuthner, 1909), pp. v–xiv. It is worth noting that in studying Chaucer's use of his sources here, Lowes was so struck by Chaucer's artistic agility in handling his material that he cast a jaundiced eye on the literal or Lounsburian reading of this passage: "It is hard to resist the suspicion, in view of the skill with which the dovetailing is done, that Chaucer's protestation of weariness 'of [Tereus] for to telle' is not to be taken with too great seriousness. It smacks strongly of the literary artifice." See "Chaucer and the *Ovide Moralisé*," *PMLA*, 33 (1918), 318n. The artifice is specifically, of course, *occupatio*.

cerian *topos* at the very least, and may possibly be more general. Such force as the language does have re-emphasizes an attitude toward the villain of the story, Tereus ("For I am wery of hym for to telle"), an attitude already established by an authorial reaction a few lines earlier in the opening of the tale:

> And, as to me, so grisely was his dede
> That, whan that I his foule storye rede,
> Myne eyen wexe foule and sore also.
> Yit last the venym of so longe ago,
> That it enfecteth hym that wol beholde
> The storye of Tereus, of which I tolde.
>
> (2238–2243)

The other crucial passage is the one Skeat referred to and glossed in his edition of the *Legend* in 1889, the passage which spawned the thesis that Chaucer wearied of the *Legend*. It occurs in *Phyllis*, after a diatribe against Demophoon and his father Theseus:

> This honurable Phillis doth hym chere;
> Hire liketh wel his port and his manere.
> But, for I am agroted herebyforn
> To wryte of hem that ben in love forsworn,
> And ek to haste me in my legende,
> (Which to performe God me grace sende!)
> Therfore I passe shortly in this wyse.
> Ye han wel herd of Theseus devyse
> In the betraysynge of fayre Adryane,
> That of hire pite kepte him from his bane.
> At shorte wordes, ryght so Demophon
> The same wey, the same path hath gon,
> That dide his false fader Theseus.
>
> (2452–2464)

The context is illuminating. The critical five lines (2454–2458) are clearly functional. Part of Chaucer's problem in the *Phyllis*, as I have already indicated, is to tell a story where his source (the *Heroides*) gives him very little to work with. The *occupatio* suggests the nature of Demo-

phoon's wooing and provides by implication a narrative
scene (and also avoids repetition) by reference to the story
of Demophoon's father, Theseus, which he has already told.
It is, in its language, a variation on the "weariness" *topos*
which Chaucer has used elsewhere. The "excuse" he gives
helps him solve a difficulty. It also contributes markedly to
the comic tone of the passage.

The tone of the *Legend* is a problem in itself.[33] Much of
the time it is serious, but not invariably. The fluctuation
of sober and light, the momentary breaking of a solemn
mood by a comic irreverence is characteristically Chaucerian and may well have been temperamental in basis. It may
also have grown out of a concern to keep his listening audience alert and to avoid restiveness. The potentiality for
such fluctuation, however, is also built into the situation
out of which the *Legend* develops. There are two aspects to
this. One is the overall theme, the praise of good women.
The theme is handled seriously much of the time, but consistently serious treatment of the theme will not be found
and should not be expected. The doctrine that women are
loyal and men are false inevitably has comic possibilities.
This is because, first, it does not eliminate the concept of
love as a contest, a war between the sexes, and this may always be viewed as comic. In the second place, as a generalization it is patently an exaggeration and untrue; at any
moment it can be deflated by the truth (some women are
false) or the antithetical conventional untruth (all women
are false). We see this in Francis Utley's observation that
courtly love is one of the most powerful reasons for the
flourishing of medieval satire on women: "However courtly
love deplored the satirical germ it was forced to contain
it . . . ."[34] Chaucer availed himself of these comic possibilities from time to time, in the *Legend* and elsewhere.

The second comic potential basic to the *Legend* is, of

33. On the tone of the Prologue, see Robert Estrich, "Chaucer's Maturing Art
in the Prologue to the *Legend of Good Women*," *JEGP*, 36 (1937), 326–337.

34. Francis Utley, *The Crooked Rib* (Columbus, Ohio State University Press,
1944), p. 32.

course, Chaucer's role as a man condemned for crimes against the fair name of women and obliged to do penance for his sins. Anyone who takes this fiction seriously had better throw away his Chaucer and pick up William Law's *Serious Call to a Devout and Holy Life*. The writing of the legends is comically dramatized as a burdensome penance; Alceste's injunction to him makes this clear:

> Now wol I seyn what penance thou shalt do
> For thy trespas, and understonde yt here:
> Thow shalt, while that thou lyvest, yer by yere,
> The moste partye of thy tyme spende
> In makyng of a glorious legende
> Of goode wymmen, maydenes and wyves,
> That weren trewe in lovyng al hire lyves. . . .
> Goo now thy wey, this penaunce ys but lyte.
>
> (479–485, 495)

Both parts of the joke are contained in this passage. The comic moments, therefore, which were to Lounsbury a sign of Chaucer's weariness or disgust are nothing of the kind. They are a frequent characteristic of poetry in which women are praised, and they are called for by the device which motivates Chaucer's telling of the legends. So we have from time to time the mocking remarks about the falseness of men and the comic suggestion that only Chaucer is a man to be trusted. Indeed, the fictive situation that makes the narratives a penance which he must perform demands that he shall groan now and then; it is part of the joke which accompanies the seriousness.

If we keep in mind the comic motivation established for the *Legend* and the satiric reverse side of the coin bearing the legend, "All women are true," we can see the lines from *Phyllis* for what they are. The particular language used for the *occupatio* exploits both these comic possibilities and might be paraphrased thus: "I am glutted with these stories of women forsworn, because I am writing them as a grievous penance — may God send me grace to finish it — and because I don't really believe all women are faithful or forsworn, whatever I am obliged to say!" It is quite in character for Chaucer to treat Phyllis and her story somewhat more — though not much more — seriously a few lines later. It is certainly consistent with his practice elsewhere.

If we cannot accept the lighter moments of the poem and the language which occasionally suggests that Chaucer is a burdened man, then we must hold that Chaucer began in the Prologue with some intimations of comedy and established a comic motivation which he subsequently ignored. It is a possibility, but what seems more probable is that he did revert to that lighter mood from time to time and made some play, now with the satiric potentialities of his lovers' martyrology, now with his pose as one forever barred from Cupid's considerations, now with his role as the suffering penitent. To assume that the *Legend* demands a solemn tone throughout and so to interpret deviations from the tragic or pathetic mood as evidence of Chaucer's contempt for his material, or to take seriously passages in which the tone lightens and treat them as literal statements expressive of his innermost feelings is to misread Chaucer badly here. There is, in fact, more comedy in the *Legend* than we have been led to believe.

There is one final argument used in support of the legend of Chaucer's weariness: the fact that the poem is unfinished. I submit that there is only one certain conclusion to be drawn from this fact: namely, that the poem is unfinished, nothing more. So is the *House of Fame*, so is the *Canterbury Tales*, so is the *Squire's Tale*, so is the *Cook's Tale*. (Lounsbury himself said "it is safe to say that no great poet ever presented to posterity so large a book of unfinished work." [35]) The evidence is unmistakable that sometimes Chaucer worked on one poem for a time, dropped it, and worked on another poem, and that sometimes at least he had every intention of returning to the abandoned poem at a later date.[36] If we say that the *Legend* is unfinished be-

35. Lounsbury, *Studies in Chaucer*, III, 431.
36. This seems to be the most reasonable interpretation of the final lines of the *Squire's Tale*.

cause it bored him, then we have to say it about the others
too.

No convincing point can be made of the fact that not only
is the project as a whole unfinished but the last tale we have,
Hypermnestra, is also incomplete. The thesis that within a
few lines of his ending Chaucer's gorge finally rose and
rather than dash off a quick conclusion he threw his pen
down never to return is not only highly melodramatic and
completely imaginary but rationally unsatisfying. He had
just written the scene of Hypermnestra alone with her sleeping bridegroom whom her father has ordered her to kill. It
is a quite magnificent scene, and he must have known it
was good. If, however, by some chance, he was resolved to
have done with the *Legend* once and for all, it seems much
more likely that he would have added his few lines and had
another finished legend to his credit. The place at which
the *Hypermnestra* ends is at least as well explained by as-
suming that he stopped writing near the end of a tale for
reasons unknown, intending to return, and for reasons unknown never did.

For, I repeat, we have the evidence of the Introduction to
the *Man of Law's Tale* to suggest that the project was something he was willing to acknowledge some time after he had
begun it and that he had a number of possible stories in
mind to tell, only some of which he used. We also have the
two Prologues. The fact that he did not complete the
Legend does not in itself prove anything, and we should
stop using it as though it were a piece of evidence.

We can conclude that Chaucer was planning to mine a
great mass of narrative, classical and other, and he chose to
make each narrative relatively brief. The technique of
abbreviatio was therefore dictated by his material and by
his plan. He used *occupatio* as a device of *abbreviatio*
throughout the poem. The passages cited as evidence of
impatience or weariness come at points in his narrative
when they clearly have a functional purpose. The *Legend*
again and again shows itself to be a brilliant work of selection, that is, of abbreviation, and *occupatio* is an important

subsidiary technique in the accomplishment of this task of selection and in the concomitant task, that of combination of the selected parts.

The tone of the poem, serious with occasional lighter moments, is characteristic of Chaucer; it is congruent with the basic situation, the praise of women, which frequently in medieval practice leads to satiric comment or comic reversals of tone, and it is congruent with Chaucer's mock role as a sinful penitent performing an act of penance. These comic aspects of the situation occasionally affect the tone of the poem and the language used in passages of *occupatio* and elsewhere.

No conclusion can be drawn from the fact that the poem was never finished, and there is no case for the thesis that Chaucer wearied of the *Legend*. This is not to deny that once he hit upon the scheme of the *Canterbury Tales* he devoted much more time and energy to it than he did to the *Legend*. From this fact we may validly hypothesize that the *Canterbury Tales*, with its possibilities for a variety of narratives, proved to be a more attractive and a more rewarding scheme. That, however, is quite a different matter from saying that the project of the *Legend* was a burden and a bore.

Index

Abbreviation, 79, 170, 194n, 199–206, 209; of Ceyx and Alcyone, 7; in *Cleopatra*, 45–46; in *Dido*, 59–60; in *Knight's Tale*, 8, 10; in *Lucrece*, 103; in *Philomela*, 138, 139–140. *See also* Brevity

Absolon: in "Balade," 190n; in *Miller's Tale*, 132

Accessus ad auctores, 16

Achates, 81n

Achilles, 197

Actium, 42

Adversus Jovinianum, 98n

Aegyptus (Egiste), 158, 159, 160, 162–163, 168

Aeneas: Chaucer's characterization of, 68, 69, 70, 73–77, 78, 118, 148, 160; in *Dido*, 59, 60, 64, 65, 66, 67, 71, 72, 81, 171, 178; earlier references to, 197; in *House of Fame*, 59, 60, 61, 178; in Virgil, 57, 63, 64

Aeneid, fourteenth-century Italian translation of, 58n

Aeneid, source: for *Ariadne*, 112; for *Dido*, 57, 58, 64n, 70n, 74; for *Phyllis*, 148n

Aiken, Pauline, 38n

Alceste, 25–26, 30, 31, 32, 33, 81, 139n, 190n, 207; allusion to, in *Troilus*, 197; dreamer's relationship to, 22n, 23–24; story of, in *Legend*, 57

Alisoun of *Miller's Tale*, 90, 132

Allegorization, 16–17; in Gower, 15, 17; of Ovid, 15, 16, 118. *See also* Moralization

Alliteration, 45n

Alliterative Morte Arthure, 43

Amis, 89, 179

Amores, 22n

Amorosa Visione, 38n

Amplification, 199; in the *Canterbury Tales*, 175, 186; in Chaucer's early poetry, 6–8, 10, 59, 170; in *Hypermnestra*, 160–161

Andrea Lancia, 58n

Andreas Capellanus, 14, 180

Androgeos, 113, 117n, 127n

"Anelida and Arcite," 3, 7, 93–94

Anna, 70

Anne of Bohemia, 11n, 22n, 39, 192, 196n

Antifeminist tradition, 190, 206

Antigone, 177

"Antiochus," 173

Antiquity, medieval attitude toward, 51

Antiromantic attitude in *Ariadne*, 117

Antony, 40, 41–42, 43, 44, 171, 180

Apostrophe, 181

Arcite, 5, 63, 116n, 117, 122, 175, 179

Argonauticon, 81n, 83, 84, 90n

Ariadne, 112n, 113, 114, 115, 117, 118, 119, 120, 123, 127, 132; characterization of, 124–126, 128–130

Ariadne, 9n, 49n, 111–133, 137n, 142n, 145, 148, 157n, 169, 172, 181, 184, 202

Ars Amatoria, 75

Artificiality, 194

Ascanius, 63, 69n, 74n
Atkins, J. W. H., 7n, 199n
Atmosphere, 100
Atwood, E.
Bagby, 58n, 68n
Audience: Chaucer's, 67, 77; problem of, 29–30
Augustine, 97, 98n

Balade in Prologue to Legend, 13, 26, 139n, 190n
"Balade of Her That Hath All Virtues," 40n
Baum, Paull F., 5n, 126, 128, 195n
Bawcutt, Priscilla, 199n
Bech, M., 38n, 47n, 58n, 81n, 98n, 111n, 137n, 148n, 157n, 158n
Bell, Robert, 191n
Bennett, H. S., 195
Bennett, J. A. W., 147n
Bergen, Henry, 40n, 93n, 189n
Berger, Harry, Jr., 9n
"Bernard the monk," 21, 133
Bethurum, Dorothy, 22n
Bilderbeck, J. B., 194
Birds, in Chaucer, 178
Bloomfield, Morton, 51n
Boccaccio: Amorosa Visione, 38n; De Casibus Virorum Illustrium, 13–14, 38, 39, 40n, 41, 189; De Claris Mulieribus, 13–14, 38, 39, 41, 47n, 49n, 58n, 81n, 98n, 157n; Cleopatra mentioned by, 37; his defense in Il Decamerone, 29n; Il Fiammetta, 38n; Il Filostrato, 7, 30; Il Teseide, 31, 112, 116–117
Boece, 31
Boethius, 31, 144n
Book of the Duchess, 2, 3, 5, 7, 26, 31, 49n, 146, 197
Books, 13, 33n
Born, Lester K., 16n
Bradley, D. R., 58n, 68n
Brevity, 62, 174, 183; formula, 202n, 203
Brewer, D. S., 93n
Brock, Edmund, 43n
Bronson, Bertrand, 29n
Browning, Elizabeth Barrett, 191n
Brusendorf, Aage, 13n, 195n
Bryan, W. F., 31

Bucq, Sir John de, 42
Bush, Douglas, 134n, 135n, 195n
Byblis, 197

Calkas, 176
Callan, Norman, 48n, 98, 99
Candace, 197
Canon's Yeoman's Prologue, 9n
Canon's Yeoman's Tale, 9n, 204
Canterbury Tales, 126n, 196, 201n, 210; characterization in, 183; complex vision of, 186; dream vision abandoned in, 12; existing narratives used in, 175; ironic juxtaposition in, 88; Legend as preparation for, 35; pathetic tales in, 94; short narrative in, 170, 173; tale length in, 8, 9n, 10; treatment of audience in, 29n; unfinished state of, 208; variety of experience in, 133; work begun on, 2, 169
De Casibus Virorum Illustrium, 13, 38, 39, 40n, 189
Catalogue, 45, 61
Ceyx and Alcyone, 7, 49n, 139n
Characterization: in Ariadne, 114–115; in Hypermnestra, 160–161, 164; in the Legend, 176–184; in Lucrece, 103–104; in Thisbe, 50; in Troilus and Criseyde, 62
Chaucer: concern as artist, 27; development as narrative poet, 60; as inventor of plots, 91, 175; relation with audience, 29–30; role as poet in House of Fame, 25; role as poet in Prologue to Legend, 24, 34
Chevre d'Or, see Simon Aurea Capra
Child, Clarence G., 112n, 148n
Chivalry, 40, 43, 62; code of violated, 105–106
Chrétien de Troyes, 15, 134–135, 137, 144, 180, 204n
Christianity, 34
Christine de Pisan, 200
"Chronycle Made by Chaucer," 93n, 139n
City of God, 97n
De Claris Mulieribus, 13, 38, 39, 47n, 49n, 58n, 81n, 82, 98n, 157n
Clark, Charles Cowden, 191n

Cleopatra, 14, 39, 41, 42, 43, 44, 47, 171, 180, 197; debut in English literature, 37–38, 39

Cleopatra, 9n, 37–46, 58, 79, 80, 81, 139n, 170, 171, 185, 195, 201

Clerk's Tale, 8n, 93, 143

Colatyn, 98n, 99, 100, 101, 171

Complaint, 61, 95; in "Anelida and Arcite," 94

Concerning Famous Women, 49n. See also *De Claris Mulieribus*

Confessio Amantis: Cleopatra in, 40n; moralization in, 185; narratives as *exempla* in, 15; problem of reading, 172; relationship with *Legend*, 9n; story of Ariadne in, 113; story of Lucrece in, 98n, 102n; story of Philomela in, 134, 135–137; story of Phyllis in, 147; story of Thisbe in, 47n, 48n; vision and narratives in, 4, 5

Convention, in art, 194

Cook's Tale, 208

Corson, Hiram, 191n

Courtly literature, 20, 133, 178

Courtly love: antifeminist satire and, 206; in *Ariadne*, 131–132; characterization and, 177, 179–180; in *Cleopatra*, 40, 41, 44, 45; in *Confessio Amantis*, 15; exhaustive treatment of, 6, 10; in *Hypsipyle and Medea*, 88, 89–90; in *Legend*, 14, 34, 35; in *Lucrece*, 105; narrator in Prologue and, 22; pathos and, 95; serious treatment of abandoned, 21

Criseyde, 131, 176, 177, 179, 183

Crosby, Ruth, 29n

Cupid, 63, 74n

Curry, William Clyde, 160n

Curtius, Ernst, 199n, 200n, 202n

Custance, 95

Daedalus, 117n

Daisy, 13, 21–24, 25, 36

Damian, 115

Danao (Egiste), 157n

Danaus, 158, 159

Dante, 37, 38, 146n

David, Alfred, 29n

De Boer, C., 114n, 120n, 134n, 204n

Il Decamerone, 29n

Decasyllabic couplet, 10, 175–176

Deiphebus, 177

Delilah, 197

Demophoon, 146, 152, 153, 154, 171, 205; characterization of, 147, 148, 149, 151, 182, 203; earlier references to, in Chaucer, 197

Dempster, Germaine, 31

Didacticism, 15, 16, 19, 21

Dido, 13, 58n, 74, 75, 76, 93n, 98n, 171, 184; Chaucer's technique with, 63–73, 180; earlier references to, in Chaucer, 197; in *House of Fame*, 59, 60, 61, 178; Phyllis paired with, 147, 148; reputation in Middle Ages, 57; role as tragic heroine, 77, 78

Dido, 9n, 57–78, 79, 80, 81, 112n, 118, 156, 157n, 171, 175, 184, 202

Diomede, 177

Dorigen, 125

Double time in *Dido*, 65–66

Douglas, Gavin, 199

Dramatization in *Ariadne*, 114

Draper, J. W., 116n

Dream garden, 133

Dream vision, 3, 4–5, 12, 20, 25

Dronke, Peter, 22n

Eagle in *House of Fame*, 178, 179

Echo, 197

Effictio, 135

Emelye, 122, 179

Eneas, 74n, 201n

English naval victory (1387), 42

L'Epistre au Dieu d'Amours, 200

Epitome Rerum Romanorum, 38

Estrich, Robert, 206n

Excidium Troiae, 58n

Exclamatio, 75

Exemplum, 59n, 75, 173, 174

Exoticism: in *Cleopatra*, 40, 44; in *Hypermnestra*, 162

Expolitio, see Amplification

Fabliau, 155

"Fabula Duorum Mercatorum," 201n

Fabulae of Hyginus, 81n, 112, 157n, 158n

Fall of Princes, 40n, 93n; Prologue to, 189
"False" *occupatio,* 202–203
Fame, Goddess of, 178
Faral, Edmond, 7n
Fasti, 98, 101, 105n, 202
"Feasting" *occupatio,* 201n
La Fiammetta, 38n
Filippo (Ceffi?), 16n, 58n, 82n, 111, 112n, 113, 147n, 157n, 158n, 160n
Il Filostrato, 7, 30, 32
Fins amors, 180
Fisher, John, 9n
Five-stress couplet, 5
Flamenca, 48n, 124n
Florus, 38
"Floure of Curtesye," 40n, 98n
Flower and the leaf, 21
"Foreyne," 115–117
Forster, E. M., 185
Fortuna, 178
Franklin, 203n
Franklin's Tale, 9n
French invasion threat (1386), 42
Friar's Tale, 9n
Friend, Albert C., 58n
Froissart, 26, 43n, 69, 180
Frye, Northrop, 96
Furnivall, F. J., 93n, 139n

Game of love, 77
Garrett, Robert Max, 126
Gawain, 119
De Genealogia Deorum, 81n, 112, 148n, 157n
General Prologue to the *Canterbury Tales,* 9n, 29n, 75, 88, 183
Gentilesse, 67, 88
Gerould, G. H., 31
Gesta Romanorum, 97n, 98n
Ghosh, P. C., 38n
Giardin-o, 116n
God of Love, 12, 15, 17, 25, 26, 28, 33, 35, 39, 190, 195; in Froissart's *Le Paradys d'Amour,* 69n
Golden Legend, 184
Good Fair White, 178
Gottfried von Strassburg, 146n
Gower, John: Cleopatra mentioned by, 40n; moral poetry and narra-
tive in, 17; reputation of, 172; tale of Ariadne, 113, 118; tale of Lucrece, 98n, 102n; tale of Philomela, 134, 135–137, 138n, 140, 142n, 144; tale of Phyllis, 147; tale of Thisbe, 47n, 48n; tales as *exempla,* 15, 185; use of vision form, 5
Grave, J. Salverda de, 74n, 201n
Griffin, Nathaniel E., 82n, 83n, 84n
Griffith, Dudley David, 11n
Griselda, 95, 143n
Guarino, Guido A., 49n
Guido delle Colonne, 81n, 82, 83, 84, 90, 196
Gunn, Alan, 7n

Hall, Louis Brewer, 57n, 58n, 59n
Haller, Robert S., 9n
Hammond, Eleanor, 11n, 94n, 190n
Handlyng Synne, 116n
Hecksher, W. S., 51n
Helen of Troy, 38, 197
Hercules, 81n, 85, 87, 89, 90, 91, 184, 197
Heresy against love, 26, 27, 207
Heroic couplet, 94
Heroides, fourteenth-century Italian translation of, 16n
Heroides: catalogue in *House of Fame* from, 60, 146; Dido in, 57; Gower's use of, for tale of Phyllis, 147; lyrical quality of, 174; moral glosses to, 16; narrative thinness of, 175, 202, 205; pathos in, 93n, 95; range of experience in, 22n; source for *Ariadne,* 111, 113, 128, 129, 130; source for *Dido,* 58n, 73; source for *Hypermnestra,* 157, 159, 165, 166; source for *Hypsipyle and Medea,* 81n, 82, 90n; source for *Phyllis,* 148n, 152, 153n, 203
Hibbard, Laura, *see* Loomis
Historia Destructionis Troiae, 81n, 82, 83n, 84
History, 43
Hoepffner, Ernest, 47–48n
Holcot, Robert, 98n
Holthausen, F., 148n
Hooper, Wynnard, 97n
Horne, Hengist, 191n

Horoscope, 160–161, 164, 183
Horror, 173; sense of, in pathos, 103, 110
House of Fame, 7, 25; Ariadne story in, 112n; characters of *Legend* in, 197; Dido story in, 58n, 59–62, 63, 202n; eagle in, 178; experimental quality of, 25, 31; Phyllis story in, 146; "plot" in, 7; unfinished state of, 208
Humphrey, Duke of Gloucester, 94n
Hunting, 69
Huygens, R. B. C., 16n
Hyginus, 81n, 112, 157n, 158n
Hypermnestra, 158, 159, 162, 184, 209; characterization of, 160, 161, 167, 183; narrative treatment of, 18, 163, 164, 166, 168
Hypermnestra, 9n, 17–19, 112n, 156–168, 169, 172, 175, 183, 203, 209
Hypsipyle, 80, 81n, 82, 83, 84, 87, 89, 90, 91, 171, 197, 202
Hypsipyle and Medea, 9n, 79–92, 111, 112n, 118, 121n, 132, 157n, 170, 171, 181, 184, 191, 202

Iarbas, 76
Idealization of women, 84
Ile of Ladies, 201n
Ilias, 58n
Imagery, 49, 53, 86, 91–92, 99n, 104, 105n, 142, 164
Inferno, 38
Irony, 52, 88, 89, 90, 131
Isolde, 14, 197

Jacques de Cessoles, 98n, 102
James I of Scotland, 142n
January in *Merchant's Tale*, 116
Jason, 84, 92, 118, 148, 170, 171, 182, 184, 202; central role in *Hypsipyle and Medea*, 80–81, 82, 83; characterization of, 85–89, 91, 121n, 181; comic treatment of, 85–89; earlier references to, in Chaucer, 197
Jean de Meun, 146, 147
Jerome, 97n
Jonathas, 190n
Le Jugement dou Roy de Navarre, 48n, 112

Kingis Quair, 142n
Kittredge, George Lyman, 12n, 146n
Knight's Tale, 2, 3, 10, 12, 45; abbreviation and *occupatio* in, 8, 201n; character treatment in, 179; comparison of, with *Dido*, 62–63; courtly love in, 6, 26; decasyllabic couplet used in, 5, 175
Kyng Alisaunder, 201n

Lactantius, 47n
Legend of Good Women: early edition of, 191; first scholarly edition of, 191; number of legends planned for, 189–190n; popularity of, 174, 190; unfinished state of, 196, 208–209, 210; variety in, 75, 184, 185
Legenda Aurea, 97n. See also *Golden Legend*
Libeaus Desconus, 119
Livy, 98n
(Loomis), Laura Hibbard, 127
Lounsbury, Thomas R., 191–194, 195, 196, 204n, 207, 208
Love: fresh view of, in *Legend*, 14, 20, 22, 26, 34–35, 89–90, 131, 173. *See also* Courtly love
Love vision, 25–26
Lowes, John Livingston, 11n, 12n, 38n, 112n, 116, 117, 122, 137n, 194n, 195n, 197, 204n
Lucrece, 13, 14, 93n, 99, 104, 171, 184; Chaucer's treatment of, 100–101, 102–103 ,106–108, 109, 110, 181; pathetic elements of, 95, 96, 97, 100–101, 102–103, 108; role of as faithful wife, 98n, 102–103, 105, 197
Lucrece, 9n, 80, 93–110, 111, 113, 156, 169, 170, 172, 175, 184, 202
Lumiansky, R. M., 80
Lydgate, John, 7, 40n, 48n, 84, 93n, 98n, 142n, 146n, 189–190, 201n
Lynceus, *see* Lyno
Lyno, 17, 158, 164, 167, 168
Lyric, 173

McCall, John, 9n, 32n
MacCracken, Henry Noble, 40n, 98n, 201n
Machaut, 26, 47n, 48n, 112

Malory, Sir Thomas, 202
Man in Black, 178
Man of Law's Tale, 8n, 93, 94, 139n, 198, 204; "Introduction to," 209
Manciple's Prologue, 9n
Manciple's Tale, 9n
Manly, John Matthews, 190n
Marguerite, *see* Daisy
Martyrs of love theme, 197
Masculine poetry in *Legend*, 44
May of *Merchant's Tale*, 115, 116
Medea, 13, 16n, 85, 87, 88, 89, 90, 92, 93n, 139n; Chaucer's treatment of, 14, 80, 82, 83, 84, 91, 138, 202; earlier references to, in Chaucer, 197; Guido delle Colonne's treatment of, 82, 83, 84
Medea, see *Hypsipyle and Medea*
Meech, Sanford Brown, 47–48n, 49n, 58n, 82n, 111n, 112n, 114, 137n, 147n, 157n, 158n, 160n
Melibee, 9n
Menagier de Paris, 98n, 102
Merchant, 186
Merchant's Tale, 8n, 115–116, 175
Mercury, 76
Metamorphoses, in Ovid and Chaucer, 184
Metamorphoses, 184; and *Book of the Duchess*, 197; Chaucer's changes of, in *Thisbe*, 50, 54–56, 202; moral glosses on, 16; and *Ovide moralisé*, 15; source for *Ariadne*, 111, 113, 118n, 202; source for *Hypsipyle and Medea*, 81n; source for *Philomela*, 134, 135n, 136n, 137n, 144n, 204; source for *Thisbe*, 47, 54–56
Middle English Dictionary (MED), 89n, 116n
Miller, Frank Justus, 55n
Miller, Robin, 170, 186
Miller's Tale, 9n, 29n, 88, 89n, 90, 174, 177, 183
Minos, 113, 114, 117, 118, 122, 131
Minotaur, 113, 114, 120, 123n, 127, 171
Monk's Tale, 9n, 93, 172, 173, 192
Moral poetry, 17
Moralization, 118, 173, 174, 184–185

Morland, Catherine, 126
Munari, F., 15n
Muscatine, Charles, 63n, 93n, 94, 95n
Mustanoja, Tauno F., 5n
Myth, 185

Narcissus, 197
Narrative, 4, 48, 56, 59, 150, 157, 168; abbreviation in, 8; brief poetic genre of, 172, 173; Chaucer's interest in, 10, 17–19; and decasyllabic couplet, 5; development of, in Chaucer, 60–62; diction in, 50; emphasis in, 171; function of, as commentary, 186; length of, 174–175; lyric element of, in the *Legend*, 173–174; summary of, 157, 171
Narrative of sentiment, 59, 174
Narrator, Chaucerian, 12
Newman, F. X., 6n
Nicholas of *Miller's Tale*, 88, 90
"Nine Worshipfullest Ladyes," 93n, 139n
Nisus, 113
Northern Homily, 116n
Norton-Smith, John, 142n
Notatio, 135
Numerals in Chaucer, 126n
Nun's Priest, 186
Nun's Priest's Tale, 9n, 45, 175

Objective characterization, 183
Objectivity, 63
Occupatio, 60, 61, 153, 199–206, 207, 209, 210
Octosyllabic couplet, 176
"On Gloucester's Approaching Marriage," 98n
"Origenes upon the Maudeleyne," 32
Orosius, 38
Overbeck, Pat Trefzger, 125n
Ovid, 13, 35, 146, 196, 197; Chaucer's changes of, in *Ariadne*, 117, 129, 130n, 202; Chaucer's changes of, in *Hypermnestra*, 159, 160, 162, 165–166; Chaucer's changes of, in *Lucrece*, 99, 100, 101, 102, 104, 105, 106, 107, 202; Chaucer's changes

of, in *Philomela*, 137, 138, 139, 140, 142n, 144, 202, 204; Chaucer's changes of, in *Thisbe*, 51, 52–53, 54–56; Chaucer's use of, in *Dido*, 58n, 59; Chaucer's use of, in *Thisbe*, 47, 48, 49, 50, 171, 180, 202; Chrétien de Troyes's use of, in *Philomena*, 134, 135; Dido story in, 57; Gower's use of, 135–136, 147; in the Middle Ages, 15–16; morality in his metamorphoses, 184; pathos in his *Heroides*, 95; Phyllis in his *Remedia Amores*, 146, 147n, 148n; range of experience in, 22n; source for *Ariadne* in, 111, 118, 129; 130n; source for *Hypermnestra* in, 156n, 157n, 159, 161, 164, 165; source for *Hypsipyle and Medea*, 82, 83, 92, 202; source for *Lucrece*, 98, 99, 100, 101, 104, 105, 107, 108; source for *Philomela*, 134, 137, 142; source for *Phyllis*, 148n, 202. *See also Fasti; Heroides; Metamorphoses*
Ovide moralisé: allegorization of Ovid in, 16, 184; medievalization of Ovid in, 15; use of, in *Ariadne*, 111, 112n, 113, 114, 117, 118, 119, 120, 121n, 123n, 124; use of, in *Philomela*, 137n, 144n, 204; use of, in *Thisbe*, 47n
Oxford English Dictionary (OED), 97n

Pagan character of the legends, 34
Palamon, 5, 63, 117, 175, 179
"Palamon and Arcite," 2, 5, 31. *See also Knight's Tale*
"Palice of Honour," 199n
Pandarus, 89, 131, 176–177, 179, 183
Pandion, 135, 139, 140, 143, 172
Panegyric, *occupatio* as, 200
Panofsky, Erwin, 51n
Paradiso, 146n
Le Paradys d'Amour, 69n
Pardoner, 186
Pardoner's Prologue, 9n
Pardoner's Tale, 9n, 174, 175
Paris, 197
Parliament of Birds, 2, 3, 5, 7, 21, 31, 38, 39, 90, 131, 178, 197

Parody, 89, 126–127, 128, 132
Parr, Johnstone, 48n
Parson's Tale, 9n, 116n, 190n
Pasiphae, 114, 118
Pathos, 93–97, 110, 136, 173, 208; in *Ariadne*, 129–132; in *Dido*, 72–73, 77; in *Hypermnestra*, 167; in *Lucrece*, 97, 100–102, 103, 108, 110; in *Philomela*, 140–145; origins of, in Chaucer, 94–95; pattern of, in Chaucer, 95; religion and, 97
Payne, Robert, 27, 28, 30
Pearsall, Derek A., 21n, 107n, 134n
Pelleas, 82, 86, 87, 90, 91, 171
Penance, for heresy against love, 27, 34–35, 207, 210
Penelope, 98n, 197, 200
Pertelote, 23
Petrarch, 37, 146n
Phaedra, 112n, 114, 115, 118, 119, 120, 121, 125, 126, 127, 181, 197
Philomela, 49n, 93n, 134, 138, 139, 144, 145, 171; in Chrétien de Troyes, 134, 135; in Gower, 136; as pathetic heroine, 95, 140, 141, 142, 143
Philomela, 9n, 49n, 93, 112n, 134–145, 170, 182, 184, 202, 203, 204
Philomena, of Chrétien de Troyes, 15, 134, 204n
Phyllis, 146, 148n, 149, 150, 155, 203; earlier references to, in Chaucer, 197; in Gower, 147; unsympathetic treatment of, 151, 152, 153, 154, 208
Phyllis, 9n, 112n, 146–155, 157, 172, 182, 193, 202, 205, 207
Physician's Tale, 9n, 93
Piers Plowman, 4, 177
Plutarch, 38, 112
Portraits in *Troilus and Criseyde*, 177–178
Priam, 176
Prioress, 132
Prioress's Prologue, 9n
Prioress's Tale, 9n, 93
Progne, 49n, 134n, 138, 171, 182, 203, 204n; in Gower, 136; pathos of, 140, 141, 142n, 143
Prologue to the *Legend of Good*

Women, 11–36; as assigned task, 196n; Chaucer's reflections on his poetry in, 10, 28; comic motivation in, 208; decasyllabic couplet in, 5; discussion of new subject matter in, 28–30, 32–36, 169; F version of, 9n, 11, 24, 25, 191, 199; G version of, 9n, 11, 24, 25, 191, 199n; possible date of, 1, 191; revision of, by Chaucer, 198, 209; tone of, 206n; vision form of, 3, 25–26
Proverb, 51
Przychocky, Gustaw, 16n
Pyramus, 5, 14, 47, 48, 49, 50, 52, 53, 197
Pyramus and Thisbe, thirteenth-century Anglo-Norman version, 180

Quain, Edwin A., 16n

Raby, F. J. E., 57n
Rape, 105, 107, 108, 136, 139n, 141–142
Realism, 90, 194; in English medieval painting, 179
Reeve's Tale, 9n, 29n, 45, 183
Religious vision, 4
Remedia Amoris, 146, 147n, 148n
"Remembrance," literature the key of, 30, 32, 173
Renard the fox, 151, 182
Repetitio, 66–67
"Retractation," 190n
Rhetoric, 52, 56, 109; reliance on, 61
Rhyme royal, 5, 94, 175, 176
Rhymed Chronicle, 116n
Richard II, 39
Rickert, Edith, 190n
Robbins, Harry W., 147n
Robinson, F. N., 22n, 24n, 32n, 190n, 195n
Role: characterization and, 177–178, 179–181, 183, 183–184; importance of, in medieval world, 177
Roman de la rose, 4, 7n, 30, 32, 98n, 144n, 146, 147n, 148n
Romance of the Rose, 28, 31, 32, 126n, 147n
Romances: elements of, 126; expectations in, 118–119; Middle English,

119, 127; mockery of, 126, 128
Romans courtois, 95
Root, Robert K., 102, 146n, 194–195, 198, 199n, 201, 202n
Roy, Maurice, 200n

St. Cecilia, life of, 2, 3, 31, 96
Saint's life, 173
Samson, 197
Samuel, Irene, 48n
Satire, 208
Scaglione, Aldo, 29n
Schanzer, Ernest, 38n
Schick, Josef, 48n, 98n, 142n, 146n
Schofield, William, 42, 43n
Scipio Africanus, 178
Scylla, 113, 114, 117, 126, 197
Second Nun's Prologue, 9n
Second Nun's Tale, 2, 9n, 31, 96
Semiramis, 38, 47–48n, 50, 197
Sentimentalism, 95
Shakespeare, William, 37
Shannon, Edgar F., 38n, 47n, 48n, 58n, 81n, 83n, 98n, 106n, 111n, 112n, 124n, 137n, 142n, 148n, 156n, 157n, 159n
Sherzer, Jane B., 201n
Shipman's Tale, 9n
Shirley, James, 94n
Showerman, Grant, 148n, 165n
Simon Aurea Capra, 58n
Sir Gawain and the Green Knight, 201n
Sir Thopas, 9n, 126, 132, 192
Skeat, W. W., 38n, 47n, 81n, 98n, 111n, 112n, 116, 137n, 142n, 146n, 148n, 157n, 190n, 191, 195, 205
Smalley, Beryl, 98n
Smithers, G. V., 201n
Solacium Ludi Schaccorum, 98n
Speculum Historiale, 16n, 38, 39
Spencer, William, 160n
Spurgeon, Caroline, 190n
Squire in General Prologue, 75
Squire of Low Degree, 119
Squire's Tale, 9n, 65n, 208
Statius, 81n
Stone, Lawrence, 95n
Story: Chaucer's dedication to, 185–186

Style, 109–110, 111; colloquial quality of, 52, 56; rhetorical quality of, 52

Subject matter, 5–6, 111, 169–170, 173; medieval artist and, 28–36

Summoner's Tale, 9n

Swann, Charles, 97n

Symbolism, 63

Symkyn, 132

Tarquin, 99, 100, 107, 110, 171, 184; Chaucer's treatment of, 103, 104, 105, 106, 108, 109, 181

Taste, medieval, 192, 193

Tatlock, J. S. P., 39n, 195, 196, 197, 198, 199n, 201, 202n, 203

Temple of Glas, 48n, 98n, 142n, 146n

Tennyson, Alfred, 191n

Tereus, 49n, 141, 142n, 171, 203; Chaucer's treatment of, 139, 140, 143–144, 182, 202, 205; Chrétien de Troyes's treatment of, 134n, 135; tale of, in *Confessio Amantis*, 134

Il Teseide, 31, 112, 116

Thebaid, 81n

Theodulus, 148n

Theseus, 113, 114, 115, 117, 118, 120, 125, 126, 127, 128, 129, 170, 171, 182, 184; Chaucer's treatment of, 119, 121–124, 181; earlier reference to, in Chaucer, 197; father of Demophoon, 148, 151, 182, 206

Thisbe, 13, 14, 47, 48, 49, 50, 52, 53; earlier reference to, in Chaucer, 197

Thisbe, 9n, 47–56, 58, 79, 80, 93, 99, 109, 156, 171, 175, 180, 184, 201–202

Tone: in *Ariadne*, 115; contrasts of, in *Legend*, 111, 157; fluctuation of, in *Legend*, 206–208, 210; humor of, in *Legend*, 196, 206–208, 210; in *Hypsipyle and Medea*, 92; in *Phyllis*, 149, 150, 182, 203

Translation, 30–32, 50, 51

Trask, Willard R., 199n

Trionfo d'Amore, 38n, 146n

Trionfo della Fama, 38n

Tristram, 14, 197

Tristran of Gottfried von Strassburg, 146n

Troilus, 65, 131, 176, 177, 179, 197

Troilus and Criseyde, 2, 126n, 142n, 170, 196, 197–198; amplification in, 7, 8, 10; characterization in, 176–178, 179, 183; classical writers praised in, 13; concern for audience in, 29n; courtly love in, 5–6, 26, 35, 90; *Dido* compared with, 62–63; heresy charge against, 28, 30; *occupatio* in, 200–201, 203; portraits in, 177–178; rhyme royal stanza in, 5; as translation, 30, 31, 32; vision form abandoned in, 3, 12; vision of experience in, 186

Troy Book, 84n

Ugolino of Pisa, 93, 95, 173

Understatement, 52

Utley, Francis, 206

Valerius Flaccus, 81n, 83, 90n

Venus, 63, 64, 74n, 171, 197; planet of, 160–161; temple of, 38

Viarre, Simone, 15n

Vincent de Beauvais, 16n, 38, 39, 41

Violence, in the legends, 34

Virgil, 78, 196; abbreviated versions of, 58; comparison of, with Chaucer, 59; Dido story in, 13, 57, 58, 60, 63, 64, 68, 69, 70, 71, 73, 74; source for *Hypsipyle and Medea*, 81n; source for *Phyllis*, 148n

Virginia, 95

Virginius, 95

Vision, narrative in, 4–5. *See also* Dream vision; Religious vision

Walter in *Clerk's Tale*, 143n

Weariness *topos* in Chaucer, 204–205

Whitaker, Virgil K., 58n

Whitman, Walt, 36

Wife of Bath, 125, 149

Wife of Bath's Prologue, 9n, 175

Wife of Bath's Tale, 9n, 119, 175

Wilkinson, L.P., 15n

Wimsatt, W. K., 38n

Wood, Chauncey, 160n

Young, Karl, 16n, 144n